Christian Higher Education
in Changing China
1880-1950

By
WILLIAM PURVIANCE FENN

WILLIAM B. EERDMANS PUBLISHING COMPANY

Library of Congress Cataloging in Publication Data

Fenn, William Purviance, 1902–
   Christian higher education in changing China.

   1. Education—China—History.   2. Protestant churches—Missions—History.
I. Title.
LA1131.F44   378.51   75–43741
ISBN 0–8028–3478–7

Christian Higher Education
in Changing China
1880-1950

Foreword

The history of modern education in China would not be complete without a chapter on the role of the Christian Colleges. Beginning very humbly and remaining relatively small institutions, the Christian Colleges exerted an influence on Chinese education and Chinese society far greater than one would expect from little more than a dozen private colleges and universities established under foreign auspices and controlled, through most of their formative years, by foreign personnel. Even when they became targets of an aroused nationalism, they continued to grow and to produce graduates who won respect in positions of leadership in government, in education, and in other walks of life.

Born at a time when China was beginning to develop a system of modern education, the Christian Colleges evolved from institutions serving primarily the Church and the Christian movement into institutions of higher learning serving the needs of a young republic and developing nation. From the early status of expanded secondary schools and junior colleges, they rose to become full-fledged colleges and universities blazing new paths for higher education in China. Eventually shedding the earmarks of foreign importation and historical connection with Western imperialism, they became integrated with the main stream of Chinese life and won national prestige.

This growth did not take place without difficulties, prolonged uncertainties, and tortuous struggles. Much had to be done to overcome academic shortcomings and to adjust to the demands and expectations of a new nationalism. At a time when political instability and governmental weakness slowed down the development of public education at all levels, the Christian Colleges were outstanding educational institutions attracting young men and women of high calibre. When, later, state-supported colleges and universities began to outdistance private institutions in financial resources and academic excellence, the Christan Colleges met the new challenge with vision and courage. Meeting mounting criticism as foreign institutions negligent of Chinese culture, which tended to "de-nationalize" their students, they undertook serious self-examination. The declared intention of Christian educators to make the Christian Colleges "more Chinese, more truly Christian, and more scholarly in academic work" was indicative of an awareness of the opportunity as well as of the need of reform if the colleges were to make their maximum contribution to the Chinese nation.

The acceptance of government grants by the Christian Colleges marked a milestone. On the one hand, it signified the readiness both in China and abroad to make the colleges an integral part of the Chinese educational scene. At the same time, the grants provided clear evidence of the recognition by the government that the Christian Colleges were national institutions making substantial contributions to the nation. The Christian Colleges had attained maturity. They had won a place of honor in the national system of education, but at the same time they had preserved the spiritual values that lay at the heart of their program and that made them unique institutions.

In the history of modern education in China, the Christian Colleges led the way in the study of Western civilization and science. Their international personnel made possible interesting experiments in inter-cultural education. They were pioneers in the teaching of English, in recognizing music as a component of liberal education, in the education of women, in the emphasis on the development of the whole man, and in other lines of effort reflecting their Christian faith. They encouraged athletics and taught the spirit of sportsmanship. Their campuses were known for their architecture and their atmosphere.

In the promotion of medical education and programs of rural betterment, the Christian Colleges gave expression to their concern for the well-being of their fellowmen. The Christian spirit was also reflected in campus life. The Colleges had a high percentage of full-time faculty who devoted their full attention to both academic and extracurricular programs. The faculty and their families took pains to cultivate close personal relations with students, inviting them to their homes and developing enduring friendships. A compliment often paid to graduates of these colleges by Chinese society was that they had a spirit of service and whole-hearted devotion to duty and could be relied on for the faithful performance of tasks.

The evolution of the Christian Colleges of China from small church schools to respected institutions of higher learning, their adjustment to changes in Chinese society and national life, their response to nationalism, and their struggle to keep alive a basic core of Christian ideals while meeting Chinese conditions and needs make a fascinating story of educational experimentation and adaptation. This story must tell about failures as well as successes, frustrations as well as sustained hopes, narrow sectarianism as well as broad vision, periodic misgivings as well as steady faith. But the over-all record is one that well justifies the effort, the devotion, and the pride of those who, at one time or another, had a share in their development and their service.

Dr. William P. Fenn is well qualified to review and interpret that experience. Reared in China, he became a professor at the University of Nanking, concerned with the cultural contacts of China with the English-speaking world. During the Sino-Japanese War, as representative of the United Board for Christian Colleges in China, he served as the intermediary between Christian Colleges in Free China and their supporters abroad. In the postwar period, he played a key role in the rehabilitation of the colleges and the charting of a new course. He knew all the colleges at first hand. From 1951 to 1970 he was General Secretary of the United Board for Christian Higher Education in Asia. He has in this volume contributed substantially to a clearer understanding of a very important phase of Chinese higher education and Chinese-American relations.

Theodore H. E. Chen
Professor of International Education
University of Southern California
Los Angeles

Contents

Contents

PART FIVE: THE LAST CHAPTERS (1937–1950)

The Christian Colleges of China
(with their Chinese names)

PROTESTANT INSTITUTIONS

Fukien Christian University (Fu-chien hsieh-ho ta-hsueh)—Foochow
Ginling College (Chin-ling nü wen-li hsüeh-yüan)—Nanking
Hangchow University (Chih-chiang ta-hsüeh)—Hangchow
Hsiang-Ya Medical College (Hsiang-ya i-hsüeh-yüan)—Changsha
Huachung University (Hua-chung ta-hsüeh)—Wuchang
Hwa Nan College (Hua-nan nü wen-li hsüeh-yüan)—Foochow
Lingnan University (Ling-nan ta-hsüeh)—Canton
Moukden Medical College (Feng-t'ien i-hsüeh-yüan)—Moukden
Nanking, University of (Chin-ling ta-hsüeh)—Nanking
St. John's University (Sheng-yüeh-han ta-hsüeh)—Shanghai
Shanghai, University of (Hu-chiang ta-hsüeh)—Shanghai
Shantung Christian University (Ch'i-lu ta-hsüeh)—Tsinan
    (also known as Cheeloo University)
Soochow University (Tung-wu ta-hsüeh)—Soochow
West China Union University (Hua-hsi hsieh-ho ta-hsüeh)—Chengtu
Women's Christian Medical College (Shanghai nü-tzu i-hsüeh-yüan)—
    Shanghai
Yale-in-China (see Hsiang-Ya Medical College)
Yenching University (Yen-ching ta-hsüeh)—Peking

ROMAN CATHOLIC INSTITUTIONS

Aurora University (Chen-ta ta-hsüeh)—Shanghai
Catholic University (Fu-jen ta-hsüeh)—Peking
Tsinku University (Tsin-ku ta-hsüeh)—Tientsin

Introduction

When in 1949 the Nationalist government of the Republic of China collapsed and Communist forces set up a new People's Government, the last page was written in a remarkable and in many respects unique story, that of the Protestant colleges of China, widely and affectionately known as the China Colleges. None having covered more than the Biblical three score and ten years and some having seen no more than half that span, they had nevertheless achieved impressive stature, gained international recognition, contributed notably to China's development, and been an outstanding and effective expression of international understanding and good will. Probably no similar group of Christian institutions in a non-Christian land had achieved comparable results or had had as great an influence on its surroundings. The story of the China Colleges should not be without interest, not only for the Protestant missions which fashioned them but for students interested in China's awakening and the part the West has played therein.

The story is a fascinating one of apparently insignificant beginnings and often unachievable goals, few straight roads and some blind alleys, deep commitment and great sacrifice, human greatness and human weakness, failure and achievement. It is a tale of the birth, growth, and sometimes death of many efforts to serve the Chinese people, leading finally to a group of institutions of higher education which made important contributions to the Protestant Church and to the development of modern China. Before the story ended they had played a small but vital role in the life of that great land as it reacted to new contacts and adjusted to renewed life. They had constituted a potent force in China's own awakening and a positive expression of Western participation in that process. Despite weakness and obvious vulnerability to criticism, they had served well through many decades of internal revolution and external reaction. When, after a century of growth, these colleges and universities were taken over by the People's Government and absorbed into its system of education, the tale ended, unlikely ever to be renewed. But it is one that bears telling, and there is a final balance of achievement worth recording.

The story is one of growth. In 1882 there was only one institution which could reasonably be considered a post-secondary institution, and it had only a handful of boys. Even a dozen years later, with four institutions claiming and possibly deserving the name of college, there were probably not more than three hundred college students. At the end of seventy years a final total of fourteen institutions—twelve co-educational universities and two colleges for women—enrolled a combined total of some thirteen thousand students. Academic programs had expanded from the original basic arts and sciences and occasional elementary theology to include the social sciences, medicine, agriculture, engineering, business, law, journalism, and public affairs. Courses which had been barely at a post-secondary level had given way to undergraduate work of recognized university standard, and there were graduate courses in a number of fields.

Before the story ended, all had achieved a position of respectability in the academic life of China and were accepted and valued parts of the higher education of that land. Some ranked among the leading universities of the country. They had also as a group become favorably known in the English-speaking world, their graduates often compiling laudable records in graduate studies overseas and rendering notable service both at home and abroad. A few were respected for their contributions and standing in one or more fields of knowledge and service.

Before we examine that story or attempt to balance the books of success and failure, let us look at the *dramatis personae* involved. Who were the China Colleges? At one time or another nearly thirty institutions appeared on the stage, but not all of these survived until the final scene. Death, always unwelcome and often protracted, and marriage, usually of convenience or necessity, reduced the number until, during the last three decades, the total was sixteen and finally fifteen. These were unevenly scattered over China proper: two (Yenching University in Peking, Shantung Christian University in Tsinan) in the north; three (Lingnan University in Canton; Fukien Christian University and Hwa Nan College in Foochow) in the south; seven (the University of Nanking and Ginling College in Nanking; St. John's University, Shanghai University, and Woman's Christian Medical College in Shanghai; Soochow University in both Shanghai and nearby Soochow; and Hangchow University in Hangchow) in the east; one (West China Union University in Chengtu) in the west; two (Hsiang-Ya Medical College in Changsha and Huachung University in Wuchang) in the center; and one (Christie Medical College in Moukden) in Manchuria. This distribution, with most of the institutions either on or within a short distance of the east coast, was the result of history, this having been the chief area of Western penetration during much of the period covered by the first part of this story.

Were the story to be that of Christian rather than Protestant higher education, it would include three Catholic institutions: Aurora University in Shanghai, Catholic University in Peking, and *L'Institut des Hautes Études Industrielles et Commerciales*, in Tientsin. Aurora, opened in 1903, gave much of its instruction in French and was noted for its meteorological observatory and press and for the scholarship of its Jesuit fathers. Catholic University (Fu Jen in Chinese) did not start until 1925, but developed under the American Province of the Society of the Divine Word into one of the leading universities in the country. *L'Institut*, founded in 1922 by the Jesuits, in 1947 took the name of Tsinku University. None of these institutions survived the Communist take-over of 1950, but a decade later Fu Jen was re-established in Taiwan. All shared many of the same goals as the Protestant colleges and universities and experienced comparable difficulties and successes but followed paths separate from and unrelated to those of Protestant higher education. Theirs is a separate story.

The story of the China Colleges can be told in four chapters. First is the period of beginnings, from the first small schools in the middle of the nineteenth century to a handful of aspiring post-secondary institutions toward the end. Then, during the first two decades of the twentieth, synchronous with revolution, educational reform, and cultural renaissance, comes a period of expansion. Next, in the midst of growing xenophobia and increasing national consciousness and assurance, follows a period of growth, consolidation, maturing, and noteworthy achievement. Finally, an often nearly fatal period of underground and refugee existence during World War II is followed by a brief period of enthusiastic and hopeful reconstruction terminated by the Communist take-over in the early 1950s. By 1951–52, the Christian colleges of China were no more. In Tunghai University in Taiwan and Chung Chi College in Hong Kong, the China Colleges have two spiritual successors founded on the same principles, committed to similar ideals. But that is another story.

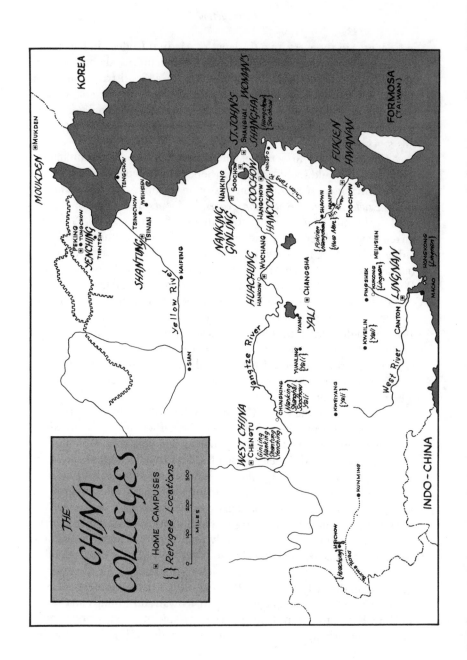

THE
CHINA
COLLEGES

▣ HOME CAMPUSES
⟨⟩ Refugee Locations

MILES
0   100   200   300

MOUKDEN
●MUKDEN

KOREA

FORMOSA
(TAIWAN)

WEST CHINA
▣ CHENGTU
⟨Ginling
Nanking
Shantung
Yenching⟩

CHUNGKING
⟨Nanking
Shanghai
Soochow
Yali⟩

YUANLING
⟨Yali⟩

HEICHOW
⟨Huachung⟩ refugee road

KUNMING

KWEYANG
⟨Yali⟩

KWEILIN
⟨Yali⟩

IYANG
⟨Yali⟩

West River

CANTON

KUKONG
⟨Lingnan⟩

PINGSHEK
⟨Lingnan⟩

MEIHSIEN
⟨Lingnan⟩

LINGNAN

HONGKONG
⟨Lingnan⟩

MACAO

INDO-CHINA

Yangtze River

YALI   ●CHANGSHA

HUACHUNG
HANKOW ● ● WUCHANG

HANGCHOW

CHIEN TANG RIVER

NINGPO

FUKIEN
⟨Wanghsien⟩

FUKIEN
HWANAN

FOOCHOW

SHAOWU
⟨Huo Mei, Foochow⟩

NANPING

NANKING
GINLING

SOOCHOW
SOOCHOW

ST. JOHN'S   WOMAN'S
SHANGHAI   SHANGHAI
⟨Hangchow
Soochow⟩

SIAN

Yellow River

KAIFENG

SHANTUNG
TSINGCHOW
●TSINAN

WEIHSIEN

TENGCHOW

TIENTSIN

PEKING
●TUNGCHOW

YENCHING

FUKIEN CHRISTIAN UNIVERSITY

GINLING COLLEGE

HANGCHOW UNIVERSITY

HWANAN COLLEGE

HUACHUNG UNIVERSITY
(Refugee Quarters)

LINGNAN UNIVERSITY

WEST CHINA UNION UNIVERSITY

UNIVERSITY OF NANKING

ST. JOHN'S UNIVERSITY

UNIVERSITY OF SHANGHAI
(Following World War II)

SHANTUNG CHRISTIAN UNIVERSITY

SOOCHOW UNIVERSITY

YENCHING UNIVERSITY

Part
1
The Beginnings
(1850–1900)

1
China in the Nineteenth Century

The century of Christian education in China was contemporaneous with the hundred years of that nation's history between the first major external threat to the Manchu Dynasty and the country's succumbing to internal collapse, between the first real pressures of foreign aggression and the achievement of equality in the family of nations. In 1851, in response to that aggression and reflecting the weakness and corruption of the government, Hung Hsiu-ch'uan proclaimed the *T'ai P'ing T'ien Kuo*, the Great Peaceful Heavenly Kingdom, leading to a decade of civil war; in 1950, after three decades of struggle, the Communists had gained effective control of the entire country. War with England (1839–42) inaugurated a series of open threats to China's weakly defended sovereignty which was to continue through the nineteenth century and well into the twentieth. In 1950 the Korean War proved China's readiness to defend herself against foreign aggression.

It was a time of political, military, intellectual, and social activity and change. Wars, civil and foreign, followed each other in rapid succession. Revolutions failed and succeeded; a monarchy crumbled and fell; a republic was painfully born, lived four decades, and gave way to a new totalitarianism. A millennium-old system of thought and expression yielded to a search for modernity, which in turn fell before a new rigidity of control. An ancient agricultural society increasingly but slowly yielded to industrialization and modern technology, and then both rural and urban societies were bound in new shackles of conformity.

The first war with Britain (1839–42) ended with the Treaty of Nanking, which provided, among other things, for the opening of five ports—Canton, Amoy, Foochow, Ningpo, and Shanghai—the ceding to Great Britain of the island of Hong Kong, and, a year later, the beginnings of extraterritoriality for British citizens. In 1844 the United

States secured similar freedom from the laws of China. These treaties made possible the entry into China proper of missionary work of all sorts, which had thus far been confined to such nearby areas as Macao and Hong Kong, Chinese-speaking but under European jurisdiction. With these beginnings there soon came into being the first missionary schools.

A second war (1856–60), in which British and French forces captured Peking and destroyed the Summer Palace, threatened the very life of the Manchu Dynasty. The Treaties of Tientsin (1858) and Peking (1860), by opening more ports to trade, the Yangtze River to navigation, Peking to foreign dwelling, and the country to freedom of travel, made possible still greater penetration of China by the West. The purpose was commercial and at times political. But Christians were given the right to propagate Christianity, and extraterritoriality affected missionaries as well as businessmen in their activities. At this time, too, began the nibbling away of China's borders which resulted in the loss of territory to Russia and of ports to other nations and ultimately to the encroachment of the second and third decades of the twentieth century and student response thereto.

For the next thirty years, up to the final decades of the nineteenth century, the country continued almost as if nothing had happened, life following long-established patterns and the government largely unaware of, or ignoring, the changes that were taking place. Yet the influence of the West was growing in many areas: missions, trade, the introduction of technology, Western books in translation, and a new type of education—all undermining the conservative and traditional ways of life, and interjecting change into a decadent civilization. Some officials saw the need. In 1866 the recently created department of foreign affairs, the *Tsungli Yamen*, presented a memorial to the Throne stating that "It is plain that it is impossible to do otherwise than to pursue the study of western knowledge." In 1871, at the urging of Yung Wing, the government began sending a group of 120 students to the United States. As early as the 1870s and 1880s, Protestant missionaries advocated the development of a modern system of education.

The Manchu Dynasty had been rudely jostled out of its deepening somnolence by the two foreign wars and one civil war of the mid-nineteenth century but had slipped again into a contented disregard of the realities of domestic and world affairs when it was shocked into startled concern by its neighbor Japan. Rivalry over Korea, where China claimed a suzerainty Japan refused to recognize, led to war in 1894.

China was quickly defeated, and, in the humiliating Treaty of Shimonoseki (1895), acknowledged the independence of Korea, ceded Formosa and the Liaotung Peninsula (later recovered), paid an indemnity, opened four more ports, and extended to Japan the extraterritorial privileges enjoyed by Western powers.

Demands from other powers followed Japan's success, with France, Britain, Germany, and Russia carving out bits of Chinese territory and securing additional concessions. With creation of foreign spheres of influence, the dismemberment of the Chinese Empire appeared under way. The Open Door Policy proposed in 1899 by American Secretary of State John Hay delayed but did not wholly avert the process.

Internal reaction to this situation took two forms: reform and conservatism, the latter in part a reaction to the former. Many Chinese became convinced that the country must adopt the methods of the West which had given Japan the ability to defeat its much larger neighbor. Reform societies sprang up, sponsored by such men as Viceroy Chang Chih-tung. Missionaries such as Timothy Richard helped with encouragement and advice. Radicals such as Sun Yat-sen, a Christian and associate of missionaries, organized revolts. Chief reformer at that time was K'ang Yu-wei, who attacked orthodox scholars for their conservatism and formulated a radical philosophy based on a new Confucianism. The Emperor himself accepted the need for change: " . . . our scholars are without solid and practical education; our artisans are without scientific instructors. . . . Changes must be made to accord with the necessities of the times. . . . We must select such subjects of Western knowledge as shall keep us in touch with the times, and diligently study and practise them in order to place our country abreast with other countries. . . ."

In the spirit of reform a number of innovations were instituted and Western-style schools set up. In the summer of 1898 the Emperor Kwang Hsü, with K'ang Yu-wei encouraging and advising, instituted a number of reforms modifying the examination system, establishing new schools, including a modern university, the Imperial University, encouraging the building of railroads, and improving army and navy. Because of the opposition aroused among the supporters of the old order, these lasted only slightly over three months—hence the name Hundred Days of Reform.

These reactionaries had the support and leadership of the Empress Dowager, Tz'u Hsi, who felt that the Emperor was moving too sharply and precipitately. She also resented his growing independence. On September 22, 1898, she seized Kwang Hsü, imprisoned him in her own palace, and assumed the regency. Most of the Emperor's edicts were countermanded and an effort was made to save the country by reaction. This took the final form of the Boxer Uprising, which tried to drive the foreigner and his ways from the country. Sporadic attacks on foreigners led to the Siege of Peking in 1900. More than two hundred foreign missionaries and several thousand Chinese Christians were killed. By the fall of 1900 Peking was in foreign hands, the court had fled, and Russia had occupied much of Manchuria. The old China had moved a long step toward ultimate collapse.

One result of the war with Japan was the impetus which defeat gave to educational reform. The conviction grew that reform in education was essential for the salvation of the country. All schools where Western language and sciences were taught were soon overcrowded. At that time China had only a handful of institutions, government or private, which could claim to be true post-secondary colleges. The earliest was the T'ung Wen Kuan, founded in 1862 by the Foreign Office for the study of foreign languages—first English, then French, Russian, and German, and finally Japanese; it was headed initially by Sir Robert Hart of Imperial Customs fame, and then by Dr. W.A.P. Martin, a Presbyterian missionary. It achieved college rank in 1866 and soon added a scientific department. Dr. Martin taught international law. The following year a training center for mechanical engineers and two naval schools (one in French and one in English) were established. In 1879 a telegraph college was started; in 1890, the Imperial Naval College; in 1892, a college of mining and engineering; and in 1893, an army medical college. What was to become Peiyang University was planned by the great viceroy Li Hung-chang as early as 1887 but did not come into being until after the Sino-Japanese War of 1894–95. Nanyang College in Shanghai was founded in 1897. Thus, at the turn of the century there were only ten government and private post-secondary institutions, and all but one of these were specialized vocational schools. The four or five Protestant colleges constituted at this stage a major force in the modernizing of China's education.

Except for this handful of modern, Western-influenced institutions, public higher education, like all education in China, continued to follow time-hallowed patterns and practices. This was a literary education, completely classical, depending largely on memory, and culminating in a series of examinations which qualified one for office. It was primarily professional in that it led to the holding of government office, and it had little vocational character other than training in the art of composition and the amassing of a store of literary references and quotations. The ladder of scholarship led, after years of non-institutional study and the passing of the requisite examinations, to the *hsiu ts'ai, chü jen*, and *chin shih* classifications, which roughly approximated bachelor's, master's, and doctor's degrees. No official position of any significance was attainable without one of these titles. Examinations were given throughout the country, those for the first degree in every prefecture twice every three years, the second in provincial capitals every third year, and the third at Peking, also once every three years. Competition was stiff and only one out of fifteen of the candidates for the *chü jen* could hope for success, while rarely more than 250 *chü jen* became *chin shih*. Theoretically admission to the ladder was open to all—and successful sons of peasants were not unknown—but practically it depended on the ability to finance many years of schooling and tutoring.

Such an education was obviously narrow and artificial. Yet its severity usually assured the selection of men of considerable ability and its uniformity contributed to a cultural unity in Chinese society. Above all, by giving the scholar official rank and popular esteem, it was largely responsible for the tremendous desire for education shown by Chinese youth throughout the days of the empire, which remained a dominant factor in the life of the republic. Yet it was clearly inadequate to meet the demands of a modern world with its growing dependence on technology, its exploding international relations, and its growing social unrest. China's education had to be replaced.

2
The First Christian Colleges

It was during this period of tottering Empire, forcibly opened doors, and increasing awareness of the rest of the world, that Christian education in China had its start and that the first Christian colleges came into being. Almost from the beginning education was an integral phase of the development of Protestant missions. It soon became an increasingly important part.

The beginnings of Christian education in China were far from impressive. Shortly before the middle of the nineteenth century three small schools (boys' and girls' boarding schoools in Ningpo and a boys' school in Shanghai) were started by Protestant missionaries along the coast, in ports opened by the Treaty of Nanking. Some fifteen years later came the first schools in the political and cultural heartland of China, the area north of the Yellow River. These were girls' and boys' schools in historic Shantung Province and similar schools in and near Peking, the capital. They were courageous but modest beginnings, the largest starting with some thirty students and some still numbering less than a dozen at the end of the first decade. It would have been difficult if not impossible for the observer to have recognized in such humble and often feeble efforts the shape of things to come. That they were future colleges and universities in embryo probably occurred to few if any of the founders.

The next twenty years, however, saw rapid growth in size and numbers. Following modest and insecure beginnings many primary schools became stronger and quickly added secondary departments known as "middle schools." Ultimately some of these undertook post-secondary work and finally could legitimately be referred to as colleges.

Public reaction to these early schools, whatever the motivation behind them, was often far from favorable. Mrs. Nevius' school for girls in Shantung in 1862 aroused the suspicion that the students were to be boiled to produce a highly medicinal oil. The boarding school for boys started by the Mateers two years later had difficulty recruiting students

24

even with the lure of free clothes, food, and instruction because those two early missionaries were suspected of seeking the boys' blood for purposes of magic. Similar suspicions of Catholic orphanages lay behind the so-called Tientsin Massacre of 1870 when a dozen sisters and priests and the French consul were killed. Both Catholics and Protestants were sufferers in the widespread riots in the Yangtze Valley in 1890 and 1891 which resulted from similar inflammatory rumors. Generally, however, suspicion ebbed and students were attracted by a type of education different from the traditional Chinese pattern and as yet available only in mission schools. These were almost the only institutions where some form of modern knowledge could be secured. Before long, most schools had all the applicants they could handle.

Not only was there no antagonism toward additional elementary schools but new secondary departments received a warm welcome. While few Chinese were yet thinking in terms of still higher modern education, the way was being prepared for the first colleges. These came into being in a climate where thirst for knowledge far outweighed suspicion of source. They were in the first instances logical additions to the elementary levels already established. Before the end of the nineteenth century, Protestant schools of all grades numbered more than twelve hundred and were enrolling some twenty-five thousand students. At the time, they constituted a very significant part of modern education in China and had laid the foundations for the national system of schools which developed rapidly after the turn of the century.

Why Christian colleges in a non-Christian land? The basic original motivation was undoubtedly evangelistic—the need, through Christian education, to provide members and leaders for the developing Christian Church. There was also the desire to continue under Christian auspices the education of the children of the Church. In some cases there may have been the natural tendency to add another stage to a structure, often denominational, which had already seen high schools erected on elementary foundations. However, the training of Christian leaders, clergy and lay, was probably dominant. The argument was early advanced that it would be cheaper to train church workers in this manner than to send out more missionaries, an argument which, however logical, did nothing to stem the flood that saw over eight thousand Protestant missionaries in China in 1927. But mission stations, increasing rapidly in number and activity, had no trouble at first in absorbing all the trained workers that could be produced.

Early missionary goals naturally focused on evangelism through conversion. Education was thought of as auxiliary. When, at the 1877 missionary conference, Calvin Mateer, that forward-looking conservative, called for a further role for education, many disagreed, some even insisting on abandonment of "secular" education. While most agreed that education was indispensable in Christianizing and enlightening the heathen Chinese, Devello Z. Sheffield, though soon to father a college himself, disagreed. During the next decade, however, he and others found themselves giving more and more time to education—partly as the result of disappointing returns from direct evangelism. By 1890 Sheffield himself was arguing for education as a missionary task and had become an enthusiastic proponent of higher education. This conversion did not, however, alter his determination that the objective should be the production of Christians who would work in building the Church. The purpose of his North China College in 1893 was given as follows: "It exists in fact as well as in name for Christ and the Church. It does not even aim to fit men for the many newly opening avenues of profitable employment under government control."

Earlier, in 1877, Bishop Schereschewsky's "Appeal for Establishing a Missionary College in China" had argued that "if education has been an element of such importance in establishing Christianity in the West, have we any reason to believe that it will be a less powerful agent in establishing Christianity in the East?" A somewhat broader goal was set in 1885 by the Reverend B.C. Henry in outlining plans for the institution which eventually became Lingnan University. He stated that "The object of the proposed Christian college is to raise up educated men to be Christian ministers, teachers and physicians, as well as for every other calling in life, . . . It will seek . . . the enlightenment and Christianization of China." The "Basis of Union in Educational Work" drawn up in Shantung in 1902 struck a similar note when it stated that "The aim of the Union Colleges shall be first and foremost the furtherance of the cause of Christ in China," but added that the purpose was "to permeate society with men and women with Christian ideals and motives."

Evangelization, however, was not the only factor. Even in the early stages education as an end in itself and a logical expression of Christian concern for the mind as well as for the body (medicine) and spirit (evangelism) also played a part. The motivation behind such a venture as the Mateer school in Tengchow was strongly educational. Especially with the development of secondary education, the early largely evangelistic concern became less than completely adequate. The Christian response to intellectual hunger and need provided part of the justification for the growing educational demands on missionary funds and personnel.

With the development of truly higher education in recognized four-year institutions, more specifically educational goals came to be powerful and clearly articulated factors. The religious motivation came to include the moral and spiritual impact on students who might never themselves profess the Christian faith. Furthermore, many soon saw that higher education was not an efficient or economical means of evangelization. Even the training of leaders for the church became of necessity a secondary objective as swelling enrolments obviously exceeded any conceivable number of candidates for the ministry. The intellectual and moral training of future citizens, whether Christian or non-Christian, began to receive increasing emphasis. A major motive came to be the broader concept of Christian service to China through the production of graduates equipped with modern knowledge and imbued with Christian ideals. The goal of something called "Christian education," "education of distinctively Christian character," which was neither wholly evangelistic nor wholly secular, was to become dominant, implicitly and explicitly, in the establishment of Protestant colleges and universities through the first half of the twentieth century.

Whatever the exact motivation in each instance, such undertakings were acts of faith, expressions of hope, and manifestations of love. However confused the immediate motives, behind each beginning lay a deep concern for the welfare of the Chinese people, a driving desire to serve, and the courage to attempt the impossible. They were altruistic and often visionary responses to human need—individual and group.

During the last two decades of the nineteenth century, missionary interest in higher education found expression in the adding of collegiate departments to middle-school foundations in five centers. Three of these were in the north, two on the east coast. In 1882, in the remote prefectural town of Tengchow, in Shantung Province, the American Presbyterians started Tengchow College. Six years later, in Peking, the American Methodists opened Peking University. The next year in the nearby city of Tungchow, the American Congregationalists set up North China College. Farther south, soon after the start of Tengchow College, the American Episcopalians developed St. John's College in Shanghai. In 1893, a hundred miles southwest of that city, American Presbyterians instituted Hangchow Presbyterian College. At the end of the century, the first four were all of full collegiate standing, the fifth still a junior college. These were the first China Colleges.

TENGCHOW COLLEGE

The first institution to achieve true collegiate standing was Tengchow College, the predecessor of Shantung Christian University. This had its beginnings in the boarding school for boys started in 1864 by Calvin and Julia Mateer of the American Presbyterian Mission at Tengchowfu in historic Shantung Province. The Mateers had difficulty finding pupils but finally succeeded in enrolling six boys, all under eleven, only one of whom could read.

In ten years, after such an inauspicious start, this school had developed into a high school which in 1877 graduated three young men who, though only middle-school graduates, came to be listed as the first graduates of Shantung Christian University. Not until after five years, however, in 1882, was the school recognized as a college and given the name Tengchow College. The locally preferred name of the College of Shantung was considered by New York to be presumptuous.

At that time, the course of study presented "such a combination of Chinese classics, Western Science, and Religious Instruction as has been found to best subserve the purpose for which the college was established. Several desirable branches, *e.g.* Mental Science and Physical Geography, have been omitted for want of suitable textbooks." The courses in the Chinese Classics followed the customary pattern except for the attention given to the writing of essays in the vernacular, an innovation dimly foreshadowing the Literary Renaissance of 1917. The Western Studies, reflecting Mateer's scientific interests, including a surprising amount of Mathematics, Physics, Chemistry, Astronomy, Physiology, and Geology, as well as courses in Universal History and Political Economy. Instruction in Religion and Moral Science covered Evidences of Christianity, *Pilgrim's Progress*, the Philosophy of the Plan of Salvation, the Epistle to the Romans, and a course in Moral Science.

Calvin Mateer, founder and first president of Tengchow College, brought to his task an extraordinary combination of talents and interests. Not at first interested in education and strongly preferring preaching to teaching, he came to be an enthusiastic educator, a pedagogical innovator, and a prolific producer of textbooks and other educational materials. He built equipment for experiments in electricity and optics while giving, in his own words, "a fuller course of experiments in philosophy or chemistry than I saw myself." Part of his first furlough, after thirteen years in the field, he spent at the Baldwin Locomotive Works. Meeting Cyrus Field, layer of the first trans-Atlantic cable, he got from him a dynamo for his school and installed the first electric lights in the area. He also found time to produce his "Mandarin Lessons," which served as the standard text for generations of students of the official Chinese language. Freed from the presidency of Tengchow College, he spent the last dozen years of his life as chairman of the Committee on Revision of the Mandarin translation of the Bible.

Tengchow College continued under the presidency of Calvin Mateer until 1895. At that time the faculty comprised four or five missionaries and five Chinese, four of whom were products of the college. Mateer was succeeded by Watson Hayes, who shared his literary productivity, authoring thirty-seven original works and translations. In 1897 Hayes was joined by the Reverend Henry Winters Luce, who was to contribute so much to two of the China Colleges. By 1900 Tengchow had nearly fifty students.

ST. JOHN'S COLLEGE

A rival to Tengchow for the title of oldest Protestant college was St. John's College in Shanghai, which, though introducing post-secondary courses in the early eighties, did not undertake a full program until some years later. This was an outgrowth of a boys' school Bishop William James Boone of the Protestant Episcopal Church of America had established in 1847. Reflecting the greater prosperity in that new treaty port area, it started with thirty-two pupils. In 1879 Boone's school and another Episcopal school in Shanghai were moved to a new site, that of the future university, and combined as St. John's College, then still a secondary school.

St. John's was very much the result of one man's vision, that of the Reverend Samuel I. J. Schereschewsky. Before leaving America in 1877 for his new charge, Bishop Schereschewsky issued an "Appeal for Establishing a Missionary College in China" in which he wrote, " . . . it seems to me that our endeavor to propagate the Christian religion among such people as the Chinese (without education) would be most unwise, for among heathen nations there are few where literature is so identified with national life." This Chinese respect for the written word is a recurrent theme in early Protestant justification of educational programs. Though his tenure as bishop lasted only until 1883, when a paralyzing stroke forced his retirement, Schereschewsky saw the "college" boasting five departments: a primary department, a "collegiate" department, a department of theology, a medical department, and a soon-abandoned Anglo-Chinese department, the main purpose of which was the teaching of English for business, a purpose which continued to influence St. John's program throughout its life. The faculty numbered five, of whom one was Chinese, the Reverend Yen Yungching, M.A. Returning after graduation from Kenyon College, he gave the president strong support as Professor of Mathematics and Natural Philosophy and translator of scientific books. All the staff except one, a doctor, were clergymen.

Succeeding Bishop Schereschewsky as headmaster was the Reverend Francis Lister Hawks Pott, destined to be the leader of St. John's throughout most of its development. None of the early Protestant colleges was to become more the lengthened shadow of a great personality than was St. John's, where Pott was to give form to Schereschewsky's vision of a great Christian university. Arriving on the field committed to a life of evangelism, he was not too pleased at being made, by episcopal direction, an educator, but soon developed into an able administrator, a firm disciplinarian, and an admired educational leader. Though a theologian by training, he believed in the teaching of natural sciences "for understanding the unity and revelation of God." "Scientific training," he felt, "is the enemy of superstition and the best form of mental training one can give." He was to serve St. John's for forty-eight years.

During the last decade of the nineteenth century, one of unrest and turmoil which threatened at times to interrupt its program, the institution's development continued, with acquisition of land, expansion of the physical plant, and strengthening of the academic program. The collegiate, theological, and medical departments all soon offered some post-secondary courses though continuing to be partly pre-collegiate. In 1899 the college consisted of three departments: Arts and Sciences, Medicine, and Theology. It enrolled sixteen students.

PEKING UNIVERSITY

Farther north, in and near Peking, there were other early beginnings. In 1862 the London Missionary Society and the American Presbyterians both started schools for boys. In 1864, Mrs. Eliza J. Bridgman, widow of the first American Protestant missionary to China, began what later developed into Bridgman Academy. In 1870, the

American Methodist Mission opened a small day school with three boys enticed by the offer of a bowl of rice at the end of each day. These four schools were all in Peking. In 1867, at Tungchow, fourteen miles to the east, the Reverend Lyman D. Chapin of the American Board Mission opened a boys' boarding school without mission approval or support. Out of these and other beginnings, ultimately grew six institutions of higher education, four of which were to unite, after years of not always harmonious discussion, to form Yenching University. The earliest of these were Peking University and North China College.

First to achieve collegiate status was the Methodist institution, which became a secondary school in 1876 and "Peking University" in 1888, when four-year post-secondary work commenced. The intention was to develop a university with colleges of liberal arts, science, theology, and medicine, in addition to preparatory and industrial schools. A board of trustees was organized in America and incorporated in 1890 under the laws of the State of New York. In 1892 a field Board of Managers included such distinguished members as the American and Dutch Ministers, the Inspector General of the Chinese Imperial Maritime Customs, and the President of the Imperial T'ung Wen College, as well as representatives of the Methodist Mission. It was assumed at that time that the university had been granted a charter. Actually the New York legislature had merely approved the filing of a certificate of incorporation. Unaware that the trustees had not been given the authority to grant degrees, the university conferred the A.B. degree in 1892 on the first five graduates from the Arts College, and M.D. degrees as early as 1898. This situation was not fully corrected until a quarter of a century later.

A single two-story building provided administrative space, classrooms, and dormitory for an enrolment that soon exceeded one hundred. The faculty included a number of able men and women. The first president died shortly after assuming office. His successor, Dr. Hiram H. Lowry, was another theologian turned educator. A man of vision and statesmanship, he was firmly committed to the concept of non-denominational Christian higher education. The extent of that vision is suggested by his having urged plans for an assembly hall seating twenty-five hundred. That he taught both theology and astronomy suggests his versatility. Associated with him was Frank D. Gamewell, A.M., S.T.B., Professor of Chemistry and Physics, who had had two years of engineering before taking a degree in theology. He won fame through his skill in superintending the construction of fortifications during the Siege of Peking. Later he became superintendent of all Methodist educational work in China and General Secretary of the China Christian Educational Association.

NORTH CHINA COLLEGE

The second school in the Peking area to achieve collegiate status was the boarding school at Tungchow, an important port on the Grand Canal, through which passed both tribute rice and expectant scholars on their way to the capital until the railroad built in 1897 bypassed the city and siphoned off its trade. By 1886 this had become a high school to which were sent selected students from all American Board mission stations in North China. In 1889 it added a four-year college for which students would prepare through five years of elementary school and four of secondary.

This institution was largely the work of the Reverend D. Z. Sheffield, D.D., one of the great personalities of early Protestant education. Though not a college man himself, he became so competent a Chinese scholar that he was appointed chairman of a committee to revise the *wen li* (literary language) translation of the Bible, produced in literary Chinese a widely read *History of the World*, and built a Chinese typewriter with five thousand characters. He was ahead of his time in seeking to adapt the Chinese language to the needs of modern education and modern society. Chinese scholars and officials held him in the highest esteem. From him came the proposal for a united program of higher education in the Peking area, involving four missions and ultimately resulting in Yenching University.

As early as 1882 the Reverend Charles A. Stanley had proposed for North China an American Board-sponsored "Anglo-Chinese College," especially for the teaching of Western science and English and following "the standards which prevail in European and American Colleges." Neither his colleagues nor his board shared his enthusiasm, and the plan fell through. His thinking that the college should produce leaders for China in all fields, some of whom might be Christian, was diametrically opposed to Sheffield's insistence that it be a "mission college" producing Christians for the building up of the native Church. Sheffield secured board and North China mission approval, and the college was organized in 1889. Funds for the securing of land and the erection of buildings came from such diverse sources as the plates of Dr. S. Wells Williams' famous

Syllabic Dictionary of the Chinese Language, the estate of the wife of a Norwegian nobleman who was herself the daughter of a Dutch general, and a Wisconsin estate. Outside the Tungchow city wall, a dormitory-classroom building and several residences were erected on a ten-acre site.

The purpose of the institution was clear: "It lends all its energies to the training of a group of young men so thoroughly Christian in spirit that they cannot but give their services to the Church to whose life they owe their educational opportunity and for whose need they have received their training." In contrast to Peking University, which insisted on a knowledge of the English language, the North China College carried on exclusively in Chinese, both because development of that language was necessary for national self-respect and because English, it was felt, would lead away from service to the Church. The conviction was probably strengthened by the fact that the founders were themselves Chinese scholars of note.

Dr. Sheffield was the first president. He was assisted by such men and women as Dr. Chauncey Goodrich and Miss Luella Miner. Dr. Goodrich, also of the American Board, was a member of the committee revising the Mandarin translation of the Bible, a hymnologist who produced the Protestant hymnbook which was to remain the standard for half a century, and editor of a widely used Chinese-English Dictionary. He later became Dean of the new North China Union Theological Seminary in Peking. Miss Miner, a geologist who produced a Chinese textbook in that field, was to become a leading figure in the development of higher education for women.

In 1891–92 there were ten college students in a combined student body of sixty-two. The faculty consisted of five Westerners—three men and two women—and two Chinese. In 1893 the institution became two separate units: the North China College (including the "Academy") and the Gordon Memorial Theological Seminary. By 1899–1900 the college had twenty-five students.

HANGCHOW CHRISTIAN COLLEGE

Another institution with early antecedents was Hangchow Christian College. In Ningpo, a treaty port one hundred miles south of Shanghai, a boarding school had started in 1846. Twenty years later, following the Taiping Rebellion, this had moved a hundred miles west to the more important city of Hangchow, long famed for its beauty—in

Chinese proverb, one of two choice places under heaven—and praised by Marco Polo for its magnificence, but only recently opened to foreign residence. Here, what was quickly named the Hangchow Presbyterian Boys' School flourished.

In 1893, by adding two classes beyond the middle-school level, this developed into a junior college. Four years later, though it was still two years short of being a full four-year post-secondary institution, it assumed the title "Hangchow Presbyterian College." One specialty was a six-year course in English. It could report many seeking admission—"most of them from Christian families, and many of them would pay the tuition if we had room to receive them. If we had more room we could take in a larger number of men from the best families in Hangchow, who would thus come in contact with the truth and influence of the Gospel."

Two outstanding educators contributed to the early development of the college. The Reverend Junius H. Judson, who arrived in 1880, was one of the first educational missionaries in China in the sense of having been trained as an educator and assigned full time to educational work. Interested in mathematics and physics, he built up a very creditable collection of apparatus, homemade and imported, and did much to develop the work in science which laid the foundation for the future college of engineering. In 1893 the Reverend Elmer L. Mattox, M.A., joined him. Both Judson and Mattox served at times as president, and each was associated with the college for forty or more years.

The men and women to whom these institutions owed their conception and early development were an extraordinary group, most of them theologians turned educators, somtimes with reluctance but often with marked success, many of them scholars of the first rank, and all of them with considerable and often surprising talents. Deeply committed to the spiritual message which had brought them to China, they were also possessed with strong educational, scholarly, and practical concerns. They were strong-minded, even imperious, but also intensely human.

Few of the early members of the faculties of the colleges were, either by training or by first choice, educators. Most were clergymen recruited by circumstance from the sharing of their faith through evangelism into the less direct approach of education. To this group belonged the presidents of the five pre-1900 colleges and of most of those which sprang up during the next two decades. At St. John's in the late eighties, four out of five of the faculty were clergymen. Of eight men involved in the early development of what became Shantung Christian

University, only one was a layman, a civil engineer who gave up a promising career in the United States to teach in Tengchow College. And he was almost immediately transferred to other work.

Lack of specialization in other areas than theology did not, however, prevent these early theologian-educators from undertaking difficult assignments and achieving remarkable results, even in the sciences. Theologians produced or translated essential textbooks in arithmetic, algebra, geometry, chemistry, physics, astronomy, physiology, geology, history, and political economy, as well as in religion and moral science. They prepared Chinese versions of the Bible, hymnbooks, and dictionaries of the Chinese language, and even an encyclopedia. They initiated creative developments such as museums. They were early participants in archaeological research.

They also undertook incredible teaching assignments. At Hangchow, Mr. Mattox taught courses in Plan of Salvation, Organic, Inorganic, and Analytical Chemistry, General History, Arithmetic, and English. He later added Political Economy. At Shantung, the Reverend Paul D. Bergen taught Old and New Testament, Zoology, Botany, and Comparative Religion, while his colleague, the Reverend E. W. Burt, undertook Psychology, Logic, Economics, History, and Life of Christ. The Reverend Henry W. Luce, whose real interest was New Testament and who had been charged with English, was at times saddled with History, Pedagogy, Physics, and Mathematics. Obviously, in China as in the United States, over-specialization was at that time no threat.

Thus, as the nineteenth century drew to a close, Protestant missions in China could boast five institutions clearly engaged in higher education: three in North China—one each in Peking, Tungchow, and Tengchow—and two in East China—one in Shanghai and one in Hangchow. There were other institutions which claimed collegiate status and many which were called colleges—two even assuming the title of university. One of the problems in recounting the beginnings of Protestant higher education in China derives from the British practice of referring to university-preparatory schools as colleges. From the start of missionary secondary schools there were many "Anglo-Chinese" and other "Colleges" which made no pretense of offering more than a secondary education and were simply high schools or, to use the Chinese term, middle schools. Even Tsinghua College, established in 1911 with American Boxer Indemnity Funds, was first a high school and then, for a time, a junior college preparing for American colleges. Some, to be sure, did add a few post-secondary courses, but true college-level work appeared only with the development of four-year institutions designed to give a B.A. or equivalent degree. Even theology and medicine, as offered by these early "colleges," were taught at a secondary level. Nanking University, despite its name, made no pretense of offering college work until after 1900. Canton Christian College, with a New York charter which classified it as a university, had no students in its collegiate department until well into the twentieth century.

The five institutions meriting college status at the end of the century were far from impressive. All five together could muster only a little over one hundred students. However, Peking University claimed with some justification that its standards were "as high as in the Occident." Considering the standards of many American institutions of that era, this may not have been either an unfounded or a particularly boastful claim.

At the same time these five institutions constituted a not unimpressive development from the tentative elementary stirrings in the mid-nineteenth century, and a truly significant contribution to Chinese education both in quantity—roughly half the total higher education available—and as pioneer and pattern-setting institutions.

Part
2
The Colleges Take Shape
(1900-1920)

3
Revolution and Change:
China 1900-1920

The year 1900 provides a convenient landmark in both political and missionary history, but the Boxer Uprising caused only a brief interruption in either the process of political and cultural change or the work of missions. Revolutionary movements grew in strength as the empire slowly collapsed. Very soon educational reform and the development of mission education at all levels were proceeding at a greatly accelerated pace. The next twenty years were to bring in a modern and tremendously expanded system of public education and to see both an eager proliferation and a painful concentration of Protestant higher education.

Politically, the tottering dynasty undertook reorganization in an attempt to suppress revolution. A constitution was promised and a national assembly was even convened. But adequate leadership was lacking, especially after the death of both the Empress Dowager and Emperor Kuang Hsü in November 1908. When the long-simmering revolution finally boiled over in Central China in October 1911, it took only four months for the Ch'ing Dynasty to fall. The monarchical form of government which had unified China through many centuries was suddenly replaced by a weak and inexperienced republic.

The new Republic was to have an unhappy and sickly childhood. The Revolution had opened a new era of potential progress—political, social, economic, and intellectual. Hopes were high and enthusiasm was rampant among the young and liberal. It was a time of ferment and of movement. But not all ferment was constructive, and not all movement was to be successful or even forward. The problems involved were too great for the easy fulfilment of expectations. Numbers were too vast— and too largely illiterate. For masses of the people, living continued little if at all above the famine level. The country was fragmented by provincial self-interest and individual loyalties. Aside from a few such as Dr. Sun himself, who had received most of his formal education in mission

39

institutions, leaders had little conception of and no experience in dis-
interested public service. Rebellion succeeded rebellion, with two brief
restorations of the monarchy. Warlords became dominant, and cliques
controlled the government. By 1920 the country was divided, not only
into North and South but among many warlords.

To these domestic problems was added the impact of World War I
and of the encroachment of foreign powers. With Japan's entry into the
war and her capture of the German-controlled port of Tsingtao, came the
notorious Twenty-One Demands of 1915, which threatened to subject
China to extensive Japanese control and exploitation. With the government's final capitulation, storms of protest swept the country. May 9,
the day on which the demands were signed, became a national day of
humiliation. In 1917 a secret agreement among the great European
powers assured Japan in her claim to German holdings in Shantung
Province, a claim confirmed by the Treaty of Versailles in June 1919, a
treaty which China refused to sign.

With these events, the Student Movement began to play the active
role which was to be so important a factor in the history of the next
decade. With industrial development, further revolutionary forces
appeared in the form of striking factory workers, many of them former
farmers who had served during the war in the labor battalions in Europe.
In 1920 China was seething with frustration and impatience and with
revolutionary movements among both intellectuals and workers.

One of the most striking changes during this period, and certainly
one of its most important developments, was the sudden and startling
outburst of modern education, which has been described as "the greatest
revolution in education the world has ever witnessed." A revolution in
itself, it contributed greatly to the success of the political revolution. The
Boxer outbreak had brought about the temporary abandonment of all
modern schools and colleges in the north. The aftermath, however, saw
even the Empress Dowager advocating reform and reviving many of
Kuang Hsü's edicts. Modern education was soon making rapid progress.
In 1901 recognition of modern schools by the government permitted
graduates to move, through a series of examinations at Peking Government University, up the ladder of civil service degrees. The members
of the Hanlin Academy, usually winners of distinction in the highest
official examinations, were ordered to study ancient and modern history,
politics, and Western learning to prepare themselves for government
service, and encouraged to take courses at Peiyang University and
Nanyang College. Fresh impetus to study abroad came when returning

students became eligible for official appointment. A plan for the first modern educational system in China, copied after Japan, stirred change throughout the country. In 1905 an edict abolished the system of examinations which had been the mark of Chinese education for two thousand years.

The last six years of the Manchu Dynasty saw both introduction of a modern educational system and unprecedented expansion of modern learning in China. The first system, in 1903, set sights too high, calling for an impossible program of seventeen preparatory years prior to a three-to-four-year university. On top of this life-consuming sequence, was further imposed a five-year "school of research." Reorganization along European rather than Japanese lines resulted in substantial reductions of time: lower and higher primaries totaling seven years, a middle school of four, and three years of university "preparatory"— altogether fourteen years of preparation. Further American-modeled revisions produced by 1922 the pattern followed throughout the rest of China's republican history: six years of primary school and six years of secondary leading to four years in the university. The response to this new program was startling. By 1910 there were over fifty thousand government, public, and private schools in the country. Students in modern schools numbered over a million and a half. And numbers continued to soar. Enrollment in mission schools also mushroomed. By the end of the period Protestants and Catholics could claim a combined total of more than a million students.

Among the first developments was the establishment of government colleges and universities. By the time of the Revolution three imperial universities—the Imperial University in Peking, established by the Emperor in 1898, Peiyang University in Tientsin, and Shansi University in Taiyuan—had a total of nearly four thousand students. The last had been founded with funds provided by the provincial government, but declined by the missions, as indemnity for the lives of missionaries killed in 1900. A number of provincial colleges had also developed. At the same time, as many as thirteen thousand students were studying in Japan, many in colleges and universities. Ten years later, institutions of higher education of all types numbered nearly a hundred.

That in the early stages of this development the Chinese government turned for leadership to the ranks of the missionaries constitutes a striking commentary on both the lack of trained Chinese and the standing of missionary educators. Prior to 1900, Dr. Charles D. Tenney, an American missionary, had been head of Peiyang University, and Dr. John C. Ferguson of Nanking, President of Nanyang. In addition, Tengchow College had provided thirteen Chinese professors, all Christian, for the new imperial institutions at Peking, Nanking, and Shanghai, while St. John's had contributed three to Nanyang. For the post-1900 institutions the government called upon Dr. W.A.P. Martin to head the new Imperial University at Peking. The Reverend Watson M. Hayes, who had succeeded Mateer at Tengchow, was asked to start the new Shantung University. The Reverend Timothy Richard, an English Baptist, was the moving force behind the new Shansi University, while the Reverend Duncan Moir of the same society was its first president. These appointments were not made without protest, however, on the part of Chinese scholars who resented such reliance on foreign personnel.

4

The Colleges: Merger and Growth

The new political and educational atmosphere found the first Protestant colleges eager to move ahead, secondary schools anxious to become colleges, and various individuals and groups with visions of new institutions. They were encouraged by the Centenary Missionary Conference held in Shanghai in 1907, which urged the developing of the colleges already started and the founding of new ones since "the effort now being put forth is in no sense commensurate with the opportunities at our door." New centers of higher education developed in rapid succession, adding to the five in existence at the end of the century, Soochow and Nanking in East China, Canton and Foochow in South China, Chengtu in West China, and several centers in Central China.

While new institutions were springing up with varying degrees of success, older ones were undergoing transformation. For the five colleges of the nineteenth century, the twentieth century appeared, once the wounds of 1900 had healed, to offer opportunity limited only by the ability to respond. Those associated with them shared the excitement and optimism of the new day. The process turned out to be slow and often painful, and dreams were by no means all fulfilled. But the results achieved were considerable and, all things considered, highly commendable. Tengchow College, after two moves and a merger, became Shantung Christian University; North China Union College and Peking University, with help from North China Union Women's College, became a new Peking University; Hangchow Presbyterian College became Hangchow Christian College; and St. John's College grew in size and quality into St. John's University.

Not all the other colleges survived. Opportunity was unlimited, ambition and hope were great, dedication and devotion were marked, but resources were often inadequate, while human weakness proved a serious obstacle. By 1910 there were eighteen institutions with a combined enrolment of one thousand. By 1920 some thirty institutions had achieved at least junior-college standing, though only sixteen, with a total of sixteen hundred students, were functioning as four-year colleges. During this time, in spite of their weaknesses, while national and other secular institutions were developing, they provided a considerable portion, and some of the best, of all opportunities for higher education.

SHANTUNG CHRISTIAN UNIVERSITY

For Tengchow College, though it had suffered only temporary suspension of activity during the Boxer days, the first years of the new century brought great change. Although the college reopened in Tengchow, by 1904 it had moved to a new location and had become part of a new union enterprise in education. From the remote and backward provincial town which had been its birthplace because of the chance presence there of the Mateers, it had been transferred to Weihsien, an important city in the heart of Shantung Province. Weihsien was a compromise between remaining in Tengchow and moving to Tsinan, the provincial capital, both of which places had their warm advocates.

The idea of cooperation in Shantung had been set forth in a 1902 statement on the "Basis of Union in Educational Work," in which the American Presbyterian Mission and the English Baptist Mission in Shantung agreed to unite in organizing three colleges—arts, theology, and medicine—with each mission retaining ownership of its own campus but sharing equally in the current expenses of all schools. Opposition was not lacking, but the agreement was carried out. At Weihsien, eighty-five students from Tengchow were joined by thirty from the Tsingchow High School, an English Baptist boys' boarding school. These constituted the arts college, named Shantung Union College. Presbyterian students from Tengchow joined Baptist students at Tsingchow, a short distance away, to form Gotch-Robinson Theological College. A scheme of peripatetic medical training under four mission doctors in four centers provided the start of the Union Medical College.

Four missionaries, two English and two American, and ten Chinese constituted the faculty at Shantung Union College in 1904. Among the Westerners were such men as the Reverend Samuel Couling, an English Baptist who in his spare time compiled an *Encyclopedia Sinica* which was published by the Oxford University Press, and who was one of the first to collect the archaeological objects known as oracle bones; and Henry W. Luce, an American Presbyterian, one of the great modern missionary educators who was to be instrumental in the development of two universities. Paul D. Bergen, another Presbyterian who was affectionately known to the Chinese as "Chün-tzu," the princely man of Confucian thought, was elected president, a post he held, except for a brief period, until 1913, when ill health forced his return to the States.

The College of Medicine, which had such a modest and homeless beginning, soon secured a firmer base. In 1910 it opened in Tsinan in its own building, erected with funds from England. Support came from the Baptists, who also sent Harold Balme, F.R.C.S., D.P.H., who was later to serve as President of the University. Under the leadership of such men as Dr. Randolph T. Shields of the Southern Presbyterians, Dr. William McClure of the Canadian Presbyterians, and Dr. Thomas Gillison of the London Mission, the college soon became the strongest part of the institution, a position it held until the end.

The advantages of a common site for the educational activities carried on at Tsingchow, Weihsien, and Tsinan had been increasingly apparent even before the Oriental Education Commission headed by Professor Ernest D. Burton of the University of Chicago had in 1909 inspired a recommendation that the university be concentrated at Tsinan, the capital and cultural center of Shantung Province. A site was selected just outside the wall surrounding the Tsinan city suburbs and close to the Medical College and the Institute, and Henry W. Luce was called on to find the needed funds. Leaving in 1912, he spent the next three years in the arduous but ultimately successful task of raising a total of $305,000.

In 1917 the College of Arts moved from Weihsien, and the College of Theology and the Normal School from Tsingchowfu, the last becoming part of the new College of Arts and Sciences. Few buildings were ready, construction having been delayed by World War I and the resulting depreciation of the American dollar from over two dollars in Chinese currency to practical parity. Only the smallness of the student body, numbering less than two hundred, made a start possible. Coming together on one campus did not mean smooth sailing. Clashes between personalities and friction between national and denominational groups shortly came to a head. Difficulties in administration resulted in a change in the presidency, the withdrawal of most senior officers, and the departure of all eighteen Presbyterian theological students, who followed Watson Hayes back to Weihsien.

One issue which continued lively throughout Shantung's history involved the emphasis on the Chinese language which constituted one of

45

the institution's claims to uniqueness. The constituent colleges had all concentrated on instruction in Chinese. With the nation-wide interest in foreign laguages, however, this policy came to be questioned. In 1906 a student strike had as one of its demands the teaching of English. President Bergen's·proposal for the introduction of English because "sooner or later we will have to make the concession to universal demand" was at first rejected and then reluctantly approved on a very restricted basis. English continued to be a little-emphasized elective and never became a tool of instruction until the first Chinese chairman of the field board insisted on greater freedom. The College of Medicine ultimately became practically bilingual, but Shantung as a whole maintained its emphasis on instruction through the medium of Chinese.

Through the years of the Chinese Revolution and the First World War, the college continued to develop, with further additions to its interdenominational character taking place. The Anglicans in 1909 sent a teacher and eleven students from their two schools. In 1916 the Canadian Presbyterian Church became interested in the medical college. The next year the transfer to Tsinan of the Nanking Medical College and the Union Medical College of Hankow brought the Southern Presbyterians of the United States and the London Missionary and Wesleyan Methodist Missionary Societies of England into the picture. The English Presbyterian Church also had a small share in the support of the medical college. In 1920 the American Board (Congregational) and in 1925 the Woman's Foreign Missionary Society of the Methodist Episcopal Church joined the ranks, bringing mission-board participation to a total of eleven societies—five British, five American, and one Canadian—making Shantung the most broadly international of all Protestant colleges in China.

NORTH CHINA COLLEGE AND PEKING UNIVERSITY

Farther north, in and near Peking, the Boxer Rebellion had brought disaster to both the North China College and Peking University, the buildings of both institutions having been burned to the ground. The new century, however, saw the slow and painful coming together of these and other beginnings in higher education in what was to prove a very strong and effective union.

Undismayed by the complete destruction of the Peking University plant, Dr. Lowry in the fall of 1900 gathered together twenty-eight former students and started classes. By the second semester, enrolment had grown sixfold. With the purchase of additional land, the erection of new buildings, the return of Western faculty members, and the recruitment of Chinese teachers, the university began a period of steady growth. Among the Americans were two men with doctorates, Isaac Taylor Headland, Professor of Mental and Moral Science and later famed for his *Court Life in China* and other glimpses of Chinese life; and H.E. King, Professor of History and International Law. At its twenty-fifth anniversary in 1913, Peking University, still unaware that it lacked power to do so, gave honorary doctorates to a number of Chinese and Westerners, the latter including Professor Paul Monroe of Columbia University and President Angell of the University of Michigan.

Development also took place in the theological and medical fields. The Wiley College of Theology, started by the Methodists before 1900, combined with the North China Union Theological College set up by the Congregationalists at the same time but shared by the Presbyterians after 1905. This became part of Peking University in 1915. Leading roles in developing this institution and bringing it into the union were played by the Reverend Chauncey Goodrich, D.D., whose scholarly achievements have already been described, and the Reverend Courtenay H. Fenn, D.D., whose *Concordance of the Bible* was the first such work in Chinese.

Destruction at Tungchow had been so great, even bricks and foundation stones having been carried away, that temporary quarters had to be found in Peking. At Tungchow a new site of seventy acres was secured; a recitation building, a dormitory, a hospital, seven residences, and a girls' school were erected. There was also an adjoining model village for Chinese faculty, with a boys' school and a church. College work resumed there in 1902. In 1903, when the London Mission joined the American Board, the North China College became the North China Union College. To the staff came Charles H. Corbett in physics and chemistry and Lucius Porter in education, both of whom were to play activ : roles in the development of the future Yenching University.

In view of the fact that no one mission had the resources to maintain a high-grade university, Dr. Sheffield proposed to the American Board and the London, Methodist, and Presbyterian Missions a united program of higher education. A field agreement for a confederation was reached in 1903 but was turned down by two boards, in part because of doubts that Methodism and Calvinism would mix. Other negotiations resulted in 1904 in the formation of the North China Educational Union, involving three missions: the American Board, responsible for the North China Union College at Tungchow and the North China Union Women's College in Peking; the Presbyterian Mission, for the North China Union Theological Seminary in Peking; and the London Mission, for the North China Union Medical College in Peking. For some years institutional loyalties, strong personalities, denominational differences, and opposing educational theories stood in the way of more complete union.

Medical education in North China started well before the end of the nineteenth century with the opening by the Methodists of a medical department in Peking. This labored under the handicap of limited resources and staff and, when the London, American Board, and Presbyterian Missions organized the Lockhart Union Medical College, it united with that institution to form the first (Peking) Union Medical College. Dr. Thomas Cochrane of the London Mission, who had been largely responsible for organizing the new college, became its president and provided wise and energetic leadership. A North China Union Women's Medical College started in 1908 as a joint enterprise of the Methodist Women's Foreign Missionary Society and the American Board and Presbyterian Missions. However, the future Peking University was not destined to have a medical department. In 1915 the Lockhart Union Medical College was taken over by the China Medical Board of the Rockefeller Foundation for its proposed Peking Union Medical College, and nine years later the Women's Medical College joined the Medical School of Shantung Christian University.

Renewed consideration of one strong Christian university for North China had followed the Edinburgh Conference of 1910. A statement of principles was submitted in 1912 to the boards of managers of the North China Educational Union, the Peking University, and the Peking Union Medical College. Peking University responded with an offer of its campus and articles of incorporation; the American Board and Presbyterian Missions gave hesitant approval; but the London Mission rejected the offer on the grounds of propinquity to lesser schools and to the compound of one mission. The cause of union seemed about to fail when Dr. Lowry submitted a proposal relaxing Methodist ties. This was quickly approved by the first two missions and two years later by the London Mission, bringing together three institutions in a new Peking University. In December 1915 the University of the State of New York added the necessary amendment to the charter of the first Peking University.

The university's first year saw an acting president and three deans, a teaching staff of twenty-nine, and 178 students. At commencement in 1917 the university conferred thirty-four bachelor's, one master's, and three honorary degrees—still without realizing the inadequacy of its charter. The separate campuses continued until the fall of 1918, when the two men's units both moved to a site just to the east of the Methodist campus. There they were to function for the next eight years. Dr. Lowry's advanced age made necessary the finding of another president. In December 1918 the Trustees elected the Reverend John Leighton Stuart, D.D., of the Union Theological Seminary in Nanking. He assumed office in the fall of 1919.

Among alumni of the two earlier colleges were such well-known men as Shaowen James Ch'üan, active in student work and secretary to the Managing Director of the Chinese Eastern Railway and finally controller of Yenching University; Fei Ch'i-hao, government official and YMCA secretary; Dr. H.H. Kung, head of several government ministries and chairman of the boards of both Shantung and Yenching Universities; and Dr. C.C. Wang, director of several of China's railroads.

ST. JOHN'S UNIVERSITY

With the more stable conditions that followed the collapse of the Boxers, the demand in Shanghai for Western education exceeded the ability of St. John's to meet it. In 1900 St. John's could accept fewer than a third of its applicants, who included sons of officials and of holders of classical degrees. Four years later, total enrolment was 187, of whom forty-eight were in the collegiate department. Of thirteen graduates, four remained to teach at St. John's, two entered other church work, three became teachers in government schools, and four entered business. The Medical School had five students.

In 1905, Articles of Incorporation issued by the District of Columbia entitled St. John's to grant degrees. The conferring of bachelor of arts degrees on four graduates in 1907 was the first time that such degrees had been legitimately conferred in China. Among the four were Andrew Yeu-Yi (Y.Y.) Tsu, who was to become a bishop, and Ts-zong (T.Z.) Koo, for some years Associate General Secretary of the National Committee of the YMCA and a Secretary of the World's Student Christian Federation. With the B.A. degree, St. John's graduates had little difficulty entering graduate institutions in the

49

United States. In some fields, Yale and Pennsylvania accepted them without examination; Harvard, Columbia, Cornell, Chicago, and Michigan required some further undergraduate training. In 1907–8 more than thirty St. John's graduates were studying in the States and more than ten in Great Britain.

The second decade brought steady growth in spite of revolution, world war, and increasing student unrest. There were additions to both land and buildings, with the alumni contributing significantly to both. In 1913, after twenty-five years of service, Dr. Pott could point with pride to a student body of over five hundred, a quarter of them in the college department, and to alumni serving in high positions with government ministries, with educational institutions, and in business, with one a Justice of the Supreme Court and one the Chinese Minister to the U.S. The First World War had little immediate effect on St. John's, but the years that followed were stormy. The signing of the Treaty of Versailles brought on a number of student strikes which interrupted the work of the university. However, by 1920 St. John's University enrolled more than 250 students in its college department.

In 1912 the Medical School, which was finding it difficult to maintain itself, unsuccessfully attempted cooperation with the Harvard Medical School of China, a project of Harvard alumni but unrelated to that university. Two years later it was joined by the medical program formerly supported at Canton Christian College by the Christian Association of the University of Pennsylvania. Dr. Josiah C. McCracken, who had been in Canton since 1907, became Dean of the Pennsylvania Medical College of St. John's University.

HANGCHOW CHRISTIAN COLLEGE

At the start of the century Hangchow Christian College was still providing only a two-year college program though offering an occasional more advanced course. The number of these was to grow until, by the second decade, Hangchow was presenting the practical equivalent of a senior-college program. Its status, however, remained that of a junior college until the end of the second decade. Meanwhile the college continued to grow. By 1905 enrolment had reached 115, of whom thirty-five were in the junior-collegiate department. In 1906, the college moved to a new campus outside the city walls, where adequate space could be found at lower cost. The site chosen was on a bluff overlooking the nearby

Ch'ien T'ang River, a magnificent location. Gifts from friends abroad provided for purchase of land and initiation of a building program. By 1911 it was possible to move to the new campus, where the college became known as *Chih Chiang Hsüeh T'ang*, or Chih River School, *Ch'ien T'ang* and *Chih Chiang* being two names for the same river. That year there were 117 students.

The faculty, which numbered twelve, had been strengthened by the addition of several Americans who were to contribute to the development of the academic program and by recruitment of a number of well-qualified Chinese. Among the former were Robert Fitch, who served as vice-president and then, after a period with the Union Evangelistic Committee, returned as president in 1922; Arthur W. March, biologist, one of the first teachers of science appointed as such, who arrived in 1905 and was to serve the college, as department head and dean, for some forty years; and Warren H. Stuart, Professor of Religion, who became president in 1916. Among the Chinese was Chow Mei-kwang, teacher of Bible since 1900, who had been in charge of the China exhibit at the St. Louis World Fair, and who served as dean for many years. In 1918 the college became a union institution, the Northern and Southern Presbyterians having set up a joint Board of Directors.

By 1910, five of the earliest Protestant colleges had become firmly established and had achieved a commendable degree of academic respectability. Indeed, they constituted a considerable and important part of China's modern higher education. Joining their ranks were a number of new institutions, some destined to attain comparable quality and influence.

5
New Colleges

I. EAST CHINA

In East China the first decades of the new century saw not only the further development of St. John's University and Hangchow Christian College but the firm establishment, well before the period was over, of four new institutions: in Nanking, the University of Nanking and Ginling College; in Soochow, Soochow University; and in Shanghai, the University of Shanghai. These were all to achieve varying degrees of distinction and to continue signal service until submerged in the tidal wave of the mid-century.

THE UNIVERSITY OF SHANGHAI

The University of Shanghai was born of the need for trained Chinese leadership for the Baptist Church in China. In 1900, when Baptist missionaries gathered in the safety of Shanghai's International Settlement first proposed such an institution, not a single Chinese Baptist teacher or layman was even a full graduate of a secondary school, nor was there one fully graded Baptist middle school. Prospects, moreover, were not bright. Neither the Central China nor the East China Mission was strong, both together having only twenty churches with a combined membership of less than a thousand, served by ten ordained Chinese preachers. Furthermore, the missionaries themselves were not specifically trained for educational work, and no local funds were in sight. Finally, in 1906 when a start was made, there were already fourteen other Protestant "colleges" in China, four of them in East China. But the Baptist Church felt the necessity of meeting its needs more directly.

The two China Missions, Southern Baptist and American Baptist, agreed to cooperate, but at home the Southern board disapproved union and the Northern board advised delay. In 1905, however, Articles of

Co-operation in two institutions, a college and a seminary, were approved by both boards, which promised forty thousand dollars for land and buildings. A site of some twenty-six acres was soon secured six miles east of the center of Shanghai and on the bank of the Whangpoo, the river connecting city and sea. The Seminary opened in a rented building in the city while work proceeded on the new site.

Finally, early in 1909, the college opened its doors to forty-nine students in the academy (middle school) and seven in the freshman year of college. The faculty consisted of two Americans, one of them President J.J. Proctor, and five Chinese. The local Board of Trustees was composed entirely of Americans until 1912, when two Chinese members were added. That same year college and seminary united under the presidency of Dr. Francis Johnstone White, who was to serve for the next sixteen years. A man of great tact and wisdom—essential qualities for reconciling the divergent views of the founders—he gave the university outstanding leadership through difficult times. Committed to the Christian character of the institution while emphasizing the highest educational standards, he strongly believed in Chinese leadership. He was also a pioneer in co-education, Shanghai becoming the first Protestant institution of higher education formally to enrol both men and women.

Because the university did not have a charter, the first two graduates received only a certificate. In 1917, however, an American Board of Trustees secured incorporation from the State of Virginia. The university granted thirty-nine bachelor's degrees in 1919. In 1918 the filling in of fields to the south added an area of twenty-one acres to the campus. New buildings included a science hall, three dormitories, and separate buildings for the middle school. By that time enrolment in the college exceeded one hundred.

SOOCHOW UNIVERSITY

The new century had barely begun when Soochow University took the place of three Southern Methodist-related institutions, each of which had aspired to college status but had failed to achieve it. Buffington Institute in Soochow, a day school started thirty years before by a young Chinese recently returned from the States, had grown into a successful primary and middle school. The Anglo-Chinese College in Shanghai had developed out of plans for an "intercultural university" into what was primarily a secondary school attracting students eager to learn English for business purposes. In 1899 Buffington was merged into the Anglo-Chinese College, freeing the campus in Soochow for the third institution, the Kung Hung School. This had been started just before the end of the nineteenth century by D.L. Anderson in response to a request from young Chinese scholars seeking a command of English as a means of helping China to learn from the West, as Japan had done. Enrolment had rapidly risen from an initial twenty-five to over a hundred.

Plans for the educational work of the China Mission of the Methodist Episcopal Church, South, included a university in Soochow, and Kung Hung School provided the foundation for the new institution. Late in 1900, the State of Tennessee granted a charter, a board of trustees elected Anderson president, and the institution adopted the name of Tung Wu College. The name reflected the fact that Soochow was in what had been known in ancient times as Eastern (Tung) Wu. Hopes for success were encouraged by gifts and promises from America of $150,000. The first real college work began four years later, with a dozen students enrolled. The first bachelor's degree was conferred in 1907.

On the death of Dr. Anderson in 1911, Dr. John W. Cline, President of Anglo-Chinese College, became president. Students from Anglo-Chinese College, which had also developed some post-secondary courses, joined Tungwu College to form the College of Arts and Sciences of what was to become known in English as Soochow University. Following this move, Soochow had some fifty students in college courses. In addition to the original Buffington buildings, a second academic building and several residence halls and dormitories rose to meet the needs of the growing institution.

The curriculum followed the pattern of the times, with emphasis on English and science. It was in the latter field that Soochow ultimately made one of its greatest contributions, setting up a program comparable to that of standard institutions in the West and producing a considerable body of recognized scientists. The groundwork in this field was laid by two very able graduates of Vanderbilt University, Professor Nathaniel Gist Gee, biologist, and Dr. Ernest Victor Jones, chemist. The quality of these two men is indicated by the posts which they later held: Professor Gee as field agent in China of the Rockefeller Foundation's China Medical Board; Dr. Jones, professor at the University of Alabama engaging in atomic research at Oak Ridge. It was possible for B.A. graduates to take additional courses and receive the B.S. degree as well. Graduate work started in the middle of the second decade, with the first master's degree being conferred in 1917, probably the first advanced degree in chemistry awarded in China. In biology connection was established with the United States Department of Agriculture, and notable research was carried on in fresh water biology, ornithology, and entomology. The Centenary of Missions of the American Methodist Church (North and South) in 1919 brought Soochow a large and well-planned science building.

In addition to a college of liberal arts, Soochow's Tennessee charter authorized it to operate colleges of theology and medicine. Beginnings were made in both fields but full-fledged work never developed. After the establishment of a theological seminary in Nanking, Soochow limited its efforts to pre-theological courses. Similarly, the establishment of the Union Medical College in Nanking in 1912 relieved Soochow of the burden of the medical school started in 1904 and staffed by the personnel of two local hospitals, and the university limited itself to premedical training. In 1915, with ten students and more than that number of teachers, began what was to prove, along with its work in science, Soochow's greatest contribution, The Comparative Law College of China. A first class of seven were awarded the LL.B. degree in 1918.

THE UNIVERSITY OF NANKING

A hundred and fifty miles up the Yangtze River from Shanghai, the old Ming Dynasty capital of Nanking, never fully recovered from the effects of the Taiping Rebellion but destined in 1928 to replace Peking as the capital of the Chinese Republic, had long been the home of a Christian university in name if not in fact. In 1888 the Methodist Episcopal Church had appointed the Reverend John C. Ferguson president of the yet-to-be "Nanking University." There were no buildings, courses, faculty, or students; only an awareness of need. The next year the president started a small school in his home. The following year a medical department opened in connection with the mission hospital. A theological department followed. By 1907 there were three school buildings, a chapel, and over two hundred students. A few "advanced" courses were offered but fell far short of a full college program. Dr. Ferguson served as president until 1897, when he left to become head of Nanyang College in Shanghai. Later years brought him a succession of government posts and honors and an international reputation in the field of Chinese art.

The University of Nanking, a different institution from Nanking

University, had its real beginning in 1910 with the union of this Methodist "university" and the educational programs of the Disciples and the Northern Presbyterians. The former's Nanking Christian College and the latter's boys' school, both started in the late eighties but still almost wholly secondary schools, had combined in 1906 to form the Union Christian College. This too offered only a smattering of junior-college courses. The new institution took the name of *ta hsüeh*, or university, and set out at once to be a truly post-secondary institution.

Dr. Arthur J. Bowen of the Methodist Mission, head of Nanking University since 1908, was elected president; Dr. John E. Williams, founder and principal of the Presbyterian boys' school, vice-president. Bowen, a graduate of Northwestern University, was to continue as president of the University of Nanking until the appointment of the first Chinese president in 1927. Williams, a graduate of Marietta College and Auburn Theological Seminary, who had come to Nanking in 1899, had early committed himself to the uniting of all the Protestant efforts in that city into one strong Christian university and had, during two years in America, devoted himself to promotion of the idea.

Each of the three denominations had agreed to provide forty thousand dollars in cash, land, or buildings, as well as to share in staffing. Methodist and Disciples properties met this requirement but the Presbyterian assets were valued at only a quarter of the necessary amount. Dr. Williams' first task, therefore, was to raise the balance. This he succeeded in doing in time for the first meeting of the Board of Managers in 1910. The next year the home board in New York secured incorporation by the University of the State of New York. Efforts to bring into the union the new Baptist college and seminary in Shanghai failed. The field was in favor but the home board agreed only to send professors, a participation later limited to the college of agriculture and forestry.

The university had been using the land and buildings of the former Nanking University. Gifts of funds for a dormitory and a science building made possible the beginning of a new campus on Disciples land near the Drum Tower, leaving the old site to the University Middle School. In these two buildings the university was one of the first to adapt Chinese architecture to modern educational needs. At this time it numbered something over fifty students. Not until after 1920, when the figure was just under one hundred, did it begin a rapid growth in numbers.

The young university quickly extended its activities beyond the customary basic arts and sciences. In 1912, a pioneer in the field, it developed a modern language school and missionary training center which was to be an important factor in the mission work of the entire East China area. The following year the East China Union Medical College, supported by seven American missions, became a part of the university. This was an outgrowth of the medical training initiated at the time of the setting up of Nanking University. The Disciples hospital became the University Hospital. The Church Missionary Society-supported Hangchow Medical College also joined. Medical education, however, was to continue only a few years, the medical school moving in 1917 to Tsinan to become part of Shantung Christian University. In connection with the hospital, however, a School of Nursing was started in 1918.

A longer-lived development was that in agriculture and forestry, which involved several very able men. The great famine of 1911, which brought tens of thousands of destitute farmers to Nanking, stirred Joseph Bailie, then a teacher of mathematics in the University Middle School, to seek a constructive means of assisting them. Gathering a few hundred men together, he set them to work clearing land, planting potatoes and beans, and making roads. On land outside the city, turned over by the controlling temple, he settled other hundreds. Later, in a longer-term development, thousands of fruit trees were planted on the slopes of Purple Mountain, just beyond the city walls. Bailie's "Colonization Scheme" received financial support from local merchants as well as from the Central Famine Relief Commission and the endorsement of such Chinese leaders as President Sun Yat-sen, Prime Minister Tang Shao-yi, the Viceroy, and the Minister of Communications and Agriculture. Out of Bailie's enthusiasm and these rough beginnings, a department of agriculture developed in 1914. The following year it was joined by a department of forestry. Shortly thereafter the Department of Industry and Agriculture of the Chinese Government closed its own school and sent the students to the University of Nanking.

II. SOUTH CHINA

The term "South China," covering that great extent of coast south of Shanghai on which most early treaty ports were situated, has a certain geographical and historical usefulness but represents little physical or cultural unity. The provinces of Kwangtung and Fukien, with Canton and Foochow as their respective capitals, spoke widely differing dialects,

SHORT

as indeed did different parts of Fukien, and their inhabitants had long had strong provincial loyalties. One institution could hardly serve both areas, and Protestant colleges developed in both Canton and Foochow.

In Canton, the original port of entry of foreign missions and center of the area from which the main stream of Chinese emigration took place, Canton Christian College, which had long held a charter as a college but had had only a few post-secondary courses and still fewer students, finally achieved a condition matching its title. Though it was one of the first of the China Colleges to be incorporated, the New York Regents granting a charter in 1893, a quarter of a century passed before it actually became a four-year college in 1910.

Fukien Province, shut off from the rest of China by high mountains and using dialects relatively unintelligible to speakers of both Mandarin and Cantonese, looked upon itself, and indeed was often looked upon, as little affected by what went on elsewhere. Though many of its students did find opportunity for education in other parts of the country, missionaries were convinced of the need for higher education in Fukien for Fukienese. The result was an absence of interest in educational developments elsewhere and a concentration on local needs. Efforts and problems in higher education were domestic. To meet these local needs, two institutions developed in the middle of the second decade of the twentieth century. There had been stirrings much earlier and some tentative explorations. Two "colleges" had attempted some post-secondary instruction and were not without ambition to rise in status. Finally, at Foochow, a port which had been the destination of many a New England clipper ship, colleges for women and men started in 1914 and 1916.

FUKIEN CHRISTIAN UNIVERSITY

Unlike many of its sister institutions, Fukien Christian University did not develop gradually from earlier primary and secondary schools, though existing "colleges" did share temporarily in its start. Neither did it spring in any sense full-grown but went through protracted planning and slow development. But it was more clearly a new institution designed for higher education. To some extent it was the result of the Edinburgh Missionary Conference of 1910, that conference's Commission on "Education in Relation to the Christianization of National Life" having sponsored a plan calling, in the case of China, for institutions in four centers, one of them Foochow. In 1911 the chairman of the

Commission's Sub-Committee on Higher Education, John Goucher, arrived in Foochow.

Sixty-six at the time, John Goucher had served from 1890 to 1908 as president of the Woman's College of Baltimore, later called Goucher College in his honor. Christian statesman of high standing, he issued the call for the meeting at which Fukien Christian University was conceived, and continued to maintain a deep interest in its development as a trustee and frequent visitor. The meeting was held at the home of John Gowdy, later to become one of the most influential figures in Fukien's history and its second president. A man of vision, courage, and administrative skill, he contributed much to the university as founder, teacher, president, and friend.

Those assembled at the meeting voted unanimously: "We consider it not only desirable but essential to establish in the Province of Fukien a union university in which all the Protestant denominations may join and which shall include bachelor, post-graduate and professional courses." The six missions in the province—American Congregational, Church of England, American Methodist, American Reformed, English Congregational, and English Presbyterian—entered upon discussions which for some years produced little result. However, strong and able personalities were at work. In addition to Goucher and Gowdy, two outstanding missionary leaders, one in Foochow and one in Amoy, were constantly pressing for implementation of the vision. One was Dr. Abbe Livingston Warnshuis of the Reformed Church in America, later to become Secretary of the International Missionary Council; the other, Dr. Lewis Hodous of the American Board Mission, ecumenical-minded worker for union in mission work. To these men was largely due the fact that the American missions joined in the task and that Foochow was chosen for the site.

Mission boards were slower than the field to act, and two of the British groups withdrew, largely for financial reasons. It was not until 1915 that the Board of Managers had its first meeting, at which Edwin Chester Jones was elected president. The next year Fukien Christian University opened with eighty-six students in an old Russian tea warehouse rented for the purpose. This was largely the uniting of the two upper classes of three junior colleges: Anglo-Chinese College (Methodist), founded in 1885 and largely Chinese financed; St. Mark's College (Anglican), established in 1906; and Foochow College (Congregational), dating from 1853 and entitled to give degrees under a charter from Massachusetts. The first made its science laboratories available to the new university; the last lent its library. The students, however, soon insisted on returning to their first alma maters, although these never went beyond a modest junior-college level, and the future university carried on thereafter with its own students. By 1920 these numbered over one hundred.

Abroad, a Board of Trustees was set up in New York in February 1918; a provisional charter was granted by the University of the State of New York that June. The next year the Board of Trustees elected Edwin C. Jones, who was already serving as field-appointed president, the first official president of Fukien Christian University. Though he served only four years, dying while home on a health furlough, he was largely responsible for the early success of the university and was one of its best-loved personalities. A chemist (M.A., Yale) and an amateur musician, he taught science and conducted choruses in addition to carrying heavy administrative responsibilities. He was a man of vision, understanding, charm, and great spiritual strength.

LINGNAN UNIVERSITY

The childhood of what was eventually to become Lingnan University, born in the mind of one of the first American missionaries in that area, had been long and precarious. Unusually well educated, the Reverend Andrew P. Happer, M.D., D.D., had early dreamed of erecting on the foundation of the lower schools already established "an exact duplication of the Protestant Syrian College" (later known as the American University in Beirut). In 1887 he organized a Board of Trustees committed to establishing a college with preparatory, collegiate, and medical departments. The Chinese Minister to Washington, the former United States Minister to Peking, two judges, a former United States Commissioner of Education, six college and university presidents, seven editors, twelve clergymen, and four professors of medicine authorized use of their names in fund-raising. A petition signed by more than four hundred Chinese outside the Christian church requested establishment of a scientific school in Canton. Elected president and with one hundred thousand dollars in hand, Dr. Happer opened his school and accepted thirty students in 1888.

With Dr. Happer's serious illness in 1890, the school closed. It reopened, however, in 1894 under a charter from the University of the State of New York with the Reverend Benjamin C. Henry, D.D., as president. A faculty of six, four of them Chinese, taught 150 students, of whom only twenty-two were in the collegiate department, which consisted of a few post-secondary courses. The campus was that of the Pui Ying School of the American Presbyterian Mission, which had been temporarily absorbed by the college. At this time the college was known as the Christian College of China.

The Pui Ying property was soon repurchased by the Presbyterians and Pui Ying re-established as an independent institution, and in 1899 the college opened in a single room behind a chapel in Canton. The next year, because of anti-foreign activities, faculty and students transferred to Macao, where the school remained until 1904, when a suitable permanent site had been found. There had been considerable sentiment in favor of Hong Kong as the location, but Canton had been chosen as offering greater possibility for influencing the development of higher education in China. On some thirty acres on Honam Island, a few miles east of Canton city, the buildings of what had become, in Chinese, Ling Nam School and, in English, Canton Christian College, were soon rising.

Enrolment increased but the collegiate department still consisted, in 1906, of only a freshman year with three students and, in 1910, of but two years with ten students. It was not until 1918 that a first class of three was graduated from what was now a college of arts and sciences. A medical department had become a part of the institution in 1910, when the University Medical School supported by the Christian Association of the University of Pennsylvania affiliated with the college. However, this relationship did not last, for in 1914 the medical school withdrew from Canton to Shanghai. Lingnan was not to have a medical college until many years later.

In 1908 Dr. Charles K. Edmunds, Ph.D. in physics from Johns Hopkins, was elected president. A man of brilliance and leadership, he devoted his great ability both to securing necessary funds and to development of the academic program, gathering around himself a goodly number of able Chinese and American educators. Disliking administrative work, he attempted several times to resign, ultimately succeeding in 1924, only to become Provost of Johns Hopkins University and later President of Pomona College, between which two appointments he served Lingnan again as Director of its American Foundation. During his time at Lingnan he had found pleasure in active participation in world-wide magnetic surveys. Among the men associated with him were several who were to play important roles in the institution's development: James M. Henry, who succeeded him; George Weidman Groff, who was to achieve fame in horticulture; and Chung Wing-kwang, teacher, dean, president, and at one time Commissioner of Education of Kwangtung.

III. CENTRAL CHINA

Central China was a name applied to an area including roughly the three provinces of Hupeh, Hunan, and Kiangsi, with a combined population of some seventy million, and having as its unofficial center the Wu-han cities of Wuchang, Hankow, and Hanyang. In the early years it was the scene of great educational activity and planning. A half-dozen mission schools aspired to become colleges if not universities, and ambitious plans were early sketched, allowed to gather dust, and then revived for a great Central China University. Actual achievement was limited but foundations were laid for one of the last of the fourteen China colleges.

The first of these educational efforts to materialize was Boone University at Wuchang, five hundred miles up the Yangtze River from Shanghai. This was sponsored by the American Protestant Episcopal Church, whose major educational concern was St. John's University in Shanghai. Though it could claim antecedents dating back to 1871, it was not until 1903 that Boone attempted post-secondary courses covering two years of college work. It added a medical school in 1907, and somewhat later a training school for librarians. Incorporation as a university followed in 1909, and the first B.A. degrees were awarded in 1911. This degree-granting power, secured from the University of the State of New York, was to play an important part in plans for a great Central China University and in the actual development of Huachung University. In 1920 Boone had seventy students.

The idea of an undenominational Christian university in Central China, based on the argument that a number of weak colleges could not hope to command the respect needed to make an effective impact on the new China, had been proposed by the London Missionary Society in 1907 and supported by the commission appointed by the China Missions Emergency Committee, which went to China to study the situation. The plan was then enlarged into a United Universities project in which Americans would also participate. Teachers were sent out to existing institutions, and a president was elected. Unfortunately lack of the necessary funds led to abandonment of the project. However, such money as had been appropriated was used for the purchase of land and the rest for construction of buildings, both of great help to Boone and to the second, post-1920, Central China University.

While these developments were taking place, in addition to Boone there were five other denominational attempts to meet the need for Christian higher education in that area. In Kiukiang, Kiangsi Province, a hundred miles downriver from Wuchang, William Nast College, an American Methodist institution, enrolled a dozen junior-college students in 1912. Across the river from Wuchang, in Hankow, Griffith John College, set up as a secondary school by the London Missionary Society, undertook some post-secondary courses in 1914 with only five students. A hundred miles southwest, on the great Tungting Lake, the Reformed Church in the United States had Huping (Lakeside) College, a secondary school which by 1920 was beginning to develop college courses. The American Methodists were planning a college at Nanchang, a hundred miles to the southeast. In Wuchang itself, the English Methodist Mission had its Wesley College with a long and successful history as a middle school but with only a handful of students at a higher level. None of these was to achieve full post-secondary status but all were to be involved in the later development of Huachung University.

What proved to be a more successful beginning was an outgrowth of the intercollegiate religious movement in North America at the end of the nineteenth century. In 1902 Yale's Student Volunteer Band organized the nondenominational Yale Foreign Missionary Society and sent Lawrence Thurston, '98, and his bride to China as its first missionaries. Less than a year after its incorporation the society received from a conference of Protestant missionaries in Hunan Province an invitation to establish an education center in Changsha, the provincial capital. Relatively inaccessible, largely untouched by new ways, strongly anti-foreign, Hunan Province, with its twenty million inhabitants, offered a dangerous challenge, but the invitation was quickly and enthusiastically accepted. Thurston did not live to see the new structure, but his place was taken in 1904 by Mr. and Mrs. Brownell Gage, Warren Seabury, and Dr. and Mrs. Edward H. Hume, first in a long line of Yale men and their wives who were to build and help carry on Yale-in-China. By 1906, a secondary school, known as the Yali Middle School, had started at Changsha.

The first years were not easy, the independent Hunanese temperament resulting in frequent disciplinary problems and even violence and temporary closing, but by 1910 the original house was bursting with fifty-seven boys, and applicants were more than Yali could handle. In 1909, with appointment of Dickson Leavens, was inaugurated the "bachelors" program which ultimately took more than seventy Yale graduates to Yali for terms of one or two years, chiefly in the middle school. Leavens himself continued to serve for nineteen years. In 1911 the staff was briefly strengthened by the arrival of Kenneth S. Latourette, '06, who was to become the great historian of missions and to serve Yale-in-China as trustee for forty years.

In 1913 construction started on a group of buildings on twenty acres of land outside the north gate of Changsha. In 1916 the middle school moved into these new quarters, where it was soon joined by the college department. The next year the medical department, consisting of a hospital started in 1908 and a medical college added in 1914, moved into new buildings next to the school campus. From the start one of the Mission's primary objectives had been a college department. This was inaugurated in 1914. In 1917 a first class of eight students was graduated from the College of Arts and Sciences. In 1919 the college was incorporated under the laws of the State of Connecticut. It grew slowly and in 1919–20 numbered only forty students, but at that time Yali had the most modern campus and probably the strongest academic program in the Central China region.

IV. WEST CHINA

West China was the last of the great areas of the country to see the development of Christian higher education. The coastal regions had naturally been the first, the less readily accessible interior the second. Not that Christian education had been slow in penetrating Szechwan Province. Missionary efforts had established primary schools almost as soon as missions had entered the area late in the nineteenth century, and had started middle schools early in the twentieth. Even before the establishment of the West China Educational Union in 1906, a Committee on Primary and Secondary Education had urged upon the various missions in West China the development of a Christian university. The growth of the Church, the increase in schools and hospitals, and the awakening of Chinese education all argued for such an institution. The spirit of the missions, unlike that in some regions, favored its being a union institution.

The first proposal for higher education came from the Canadian

Methodist Mission which, in 1903, considered the possibility of a Canadian Methodist college providing arts and theology as well as medicine, which had been its first concern. The American Methodist Episcopal Mission began in 1904 a "college" with a faculty of three missionaries and two Chinese and started to raise fifty thousand dollars for a building. Realization of the impracticability of a number of small independent colleges brought together a group of men representing the different missions. Outlining a proposed union institution, they submitted the plan to Professors E.D. Burton and Thomas C. Chamberlain of the University of Chicago, who were on a fact-finding tour, and then, in April 1905, presented it to representatives of the four missions chiefly involved—the Methodist Episcopal, the American Baptist, the Canadian Methodist, and the British Friends. In 1918 the Church Missionary Society of England became the fifth cooperating body in the university.

This scheme was at once submitted to the home boards. The response was largely discouraging, the boards neither sharing the dream nor prepared to invest in such an expensive undertaking. Though the Canadian Board showed some interest, the proposal was turned down in London, New York, and Toronto. However, continued discussion led, in 1910, to a constitution and basis of union which was to serve the university throughout its life.

In the meantime, in Chengtu, capital of populous Szechwan Province and cultural center of the west, the missions had purchased some sixty acres of land south of the city, drafted architectural designs, and begun construction of buildings. Even before approval of the constitution, West China Union University opened with eleven students selected from the Union Middle School. The faculty numbered eleven instructors, clearly not all full-time. The curriculum consisted of basic courses in English, chemistry, physics, Western history, Chinese, and religious knowledge. However, the opening of the second year was interrupted by the Revolution of 1911, all foreigners being forced to seek safety in Shanghai, and it was not possible to reopen the university until the spring of 1913.

With reopening, expansion of plant and equipment became imperative. Within a few years some forty buildings had been added, largely given by individual donors in Canada, Britain, and the U.S. Local enthusiasm was such that, when the strain of World War I led home boards to order stoppage of work on the Administration Building, members of the community underwrote the needed funds. Early efforts to affiliate the university with either the University of Chicago or Oxford

University proved unsuccessful. It was not until 1922 that it received a provisional charter from the University of the State of New York.

Leadership during the years of planning had been in the hands of a number of such creative and dynamic missionaries as Omar L. Kilborn, M.D., and Joseph Beech, D.D., of the Canadian and American Methodist Missions respectively. With actual operation single leadership was essential and in 1914 Dr. Beech was elected the first president, a position he held until appointment of a Chinese president in 1931. Though assisted by a number of very able colleagues, he provided the leadership which guided West China's rapid growth.

From the beginning the founders sought a system of education not too American, Canadian, or English, but adapted to the needs of China. To the initial faculties of arts and sciences, a normal school was added in 1912, a faculty of religion in 1915, a faculty of medicine in 1914, and one of dentistry in 1917. Chinese studies were early given special emphasis. By 1920 West China had nearly a hundred students.

V. COLLEGES FOR WOMEN

The early twentieth century also saw the sudden and rapid emergence of higher education for women, a field in which Protestant missions pioneered. From the start Protestant education had included both sexes. A girls' boarding school had opened in Ningpo by 1846, and later developments elsewhere usually saw schools for boys matched by schools for girls. As time went on and high schools grew out of primary, the foundations were laid for such outstanding girls' secondary schools as Bridgman Academy in Peking, and St. Mary's Hall, McTeiyre School, and Mary Farnum School in Shanghai.

These developments, particularly at the elementary level, constituted not too abrupt a break with the past or too threatening a portent of the future. Though traditional public education had made little provision for the intellectual training of women, feminine literacy was by no means unknown and moral training for women held high place in Chinese society. Chinese history and literature tell of many women who distinguished themselves as poets, teachers, historians, reformers, and even inventors, or who quoted as freely from the classics as did their brothers. But the formal education of women was exceptional, Girls' schools established and directed by the Chinese themselves appeared just before 1900.

Even after 1900 the educational system established by the tottering Manchu regime had no clear place for the education of women. It was not until 1907 that regulations provided for elementary and normal schools for girls, both at a lower level than similar schools for boys. These included neither middle schools nor colleges for girls. Five years later, in the new educational system, the education of women had, at least theoretically, an equal status with that of men, but time was needed to provide equal opportunity. Even by 1919 girls constituted only five percent of all non-mission primary students, and there were less than a thousand girls in non-mission middle schools.

Higher education was quite another matter. Conservative society saw little or no need for highly educated women though, even in the nineteenth century, an increasing number of girls sensed the dawning of a new era and felt the call of greater learning. By the second decade of the twentieth century, however, this was a call which even government institutions felt compelled to answer. In 1924, when there were already two independent Christian women's colleges—Hwa Nan and Ginling—and two affiliated colleges—West China and Yenching—the only government institution of the sort was Peking Teachers College for Women. But a number of private and government universities and colleges had become co-educational, a pattern soon followed by almost all institutions of higher education. At the end of the second decade, however, numbers remained low, with women constituting less than four percent of the total enrolment in higher education in the country.

For Protestant missions, the new century brought a growing interest in higher education for women. The first college for women was the North China Union Women's College organized in 1905 under the leadership of Miss Luella Miner, who had been on the faculty of the North China College and was to be a dominant figure in women's education for the next quarter century, first at Yenching and then at Shantung, at both of which institutions she was a highly respected dean. The college itself was an outgrowth of the school started by Mrs. Eliza J. Bridgman in 1964 when she took into her home three little daughters of a woman begging on the street. Thirty years later this had become Bridgman Academy, which lost its building while a third of its students lost their lives in the Boxer Uprising. It resumed classes in a Mongol

Palace, and in 1903 undertook a year of college work. On this foundation the London Mission, the American Board, and the Presbyterian Mission decided to develop a full four-year college for women as part of the North China Educational Union. Two years later they were joined by the Woman's Foreign Missionary Society of the Methodist Church.

A building erected on American Board property in 1905 was shared by Bridgman and the Women's College until 1916, when the latter moved to an old palace, the T'ungfu, in which the mother of K'ang Hsi, the great seventeenth-century Manchu emperor, had lived. The room in which the Emperor had held audience when he visited his mother became the assembly hall. Beginnings were modest, with only fourteen students in 1912, but by the end of the second decade the number had risen to over seventy.

The development of the new Peking University from a union of existing institutions of higher education raised the problem of the part to be played by the Women's Colleges of Arts and of Medicine. From the start the North China Educational Union favored their participation, but there was disagreement as to the nature of the relationship, whether it should be absorption into a co-educational institution or affiliation as an autonomous women's college. The example of Barnard College, which maintained its own faculty, trustees, and internal administration while its graduates received their degrees from Columbia University, appealed most to the women. In January 1920 the Women's College affiliated on a similar basis with the reorganized Peking University, the first experiment in China of including a women's college in an otherwise men's university.

The second great step in higher education for women came with the establishment, in 1914 and 1915, of Hwa Nan and Ginling Colleges. The former was the result of planning which had begun in 1904, when the Woman's Foreign Missionary Society of the Methodist Episcopal Church (U.S.A.) resolved to "authorize proceedings looking toward the establishing in Foochow of a College for Women." A year later in Shanghai, the China Christian Educational Association "Resolved that it is the sense of this meeting that ultimately we shall need to establish four woman's colleges in China—one each in north, central, west, and south," and heartily endorsed the action looking to one in Foochow. However, it favored union wherever practicable.

Though the Society's action was endorsed by the Methodist Church in China, there followed long years of preparation. For one thing, a strong high school was needed to prepare for admission to college. Miss Lydia Trimble, who had inspired the Society's action, was elected principal of what was awkwardly but descriptively named the Foochow College Preparatory of Foochow Woman's College. Evangelistic missionary appointed to a country district, she had started a girls' boarding school in a small town down the coast and had served as its principal. Her work with country women had shown her their need, and her contacts with girls had convinced her of their ability to become leaders in service to their less privileged sisters. It was this experience that led her to advocate higher education for women and to serve Hwa Nan so ably during its first ten years of life.

A site for the college was found on Nantai Island, across the Min River from the crowded city of Foochow. Construction began in 1911, but the campus was not ready for occupancy until three years later. College work started in the fall of 1914 with the offering of the first two years. In 1916, five students completed this course, four then going abroad to continue their studies, the fifth entering the Women's Christian Medical College in Shanghai. A full four-year course leading to the B.A. degree, awarded by the college itself, was first offered in 1917. Five girls entered, but after two years two accepted scholarships in the United States. One of these was Lucy Wang, later to become Hwa Nan's first Chinese president. The three who completed the course in 1921 constituted Hwa Nan's first alumnae. Growth was slow, and by 1920 enrolment in the college was only fourteen.

Another long-cherished dream began to take form in 1911–12 when representatives of eight girls' schools, meeting in Shanghai, appealed to their mission boards for a union college for women in the Yangtze Valley. Five of the boards—Northern Baptist, Disciples, Northern and Southern Methodists, and Northern Presbyterians—responded favorably, each pledging ten thousand dollars for buildings and equipment, the support of a teacher, and a contribution of not less than six hundred dollars a year toward current expenses. In 1913 a Board of Control elected Mrs. Lawrence Thurston as first president of the college to be. Mrs. Thurston had had wide experience, as teacher in Turkey and at the Yale School in Changsha where her husband had been the Yale Foreign Missionary Society's first representative, and as Secretary of the Student Volunteer Movement. She was to give the new college constructive leadership for the next fifteen years.

Nanking was chosen for the location of the college, and Ginling, the literary name for Nanking, took the place of the cumbersome early title, The Union College for Women in the Yangtze Valley. The college opened in September 1915 in two large Chinese mansions, each consisting of four courts. Thirteen students registered, five of whom were graduated in 1919. These were the first women to receive a fully accredited B.A. degree from an institution in China. The degrees were granted by the University of Nanking under its charter from the University of the State of New York. The University Trustees held in trust all property and funds of the college. They had added to their number five women representing the five supporting missions, but a local Board of Control directed most of the college's activities. By 1920, enrolment had reached seventy and the faculty numbered sixteen, of whom five were Chinese.

When the North China Union Women's College became a largely autonomous part of Peking University, it secured, in the words of its president, Luella Miner, "most of the advantages of co-education and none of its disadvantages." Whatever these latter were thought to be, co-education ultimately became a part of Christian higher education in twelve of the fourteen institutions, the pattern at Yenching and West China differing from straight co-education only in degree. Only Ginling and Hwa Nan continued to cling to single blessedness. Shanghai University was the first Christian university to adopt co-education, admitting women students as early as 1920, the same year that National Peking University accepted them. At that time, some 115 women constituted just over six percent of the total enrolment of the Protestant colleges. From then on, the doors were opened in one institution after another until, by 1936, all Protestant colleges and universities were accepting women. By then these made up more than a quarter of the total, with the ratio rising in individual instances to above one in three. Thus the higher education of women, pioneered by Protestant missions in 1905, had become an unquestioned part of education in China.

Part
3
Nationalism and Maturity (1920-1937)

6
Nationalist China

For China, as a nation and a people, the period from 1920 to 1937 was one of struggle for national unity and stability and international dignity, with relative chaos only gradually yielding to a degree of hopeful though newly threatened order. It was a time of continued revolution and of many movements, political, social, and intellectual. It saw the establishment of the government that was to rule China through the last decades of China College history, and the birth of the force that was to overthrow the government and engulf the colleges. It brought China well along the road to full autonomy in the family of nations and an end to the humiliations of a hundred years. It saw the active and sometimes bloody involvement of China's youth in the life of the nation.

It was in the early twenties that the Kuomintang, though dating back to the 1912 Revolution, came into real power. Under the direction of Russian counselors invited by Sun Yat-sen, the Party became more and more Communist in pattern and program. Sun was made national hero and his Three People's Principles the Party's bible. In 1926 the Party's armies, under General Chiang Kai-shek, began a momentous northern expedition aimed at uniting the warlord-divided country. By the spring of 1927 the Yangtze had been reached, centers such as Hankow and Shanghai had been captured, and the road to Peking appeared open. But the left wing of the Kuomintang was growing in numbers, especially among students, and in radicalism. Following the fall of Nanking in March, conservatives formed a government in Nanking in opposition to that in Hankow. By the end of the year, Communism had lost much of its appeal, an anti-Communist government with Chiang at the head was in control, the Russian advisers had left, and in June 1928 the Nationalist army entered Peking and the country was theoretically united. In 1930 Northern warlords had to be defeated, and in 1931 a Southern coalition attempted to oust Chiang. In general, however, the Nationalist government, recruiting a number of able men, many of them

73

returned students, grew in power and stability. Through the early thirties, Nanking was the center of many hopeful developments. On the basis of a revival of traditional Confucian virtues under the label "New Life Movement," the government attempted to rally the people behind a modernization of the country through Western technology and techniques.

However, China's industrial revolution had only begun, and the country, while undergoing change, continued on a largely agrarian basis. Famines took millions of lives, and the nation's economy was slow in getting on its feet. Rural reconstruction became a major goal though never carried far enough. Economic life, disorganized by contact with the West, continued in a precarious state. A factor of particular concern to foreign-supported programs was the lack of economic stability and the fluctuating rate of exchange which saw the Chinese silver dollar ranging in value from more than one gold dollar early in the 1920s to less than thirty cents even before the fantastic inflation following the Japanese invasion of 1937.

At the same time China was far from free of internal troubles. Communists and bandits, the latter often claiming to be Communists, overran large areas. Communism was still alive and growing, attracting especially students. Large sections of southeast and central China were in the hands of so-called Communists, whether bandits, hopeless peasants, or true believers. Campaigns launched against these between 1930 and 1934, when the famous Long March took the Red Army to Yenan, were largely unsuccessful.

In international relations China made considerable headway in establishing her autonomy and asserting her equality with other nations. Several foreign concessions were returned, tariff autonomy was secured, the Shanghai foreign law courts were discontinued, and progress was made in abolishing extraterritoriality, though the major powers, arguing from the social and legal chaos, remained largely unaffected in this respect for another half-dozen years. A major step was the Nine Power Treaty of 1922 (Washington), which guaranteed "the sovereignty, the independence, and the territorial and administrative integrity of China." This progress was not without tension. The years were marked by propaganda, strikes, attacks on concessions, and occasional "incidents" such as that at Nanking in 1927 when foreigners were the victims, and that at Shanghai in 1925 when Chinese students were killed.

The Japanese pressures which were to result in war in 1937 continued in spite of Japan's having committed itself to China's sovereignty and integrity. In 1932, following minor incidents, Japan seized Manchuria and set up a puppet regime called Manchukuo, under the nominal headship of P'u-i, the last Manchu emperor. Meanwhile the boycott of Japanese goods which had developed led to an attack on Shanghai and heavy damage and loss of life.

The League of Nations and its Lytton Commission condemned Japan but did not succeed in restraining her. In January 1933 Japanese troops had moved inside the Great Wall, and China bought time by tacitly accepting Japan's control of Manchuria. Japanese encroachment continued, in Mongolia and even in North China. Increasingly government efforts and student activity were directed toward preparation for what was more and more clearly an inescapable war. One move was the patching up of an armed truce between Kuomintang and Communists in 1936, leaving the latter in control of the northwestern enclave centered at Yenan, and making possible presentation of a "United Front."

Three related and largely overlapping movements were important features of the period, especially during the twenties. These were a Student Movement, an Anti-Christian Movement, and a more general anti-foreign attitude on the part of students and intellectuals. These naturally affected the work of the Christian colleges, as they did that of all foreign-related activities. They were all expressions of reaction to the treatment to which China and its people had been subjected for nearly a century. The roots of each were deep. And each was finding willing hands to water it.

The causes of anti-foreignism were obvious. On the one hand Western imperialism, openly expressed in concessions, extraterritoriality, and even attitudes of superiority, had long been a source of humiliation. On the other, China's awakening and its embarking on a new course as the result of revolution had resulted in an upsurge of racial pride and a developing nationalism. Feeding these emotions and adding to anti-imperialism the economic factor of anti-capitalism, was Russian-encouraged Communism. Although reaction was often extreme and issues were confused, the movement had a positive element of concern for China. It was supported by Chinese of all ages but was given voice and cutting edge by students. The modernization of China during the first quarter of the twentieth century was in no small measure due to the efforts of these students. They were powerful factors in the changes from despotism to elements of democracy, from conservatism to liberalism, from apathy to action.

Students had begun to play a part in public affairs early in the life of modern China, but after the Revolution they engaged more and more in political agitation. An organized Student Movement can be said to have started in 1919 with the patriotic reaction to the terms of the Treaty of Versailles which made the Fourth of May a day of humiliation. Demonstrations resulted in the arrest of fifty students, strikes, and a lasting boycott of Japanese goods. Japanophile officials went into hiding. Nationalistic fervor was intensified with the massacre of unarmed students in Shanghai on May 30, 1925. In their enthusiasm, many students became propagandists for Communism and many were executed in the reaction of 1927. Though the Student Movement advocated direct action against Japan and had a part in the 1931 reform of the Nanking government, it had little influence in the thirties and was largely supplanted by the Kuomintang-backed Youth Corps.

Something of an offshoot of both the anti-foreign sentiment and the Student Movement was the Anti-Christian Movement of the twenties. Christianity came to be looked upon by many students and other intellectuals as the "running dog" of Western imperialism and a superstition threatening the Chinese way of life. Such an attitude was of course long standing, but the movement took shape in the twenties. An early move was an unsuccessful attempt to disrupt the 1922 Peking conference of the World Student Christian Federation. Anti-Christian federations were organized and a nation-wide movement was started to secure Chinese control of mission schools, which, at all levels, were branded as a threat to Chinese education, "denationalizing" students and forcing them to become Christian. This movement sought to force Christian schools to register and to give up their emphasis on religion, which was attacked as non-scientific superstition. Fundamentally anti-religious rather than simply anti-Christian, ·this movement attacked native Taoism and Confucianism and long-indigenized Buddhism as well, but agitation centered on the obviously foreign Christianity. At the same time, appreciation of Christianity's contribution to the new life in China and of the services rendered by missions in many fields was not lacking.

A more positive force was the "New Tide Movement" in the intellectual and social life of the country, although this too had its anti-religious aspects. This had started with students, had been stimulated by the lectures of men like John Dewey and Bertrand Russell, and had consolidated around Chancellor Ts'ai Yuan-p'ei of Peking National University. With the publication on January 1, 1917, in *The New Youth Magazine* of two articles, Hu Shih's "Some Suggestions for the

Reform of Chinese Literature" and Ch'en Tu-hsiu's "Revolution in Literature," was born what came to be known as the Literary Renaissance. With its emphasis on abandonment of *wen li*, the language of the classics, and the use in writing of *pai hua*, the modern spoken language, this movement was to have profound effect on education. The success of this revolution calls to mind the translation of the Bible into Mandarin as early as 1870 or 1872 and the involvement in that task of such men as Martin and Schereschewsky and, later, Mateer and Goodrich. Well before 1900, Mateer was saying that "ultimately Mandarin, enriched, corrected, and dignified will be the written as well as the spoken language of China" and requiring at Tengchow College essays in the vernacular.

By 1920 Protestant higher education had come of age. Only a few institutions continued at largely secondary levels while claiming to be colleges, and these were soon to be absorbed. Sixteen were functioning as four-year colleges, one as a junior college. These, with their nearly two thousand students, constituted some twelve percent of higher education in China. They had helped to meet an urgent quantitative need at a time when other means were largely lacking. They had done so at a respectable level and with an otherwise largely non-existent spiritual emphasis. They had set new patterns, worthy standards, and helpful examples.

Although relatively small, they had provided training for a significant number of men and women, Christian and non-Christian, well-known and unheard-of, and in so doing had contributed both to society and to the Christian Church. Well over a hundred graduates had entered the ministry; over a thousand were in the teaching profession. Perhaps a hundred could be said to be in public service, filling positions from premier down. For their size, the colleges were having a disproportionate influence on Chinese society.

Originally almost wholly Western in concept and leadership, they were becoming increasingly Chinese, though facing an era of often antagonistic nationalism. They were now part of a rapidly expanding government and private system of higher education and having to compete for students and standing with their foreignness increasingly a handicap. The process of indigenization, however, was well under way by 1920. The first Chinese president was yet to be appointed, but perhaps half of the faculties were now nationals.

There remained elements of weakness, some inherent in the nature of sponsorship, some the result of inexperience, some caused by institutional self-centeredness. Many were still weak, and all suffered from inadequacies of staff and equipment. There were more institutions than Protestant forces could expect to maintain at desirable levels of size and quality. However, while relatively small—ranging in numbers from fifteen to 250, with only six having more than a hundred students—they had established solid foundations for institutions of greater size and higher standards that were to develop during the next decade or two.

For the Protestant colleges and universities, the period from 1920 to 1937 was a difficult and often uncomfortable time of response to the requirements of a new and changing nation. At one time their very survival was threatened, when civil war resulted in the reduction of the number of Protestant missionaries by fifty percent and only ten of sixteen colleges were open. They were to be uncertain and interrupted years, testing faith, straining courage, and providing moments of despair. But out of them came a large and generally healthy segment of Chinese higher education. By 1937 enrolment in the China Colleges had grown to nearly seven thousand from less than two thousand in 1920. One-seventh of the college students of China were to be found in the China Colleges.

In 1920 the Protestant colleges faced critical issues which were to involve them in heart-searching and struggle and to result in both change and stability. These revolved around three major questions: their foreignness, their religious purpose, and their ability to maintain themselves at an adequate material and educational level. Exploding nationalism demanded greater identification with the life of the country. Antagonisms had to be faced and conquered. Basic goals and guiding principles had to be defended when valid. The demands of the new day and the great increase in the number and strength of competing institutions made necessary improvement in facilities and standards and new academic emphases. Ways and means must constantly be sought, with the issue of concentration always challenging individual aspirations.

No final answers were to be expected, but by the mid-thirties the outlook was highly encouraging. In most cases, foreignness was no longer a critical issue, and integration of Christian schools into the government system had been achieved with satisfaction to both parties. Religion was still a point of difference, but the Protestant colleges and universities had become an integral and largely indigenous part of China's higher education. And the question of physical survival, though by no means fully resolved, had not proved the millstone that had been feared. Though union, and even cooperation, had made little progress, almost all had survived and were stronger than ever.

7

The China Colleges–North China

In North China the years 1920–37 saw the growth of two very different institutions of higher education, Shantung Christian University at Tsinan and Yenching University at Peking. One was to become a somewhat provincial institution with a rural emphasis and an outstanding medical school; the other, a well-rounded institution with national outreach and even international repute.

YENCHING UNIVERSITY

The beginning of the third decade found the future Yenching not only with a new union structure and a new president but with several major problems. For one thing, the name Peking University, which had been carried for nearly three decades by the Methodist unit, was unacceptable to the other units. After a Western board of arbitration had proposed another name which also proved unacceptable, a committee of prominent Chinese scholars unanimously recommended "Yenching" (a literary name for Peking). Peking University continued as the English name until 1928, when that also became Yenching University.

Another problem was a lack of facilities. Because the merging institutions had turned over their libraries and laboratories to the academies they left behind, the new university was badly handicapped. The ituation improved when the university was allowed to share the facilities of the Premedical School of the Peking Union Medical College, and then again when that entire school, including some of the teachers, was turned over to it. Growth of a library was slow, though Chinese studies received substantial help when the Harvard-Yenching Institute was established.

Perhaps the most serious problem was that of site. In addition to being inadequate in size, the land in the southeast corner of Peking was prohibitively expensive. Land alone threatened to consume all available funds, leaving nothing for buildings. Finally, in the summer of 1920, with the assistance of two Chinese elder statesmen, a sixty-acre estate five miles northeast of Peking was secured. Two other gardens were quickly added and a fourth one was rented. By 1925, two hundred acres, of which the university actually owned 116, were available for use.

A continuing problem was that of finance. Though the four mission boards had promised eight teachers, and actually provided more, and $350,000 in capital funds, the four thousand dollars a year for current expenses was totally inadequate. The situation proved so critical that, although the Trustees had agreed that he should not be responsible for raising funds, Dr. Stuart found it necessary to devote much of his time throughout the twenties and thirties to financial campaigns. A first step was an invitation to Dr. Henry Winters Luce, who had left Shantung and was working in the China Christian Educational Association, to become vice-president with primary responsibility for raising funds in America, a task which he carried on with skill and success for many years.

The start of Yenching University came at a period of great ferment in Chinese society and in a city, Peking, that was the center of the Chinese Renaissance and of much of the student agitation of the times. Though an unusual degree of understanding was maintained between administration and students, the normal academic program sometimes suffered disruption during the early twenties. However, Yenching was fitting itself into the national system of education through registration. As early as February 1927 it was temporarily registered under the 1925 regulations, but changes in the requirements soon necessitated further negotiation. Final official recognition as a university did not come until two years later.

By this time Yenching had moved to its new site, where it started classes in the summer of 1926, while construction was still under way. The new campus was a thing of beauty, generously endowed with earlier landscaping and enriched with new buildings inspired by the palaces of the Forbidden City. That year the university had an enrolment of 542. Demand was great, but, with the limiting of the freshman class to one out of six of the candidates, the total never exceeded 880 before the War in 1937. Of 105 full-time faculty members, roughly one-third were Western and two-thirds, Chinese. Thirty-seven had their doctorates.

At the time of registration, in order to meet requirements for the title of university, the institution reorganized its two colleges of arts and of sciences into a College of Arts with ten departments, a College of

Natural Sciences with six, and a College of Applied Social Sciences with three. In the case of the last, a later shift of sociology to the College of Arts and the setting up of a Department of Jurisprudence brought a change of name to College of Public Affairs (*Fa Hsüeh Yuan*, College of Law, in Chinese). The School of Theology, which had been the first unit in the union, was renamed in 1925 the Yenching School of Religion and, because of government regulations, became a unit outside the officially recognized academic structure. In its undergraduate work Yenching emphasized both the indigenous Chinese culture and the imported Western. Able staff and a strong program provided well for both instruction and research in Chinese studies. At the same time Yenching stressed Western culture for all students, offering majors in Western languages and literatures.

Graduate work had started even before the move to the new campus, with an M.A. degree granted as early as 1922. By 1934 eleven departments were offering graduate courses. That year the Ministry refused to recognize all but four—history, biology, chemistry, and political science—and reduced the graduate school to a research institute. The seven departments not officially approved nevertheless carried on, their students receiving American degrees under Yenching's American charter. However, by 1936–37 the number of graduate students, which had at one time reached a peak of 119, had declined to forty-eight. The Yenching School of Religion remained an unregistered graduate school requiring a bachelor's degree for admission.

In addition to its purely academic concern, Yenching early undertook vocational training. A small department of education continued to grow in spite of recommendations of the Burton Commission; a full-fledged department of animal husbandry started; the Department of Chemistry undertook leather-tanning. However, animal husbandry and a pre-engineering course established in 1922 were discontinued when the university moved to its new campus. Yenching also developed the first full-fledged department of journalism in Asia. Started in 1924, this achieved in a decade an outstanding reputation. In 1929 financial security for five years was assured by gifts from half a dozen leading American newspapers. Cooperation with the School of Journalism of the University of Missouri gave the department added strength and status. During World War II the heads of the Chinese News Services at London, Paris, New York, Washington, San Francisco, and New Delhi were its graduates.

For Yenching, registration involved not only academic reorganization but drastic administrative changes. Vice-President Wu Lei-ch'uan was elected chancellor while Dr. Stuart continued as president, assisting the chancellor and acting for him in his absence. Mr. Wu, a distinguished scholar who held the highest of the old-time degrees, had become a deeply committed Christian late in life. He was concerned with the relationship between Chinese culture and Christian faith, and lectured on Confucianism and Christianity in the School of Religion as well as teaching in the Department of Chinese. Prior to moving to Yenching, he had served as Councillor in the Ministry of Education. He left Yenching in 1933 to become Vice-Minister. He was followed by a succession of acting-chancellors and then, in 1937, by Dr. H.H. Kung, Minister of Finance in the Nanking Government. The Board of Managers, originally thirty-one in number, was reduced to the prescribed fifteen, two-thirds of whom were Chinese.

Following the Manchurian Incident of 1931, Yenching came under the increasingly heavy shadow of Japanese aggression. Each act of Japanese encroachment resulted in outbursts of student protest and moves to suspend classes. Communist political activity, increasing with the growing strength of the movement, resulted in occasional serious confrontation between students and administration. But, in spite of disruptions, the work of the university continued with relative smoothness and effectiveness.

SHANTUNG CHRISTIAN UNIVERSITY

Two hundred and fifty miles south of Peking, another recent union also faced the task of establishing on a new campus a sound administration and an effective educational program. The year 1920 found Shantung Christian University struggling with serious problems of personnel and program. Though the next decade saw progress, it produced not a few moments of anxiety.

At the time of consolidation, J. Percy Bruce, a scholar who was later to become Professor of Chinese at the University of London, was elected president. Failing to get along well with either his board or his faculty, he resigned in January 1920. An acting-president and several acting-deans carried on until the appointment as president of Dr. Harold Balme of the Medical College, an efficient and respected representative of the English Baptist Mission. Among those called on for emergency service was Dr. Randolph T. Shields of the Southern Presbyterian

Mission, who had been dean of the medical department at Nanking prior to its transfer to Tsinan. At various times he served as Acting Dean of Arts and Sciences, Dean of Medicine, Vice-President of the University, and, during the first years of the war with Japan, Acting President. Probably no one was more closely or continuously identified with the life of the university for the quarter of a century following 1917.

In 1921 the Burton Commission proposed that Shantung and Peking Universities be merged to form a single institution with two campuses performing different functions. Though the possible sharpening of focus and avoidance of duplication had much to be said for it, there were so many obvious and even insuperable difficulties in the way that the plan was accepted only in part and then most reluctantly, and eventually was almost wholly ignored. One specific recommendation, however, was acted upon. The Shantung College of Arts, which was having difficulty building up enrolment—in 1920 fewer than two hundred students were occupying facilities planned for six hundred—began to place greater emphasis on the training of teachers. In spite of objections on the part of the Chinese in general and the alumni in particular, a strong department quickly developed. In a few years, however, lack of students combined with restrictive government regulations to force the giving up of the function of teacher training.

With union, the university sought to secure a foreign charter as a means of providing academic degrees and of facilitating study abroad. The first approach was to London, but there proved to be no way under British law to charter an educational institution in a foreign country. An attempt to secure a New York charter encountered the requirement that a majority of the governing body be residents of the United States, which would have been unfair to British and Canadian interests. Finally a Canadian Act of Incorporation was approved in July 1924.

Such a charter did not of course provide for official Chinese recognition. Though decision to seek registration had been reached in 1925, it was not until four years later that Dr. Li T'ien-lu was elected the university's first Chinese president. Dr. Li, who had been Secretary of the Chinese Delegation to the Washington Conference of 1921, had been called to Tsinan in 1923 as Dean of Arts and Sciences and had been Vice-President for two years. Though the requirement of Chinese leadership had been met, negotiations dragged on. It was not until December 1931 that registration was finally achieved.

Even while these matters were being considered, the university faced serious internal disturbances. The Nationalist revolution of

1927–28 brought complications, with Western faculty members forced to evacuate in both years. An unsuccessful demand for the resignation of President Li was backed by a strike and threats to burn down major buildings. A second strike hastened organizational changes, but employees of the university were induced by radical elements to form a union and to lay siege to the university, cutting power cables, picketing the campus, and seizing the chairman of the Prudential Committee. Disorder continued until orders came from the Central government in Nanking to settle the affair.

In 1930, Dr. Chu Ching-nung (King Chu) assumed the presidency. Though holder of B.A. and M.A. degrees from the States, he had earlier studied in Japan and had been a follower of Dr. Sun Yat-sen. He had held important positions in China in education and publishing, and it was hoped that his coming would bring unity, but he was called to government service and left at the end of the year. Not until 1935 was a successor found, Liu Shu-ming, a Shantung alumnus and distinguished professor at Peking National University. His coming brought renewed leadership but not complete unity, the medical faculty proposing that the university become only a college of medicine. The College of Medicine, probably the strongest of the three units which had united in 1906, had received further strength with the transfer in 1924 of the North China Union Medical College for Women, and was clearly the most stable part of the university. Through the twenties and thirties, it was under the capable deanship of Dr. Peter C. Kiang, a St. John's alumnus with specialization at Harvard and Johns Hopkins.

The rural emphasis proposed by the Correlated Program of 1928 was approved by the Board of Governors but strongly opposed by alumni, faculty, and students. These would have welcomed a college of agriculture, but that was reserved for Nanking. Though the dream was never fully given up, a rural program of sorts soon developed. A Rural Institute, started in 1927, soon developed departments of agriculture and economics, education, health, and homemaking. It did not, however, secure official recognition until 1937, when T.H. Sun became director.

The first two years of President Liu's leadership saw the university making substantial overall progress. The return of Chinese members with graduate degrees from abroad brought new strength to the faculty. By 1936 enrolment had reached a new high of nearly six hundred. The future, of what was coming to be known even in English as Cheeloo University, looked rosier than at any time during the university's first thirty years. At that moment the war in Asia began.

8

The China Colleges–East China

ST. JOHN'S UNIVERSITY

In Shanghai, the post-World War I decade was a troubled one for St. John's. The reaction following the Treaty of Versailles brought anti-government strikes and the closing of St. John's three times in 1919–20. Civil War, anti-foreignism, and student unrest continued to cause interruptions to the academic program, notably a stopping of work toward the end of the school year in 1925. Again in January 1927 the approach of the southern army forced a closing which lasted for nearly a year because of reluctance to accept the educational regulations of the new government.

The chief objection was to the requirement that all religious worship and instruction be voluntary. Here Chinese and Western educators parted company, the former almost solidly in favor, the latter divided. Both bishop and president preferred closing to compromise. Another concern was the requirement that a university be under Chinese control and administration. It was felt that there were not as yet enough Christian Chinese of adequate educational experience to serve as presidents. Dr. Pott continued to direct the development of St. John's through the twenties and thirties, and it was not until 1939 that he retired and was succeeded by a Chinese president. By that time he had served St. John's forty-eight years. A hesitant application for registration proved abortive and St. John's remained unregistered throughout the period. The effects of non-registration were felt most severely by the alumni, who were thereby theoretically barred from official service. Actually many were employed because of their qualifications, especially their command of English. Even graduates of the medical college were granted licenses to practice.

St. John's entered the twenties a "university" with a "collegiate department" and an associated medical school. In addition to the usual departments in the School of Arts and Sciences, a Department of Civil Engineering was in the process of development. Under Dr. John E. Ely, who had been Dean of Arts and Sciences and was later to act for Dr. Pott while the latter was on furlough, this became a School of Engineering, which did good work within the limits of civil engineering. The Theological School, which had been one of the first units, never had many students, partly because as much teaching as possible was done in English, and was discontinued in 1933. A course in journalism offered by the English Department became, under the leadership of Mr. Maurice Votaw of the University of Missouri, a Department of Journalism. Thus, the academic program at St. John's was basically one of arts and sciences with professional emphases in engineering, journalism, and medicine. None of the latter, even medicine, constituted a major element in the university although all contributed competent and successful graduates to society.

The medical school continued small and inadequately financed. The University of Pennsylvania, through its Christian Association, provided only Dr. McCracken's salary, and St. John's neither wholly accepted the college nor gave it support. Yet somehow it managed to survive and, under the deanships of Dr. McCracken and Dr. Edward S. Tyau, to do very good work, holding to the requirements of Grade A institutions in the U.S. It produced an outstanding group of graduates, most of whom took specialized training abroad, almost all returning to practice in China and many serving in mission hospitals.

The twenties saw little growth in numbers. When the university reopened in 1928, there were only 182 students in the collegiate programs and fifteen in the medical. Three years later there were still only 270 and thirty-seven respectively. After that, however, numbers rapidly increased, with enrolment soon doubling. This was not wholly to Dr. Pott's liking, for he felt that "It is not necessary that St. John's should be a large institution, . . . The chief aim should remain . . . the development of men of Christian character and of sound intelligence."

As China's largest city and chief port, Shanghai was particularly exposed to the internal unrest of the twenties and the external pressures of the thirties. St. John's felt the effects of both. Student activities brought occasional interruptions, and in the fighting which followed Japanese seizure of Manchuria in 1932 the campus became part of the western boundary of defense. The undeclared war which broke out in August 1937 again found St. John's in the thick of things.

UNIVERSITY OF SHANGHAI

In 1920 Shanghai Baptist College was beginning, on a campus still largely undeveloped, the growth which was to produce by 1937 a sound but unspectacular denominational university with strong religious emphasis. It had come a long way in its thirteen years but was still one of the smaller Protestant colleges, with large material and academic problems ahead.

Admission policy continued to follow the Articles of Confederation, which stipulated that "the number of non-Christian students shall never exceed the number of those who are Christian added to the number whose parents are Christian, or who have spent three years in a Christian preparatory school," a somewhat complicated formula designed to assure a predominance of Christian background if not of actual current profession of faith. The Anti-Christian Movement of the 1920s affected the spiritual tone of the university but did not interfere seriously with its program.

In spite of this religious concern, Shanghai responded promptly to the requirement of registration, making religious courses and exercises voluntary, adding Chinese members to the Board of Managers, appointing a Chinese president, and reorganizing the college to conform. A majority of the teaching staff already were Chinese. Academic reorganization, conforming to government emphasis on vocational courses, resulted in colleges of arts, science, and commerce. Registration was applied for in the autumn of 1927 and approved eighteen months later. The Chinese name then became *Hu Kiang* (a name for Shanghai) *Ta Hsueh*. In 1931 the English name was changed to University of Shanghai.

Registration brought to a close the administration of President White, one of the founders of Shanghai Baptist College and Seminary, who had served the institution in some capacity for nearly a quarter of a century. During his administration, between 1911 and 1928, the campus had almost doubled in size, faculty had increased sixfold, enrolment had grown from 104 (in middle school, college, and seminary) to over nine hundred, and the budget had risen from some sixteen thousand dollars to three hundred thousand.

He was succeeded by Herman C. E. Liu, who was to prove an outstanding but tragic figure in the history of Protestant higher education. Grandson and son of Baptist preachers, he had graduated from Soochow University before going abroad for further study. With an

M.A. in education from Chicago and a Ph.D. from Columbia, where he had had Dr. Paul Monroe as adviser, he returned to China in 1922 as national education secretary for the YMCA. He also served education and government in other capacities: professor of education in two universities, research director of the National Educational Association, secretary of the government's educational commission, chief delegate from China to the world YMCA Conference of 1926. His stated goal was for Shanghai College to be a "better educational institution, more Christian and more Chinese, to meet the needs of Chinese social life of the present day." Early in the Japanese occupation of Shanghai, he was to be the victim of assassination. At his funeral, the following tribute was paid: "He was a born leader of men, all men, regardless of nationality. . . . His quick intellect, his readiness of speech in both Chinese and English, his boundless enthusiasm combined with a sane judgment. . . ."

One of President Liu's first tasks was to secure greater and more assured support for the university. From local sources he quickly raised sufficient funds to erect a new library and improve the collection of books, and the home boards soon approved a building program costing a third of a million. A major academic development was the opening in the city in March 1932 of a Downtown School of Commerce. Starting with an enrolment of over five hundred, this was to prove one of the most successful units of the university and that for which it was perhaps best known.

The Sino-Japanese Incident of 1932, with severe fighting in the eastern part of Shanghai, interrupted classes for some weeks, but the situation did not become serious until the outbreak of the Sino-Japanese War in 1937. By that time the university, celebrating its thirtieth anniversary (1936), could report an overall enrolment of 2834, of whom 627 were in the three colleges. Sixty percent of the faculty were Chinese.

SOOCHOW UNIVERSITY

Fifty miles west of Shanghai, in the city of Soochow, famed as one of the two finest places under heaven, another denominational university, this one Methodist, had embarked on development that was to bring it outstanding achievement and leadership in two fields—science and law.

For the first half of this period Soochow continued to develop under Western leadership. When ill health forced President John W.

Cline to resign, he was succeeded in 1922 by Dr. W.B. Nance, who had served Soochow and its predecessor institutions since 1899 and was to continue in an active relationship for half a century. He had been vice-president under Dr. Cline. When political and military troubles forced the closing of the university in the spring of 1927, Dr. Nance resigned, to be succeeded by Soochow's first Chinese president, Dr. Y.C. Yang.

A Soochow alumnus with graduate degrees in international relations and law, Dr. Yang had been serving on the staff of Dr. Wellington Koo, formerly ambassador in Washington and London and currently Minister of Foreign Affairs. He had been elected vice-president of the university in 1922 but had felt that he must carry on the important work of treaty-revision with which Dr. Koo had entrusted him. He was to prove an able leader for the university through the thirties, the war, and the university's last days.

One of President Yang's first tasks was to make the changes in organization and administration required for registration. Possibly because of the president's good relations with the government, the process went through without hitch in 1928. As part of the reorganization required, the College of Arts and Science separated into the College of Arts and the College of Science, which, together with Law, gave it three colleges and qualified it as a university.

The decade leading up to the Sino-Japanese War was one of steady growth both physically and academically. A number of badly needed buildings were added to the campus. The Chinese faculty was notably strengthened, and academic standards were maintained at a high level. Two elements of the academic program showed especially impressive achievement: the Colleges of Science and of Law.

After 1920 the College of Science continued the teaching and research so ably developed by Professors Gee and Jones. Extensive additions were made to outstanding ornithological and entomological collections. A number of Soochow graduates, especially in biology, attained important positions in other Christian and private institutions. One of the most significant contributions made by the college was through the Biological Supply Service which had been envisioned by Professor Gee but not set up until 1924.

Along with its work in science, Soochow's greatest contribution was through its College of Law. By 1922 eighty students were in attendance at "The Comparative Law School of China" in Shanghai, established in 1915 on the site of the Anglo-Chinese College which had moved to Soochow as part of Tungwu College. The college grew rapidly, especially after the appointment in 1927 of Dr. John C.H. Wu as principal and Dr. Robert C.W. Sheng as dean. By 1937 it had over two hundred students and a highly qualified, though largely part-time, faculty. It was widely and favorably recognized.

HANGCHOW CHRISTIAN COLLEGE

Two hundred miles to the southwest, Hangchow Christian College was responding to the opportunities and challenges brought by its acquiring, in November 1920, a charter as a four-year degree-granting college. Pressure to keep it a two-year junior college—most notably from the Burton Commission—continued, but in June 1922 two B.A. degrees were granted, one to Ku Tun-jou, who was to become Professor of Political Science and Dean of Arts at his alma mater and finally to serve as dean at Tunghai University in Taiwan. Alumni pressures in China and pressure from abroad resulted two years later in trustee approval of full-college status. In 1926, following an acting presidency by Dr. Mattox, Dr. Robert F. Fitch was inaugurated fourth president. The arrival of several Westerners and the appointment of some very able Chinese brought needed strength to the staff.

Like all other colleges, Hangchow was affected by the political turmoil and anti-foreign and anti-Christian outbursts of the twenties. Winter and spring of 1926–27 were the most critical time, with Northern and Southern armies fighting for the city, the former looting and burning on the way out. After the Nanking Incident, all Americans were evacuated, leaving the college under a committee of Chinese members of the faculty. Only ninety out of the 258 students returned for the spring term.

With the establishment of the new Nationalist government in Nanking, the question of recognition took on greater urgency. To make way for a Chinese president, Dr. Robert Fitch resigned. Dr. King Chu (Chu Ching-nung), who was later to become president of Shantung Christian University, was elected to take his place as soon as policy in regard to registration had been clarified. The process received a setback in June 1928 with disapproval of the idea by the Trustees and stipulation by the Provincial Board of Education that the local board of control be all-Chinese. The Field Board of Control voted to close the college pending settlement of these issues. This decision was in part forced by financial difficulties. The faculty scattered, most of them to other parts of China but some Westerners returning home. Not until July 1931 did Chih Chiang (Hangchow) register as a full senior college.

Hangchow College reopened in the fall of 1929 with Lee Baen acting for President-Elect Chu. A Hangchow alumnus, Lee had master's degrees in arts and in business administration from America, had recently been Chairman of the Field Board of Control, and was English editor of the Shanghai Commercial Press, China's greatest publishing house. He was to serve the university tirelessly and ably until the end. With Arthur March directing the School of Science and Dr. Mattox serving as Bursar, Acting President Lee himself looked after the School of Arts. A number of able Chinese and Westerners were found to head various departments. In May 1930 King Chu, by that time Minister of Education, tendered his resignation and Baen E. Lee was elected president.

When the college reopened in 1929, it admitted 350 out of nine hundred applicants. Not one of these was a former student, all of those having sought security in other institutions. Eighteen were girls, making Hangchow for the first time co-educational.

The early thirties were a period of difficulty, internal and external, but nevertheless a time of growth and increasing stability. Student agitations continued to disturb but not to disrupt. The flood of 1931 found Hangchow surrounded by disaster. But expansion and development of campus and program continued. The Departments of Civil Engineering and of Commerce were moving rapidly toward the status of colleges. The work in arts and sciences was also growing in strength, especially in the areas of Chinese and biology. Into this increasingly happy situation, the war with Japan interjected almost overwhelming complications.

THE UNIVERSITY OF NANKING AND GINLING COLLEGE

At Nanking, the drab and somewhat empty former Ming Dynasty capital which was soon to become the more colorful and populous capital of the Nationalist government, the twenties and thirties brought increasing political activity and new life to society as a whole and saw the growth of the University of Nanking and Ginling College into two of the most impressive and most widely known of the China Colleges.

The 1920s found both institutions facing the same political and student problems which were interrupting academic routines throughout the country. Though the Shanghai troubles of 1925–26 created a tense situation and resulted in making voluntary previously required religious training, there were no untoward events until 1927, when the Nanking Incident brought tragedy to the university campus and disruption to both institutions. A few hours after the Nationalist (Southern) army from Canton had entered the city on March 24, 1927, Vice-President John E. Williams lay dead, casually shot through the head by a looting soldier. Two days later, encouraged to do so by their Chinese colleagues, all Americans in both the University and Ginling had left. It was more than a year before all returned.

With the departure of foreigners, and after re-establishment of law and order, the university reopened under a Chinese administrative committee. Eight months later, Dr. Y.G. Chen (Chen Yu-kwan) was elected president. A Nanking alumnus, with a doctorate in chemistry from Columbia University, he had joined the university staff in 1925 after having served as dean at the Peking Normal University. He had been Dean of the College of Science for a year. A deeply religious man from a large and highly respected Christian family, he had a quiet strength and devotion that won respect and served the university well.

Registration, one of the first problems the new president faced, proved simpler for Nanking than for most of the other Christian colleges. On September 20, 1928, less than a year after Dr. Chen's taking office, the University of Nanking achieved registration, the first of the China Colleges to do so. It was recognized as a university with three colleges: Arts, Science, and Agriculture. At the time it had nearly five hundred students, with roughly one-third in each college. Among these were fourteen girls.

The work in agriculture and forestry, which was to prove Nanking's outstanding contribution, received important stimulus in 1923 from two sources. After the flood of 1922, the balance of relief funds, amounting to nine hundred thousand US dollars, was given to Nanking and Yenching Universities for work in famine prevention, Nanking receiving three-fourths of the total. In 1932, following a careful review of operations, the unexpended balance, amounting to six hundred thousand dollars, was fully turned over to the University of Nanking. Also, in 1923, Cornell University entered into a cooperative relationship with the College of Agriculture and Forestry, sending visiting professors and providing opportunities for graduate study and research by Nanking faculty. From 1917 to 1931, the college was under the leadership of Dr.

John H. Reisner, one of the great agricultural missionaries.

The College of Agriculture and Forestry became the leading institution of its kind in the country, with Departments of Agricultural Economics, Agronomy, Botany (including Bacteriology and Plant Pathology), Forestry, Horticulture, Rural Education, Sericulture, and Extension. It also offered short courses such as a Rural Leaders' Training Course, a Training Course in Sericulture, and Correspondence Courses in Forestry. It maintained crop experiment stations in various parts of the country. A notable part of its research was the study of Land Utilization in China directed by Dr. J. Lossing Buck. The first Chinese Dean, K.S. Sie, was called to government service in the Ministry of Agriculture and Forestry. His successor, C.W. Chang, became Executive Secretary of the International Rice Commission of the United Nations' Food and Agricultural Organization following the Communist take-over of 1950.

At much the same time that agriculture was receiving such substantial aid, another relationship made possible the development of instruction and research in Chinese language and culture. The designation of three hundred thousand dollars in 1928 in connection with the establishment of the Harvard-Yenching Institute provided support for the development two years later of an Institute of Chinese Cultural Studies, affiliated with the College of Arts. Through its research and publications, this gained recognition not only for itself but for college and university, and helped to correct the image of the university as a Western-oriented institution.

The College of Arts showed some strength in the teaching of English and History, in studies in local government carried on by the Department of Political Science, and in research in the field of Sociology. Under the leadership of Dr. H.R. Wei, who succeeded Dr. Chen as dean when the latter assumed the presidency, the College of Science developed strong departments of Chemistry, Physics, and Zoology, degree courses in Industrial Chemistry and Electrical Engineering, and, with government support, short courses in Automotive Engineering and Audio-Visual Education. In the mid-thirties it began offering a master's degree in Chemistry. Dr. Li Fang-hsün, head of the Department of Chemistry, became the first president of the post-1950 Nanking University resulting from the merger, by the Communists, of Ginling College and the University of Nanking.

For Ginling College the early twenties were a time for building. A total of twenty-seven acres had been acquired some three-fourths of a mile west of the University of Nanking. Plans had been drawn up, adapting Chinese architecture to modern needs, for a college of four hundred students. Ginling had joined six other colleges—two in China, three in India, and one in Japan—in a campaign to raise three million dollars, with Ginling's share six hundred thousand dollars. By 1921 enough money was in hand to justify proceeding with construction, and by the fall of 1923 six buildings had been erected at a cost of three hundred thousand dollars. In 1924–25 enrolment had reached 133.

With the departure of Western faculty members following the murder of Dr. Williams of the University of Nanking, an Administrative Committee of alumnae took over responsibility. An Executive Committee of the Board of Control recommended election as president of Miss Wu Yi-fang, a member of Ginling's first entering class. Since Miss Wu was completing work for a Ph.D. in entomology at the University of Michigan, Mrs. Thurston continued as president until her return in 1928. College opened in the fall of 1927 with only ninety-five students. The faculty numbered twenty-four, of whom eight were American women who disregarded official advice not to return at that time

One of the first problems facing President Wu was that of registration. Rules regarding a Chinese president and a board of control more than half Chinese had already been met, but rules affecting religious purpose and program created difficulties. Finally, on the basis of a statement which protected the original purpose without making it explicit, Ginling College was registered in December 1930.

The early 1930s were generally a time of growth and strengthening. Enrolment soon rose above the two hundred mark. Majors were offered in biology, chemistry, Chinese, economics, English, history, music, philosophy, physical education, physics and mathematics, political science and sociology, and premedical and nursing fields. A senior-middle practice school, with a dormitory housing seventy students, had become a model tool in the training of teachers. This wide range of a dozen majors in an institution of two hundred resulted in very small classes and a relatively costly program but a high degree of personal contact and influence. The faculty had been strengthened from both Chinese and Western sources and ranked well among college faculties. The erection of a Library-Administration Building and a Chapel-Music Building completed by 1934 the academic group as planned, resulting in one of the most attractive and impressive small college campuses. Ginling received its charter from the University of the State of New York in 1935.

9
The China Colleges–South China

SOUTH CHINA

In the northern sector of what was known as South China, in the coastal city of Foochow, the twenties saw the slow and sometimes interrupted development of two institutions: Fukien Christian University, the only Protestant university between Hangchow, three hundred miles to the north, and Canton, five hundred miles to the south, and Hwa Nan College, one of the two wholly independent colleges for women in Protestant higher education in China.

FUKIEN CHRISTIAN COLLEGE

Shortly before the end of the second decade, a gift from America made possible the purchase of a permanent site for Fukien Christian College, which had been carrying on in makeshift quarters in the city. This consisted of fifty acres of rice fields and hillsides along the northern bank of the Min River ten miles below Foochow, a site of great beauty though of relative isolation. By the spring of 1922 construction was far enough advanced to permit moving to the new campus with some 120 students. However, overly enthusiastic construction had left the college seriously in debt, and John Gowdy (later Bishop) in whose home in 1911 Fukien College may be said to have been born and who succeeded President Jones on the latter's death in 1924, had to devote much of his energy to the raising of funds. The work was complicated by widespread student troubles, especially in 1927 when a general strike was called to force the turning of Fukien into a government university. When it became clear that the government itself did not approve such a move, the effort collapsed, but the need for Chinese leadership had become clear.

Foreseeing this need, President Gowdy had tried to resign in

December 1926, but it was not until six months later that the Managers accepted his resignation and appointed an Administrative Committee to carry on. The chairman of this committee was Mr. Ching-jun Lin, lecturer in political science and economics, eventually recognized as one of the foremost Christian educators of his day. A graduate of Fukien, with an M.A. from Oberlin, he had studied at Harvard, Columbia, and Drew Universities, but had declined to take the Ph.D. he might have had because he did not wish to separate himself from the rest of mankind by a "tail to his name." He was to become the builder of the modern Fukien Christian University and a greatly loved and highly admired figure. His death from cancer in 1947 was a tragic loss to the cause of Christian higher education.

The first years of President Lin's administration were not easy. Difficulties included the total loss by fire of a new dormitory, the necessity of raising funds both abroad and in China, intermittent student troubles, and the urgent need for academic and administrative reorganization. The last need was partially met by the appointment as dean of Theodore H.E. Chen, later Professor of Education and Asiatic Studies at the University of Southern California, and, for a brief period after World War II, President of Fukien Christian University. One of Fukien's distinguished alumni, Dr. Chen has continued a respected interpreter of the Chinese scene.

President Lin's first task was to meet the requirements for registration. The major stumbling block was the limitation on the propagation of religion. Registration came early in 1931, but was only partial as Fukien did not at that time meet the requirements for a university. Division of the College of Arts and Sciences provided two colleges but not the required three. Fukien therefore continued as *Wen-Li Hsüeh-Yüan* (College of Arts and Sciences) until 1942, when a College of Agriculture finally provided the essential third college.

President Lin was very conscious of the needs of the rural community, not only in the area immediately around the college but in the whole of Fukien Province, a distinctive part of China bounded on three sides by mountains and on the fourth by the sea, and of the college's responsibility to help meet those needs. Agricultural experimentation had been carried on with considerable success for a decade and there was a strong interest in rural problems. On this foundation a Department of Rural Service was erected in 1930. Its success led in 1935 to the provincial government's transferring to the college its own nearby rural experiment station, and, the following year, to support from the Nationalist government. At that time the department became a College of Rural Reconstruction, a title which, while not meeting the requirement for a university, provided improved status. Fukien had long aspired to develop a college of agriculture but had been prevented from doing so by the Correlated Program's decision that Christian forces could support only two such colleges, those at Nanking and Canton.

Support from the Harvard-Yenching Institute enabled President Lin to satisfy another strong desire, which was to have Chinese language, literature, and culture reach a position of distinction in a foreign-supported Christian institution. This goal was achieved with considerable success. The gift of the library of a Chinese scholar who had been Grand Tutor to the last Manchu emperor helped, adding greatly to the status of the college library.

It was also in the 1920s that Fukien became co-educational. The Burton Commission in 1922 had called for cooperation between Fukien and the Women's College of South China (Hwa Nan), which would have resulted in *de facto* co-education, and the Correlated Program of 1928 had urged a union of the two institutions. The Hocking Commission of 1932 had joined the chorus. Careful and prolonged consideration was given to the idea, and tentative approval had been reached before it was finally abandoned in 1936. Meanwhile, Fukien had, in 1932, admitted its first girl students. By 1936–37 girls constituted a quarter of the total of 179 students.

HWA NAN COLLEGE

A dozen miles west of Fukien Christian College, the Women's College of South China was moving into a position of stability and distinction as a leader in education for women. In 1922 it received a provisional charter from the University of the State of New York. Consideration was given to its becoming a union institution, but neither the Anglicans nor the Congregationalists (who were heavily involved in Fukien Christian College) were prepared to support it financially, and it remained Methodist. At that time there were over two hundred students in the preparatory department but fewer than fifty in the college.

Although it experienced little trouble on its campus, Hwa Nan felt the effects of the student unrest throughout the country. The number of graduates remained small, the highest being nine in 1925. However, these set high standards, six later pursuing graduate studies. Serious trouble did come with the arrival of Nationalist troops in 1927, forcing the closing of the college for several weeks. With the political and educational revolution taking place, Hwa Nan turned to Chinese leadership.

Miss Trimble, who had led Hwa Nan through its early development, was succeeded in 1925 by Dr. Ida Belle Lewis, who had served as Associate Secretary of Education for the Methodist Episcopal Church in China. Three years later, she made way for Lucy Wang, the first Chinese president of the college. A member of Hwa Nan's first four-year class, which entered college in 1917, Lucy Wang had completed her undergraduate work at Morningside College and had taken a master's degree at the University of Michigan, where she was the first Chinese woman to be awarded a Barbour Scholarship. In 1924 she had joined Hwa Nan's Department of Chemistry. When elected president, she was again at Michigan working for her doctorate. With that achieved, she returned to Hwa Nan in 1930.

Some years before her return, consideration had been given to the matter of registration, but, in the absence of a Chinese president, actual steps had been delayed. An application was presented in 1931, but much remained to be done. Though Hwa Nan's budget and salaries were below minimal official standards, the faculty serving on a clearly sacrificial basis, the high quality of the staff was evident, an unusual proportion of the Chinese members having studied abroad. The fact that seventy-eight percent of Hwa Nan's graduates were serving their country in education, medicine, and social service also made a favorable impression. In 1933 Hwa Nan secured provisional registration and in the following year permanent registration as a college of arts and sciences. That fall the New York Regents granted it an absolute charter with power to confer B.A. and B.S. degrees.

Throughout these years pressure had continued for Hwa Nan to affiliate in some manner with Fukien Christian College. The distance between the two institutions provided one obstacle, but the main cause of reluctance on Hwa Nan's part was a deep conviction of the advantages of a small and purely women's college. Though a joint committee of the two boards tentatively approved consolidation in 1935, nothing was done and, in 1936, the Board of Trustees of the South China Women's College voted against union, stating that "Co-education is premature in China and also in America."

LINGNAN UNIVERSITY

Far to the south, Canton Christian College began a period of development which saw it grow from a very small and tentative four-year college to an established university with a varied academic program and growing local support. Enrolment, only a little over a hundred in 1920–21, had reached nearly six hundred by 1936–37. The College of Arts and Sciences had become a university with colleges of arts and science, engineering, medicine, and agriculture.

The College of Agriculture was the first to be added. This was largely an outcome of the work of Dr. George Weidman Groff, a horticulturist who had come to the college in 1908. For most of his career, his support came from the faculty and students of Pennsylvania State College, his alma mater, which continued its interest in Lingnan for nearly forty years. He had developed a model dairy, established a citrus-introduction station, and set up a herbarium which was to become outstanding. Sericulture had also received a start. The college came into being in 1921–22 with the elevation to that status of an earlier department of agriculture. A Chinese Board of Managers assumed full financial responsibility and in 1923–24 raised forty-three thousand dollars to balance its budget. However, the college never drew more than a handful of students or produced more than an occasional graduate, though it continued experimentation in such fields as horticulture, sericulture, and animal husbandry. A subcollegiate agricultural school was added in 1928 but closed ten years later.

The College of Medicine had its roots in early efforts in the field of medical education but had been slow in growing. The withdrawal in 1914 of the University Medical College supported by the Christian Association of the University of Pennsylvania had been followed by a long interval of inactivity. Finally in 1930 Lingnan accepted responsibility for the famous ninety-year-old Canton Hospital. Negotiations with Hackett Medical College for Women of the American Presbyterian Mission led to the establishment of the Dr. Sun Yat-sen Medical College of Lingnan University in 1935 in a building in Canton given by the Nanking government.

The College of Engineering was made possible in 1929 by cooperation with the Ministry of Railways, which was headed by Sun Fo, son of Dr. Sun Yat-sen, who was at that time also president of the Lingnan Board of Directors. The College later became a department of the College of Science.

In 1923 President Edmunds resigned to become Provost of Johns Hopkins University and was succeeded by Dr. James M. Henry, who had been born in China of missionary parents. A member of the Canton Mission of the Presbyterian Board, Henry had taught at Pui Ying School and at Union Theological College in Canton. He had an unusual command of the Cantonese dialect. He joined Lingnan in 1919, serving first as Executive Secretary and then as Vice-President. After the war, Dr. Henry was for a time Deputy Director of UNRRA for Kwangtung Province, then adviser to the Governor of Kwangtung, becoming an "Illustrious Citizen," and then Director of Lingnan's New York office.

Because of its location in Canton, where the Kuomintang was in control, Lingnan was the first of the Christian colleges to feel the effects of the new nationalism which found expression in the Nationalist Revolution. Beginning in 1925 it had for several years to struggle with the problems of civil war and anti-foreignism. For a week in early June 1925 the campus was involved in fighting between Cantonese troops and an army from Yunnan Province. Ten days later the college was torn apart by the turbulence and controversy resulting from the tragic ending to a patriotic parade in Canton commemorating the Shanghai "Massacre" of May 30. Responsibility for the first shot was never determined, but British and French marines had killed fifty-one paraders, including a professor and a student from Lingnan. Public statements by faculty and administration, though generally favoring the Chinese and deploring the shooting, failed to satisfy either side. For a time there was a complete strike of workmen and a taking over of the institution. One American and one British faculty member were forced to leave. Although official relations soon returned to normal, student feeling against Lingnan remained bitter for some time. However, the next year another strike was settled through government arbitration and an effort to wreck the college was thwarted by a majority of the students themselves.

In the summer of 1925 a group of alumni proposed a plan for placing the university under Chinese control. Later that year, when the Ministry of Education issued regulations governing educational institutions established with foreign funds, the university had little difficulty complying. In 1927 the new, more stringent requirements for registration were met by a plan which included a Chinese Board of Directors financially responsible for support of Chinese faculty and staff, an American Foundation responsible for support of Western personnel, a Chinese president, and a Resident Director of the Foundation, called Provost in English, Adviser in Chinese. Registration followed in 1928.

Trouble, however, continued. First a strike by the Workmen's Union and then one by the Union of the Non-Teaching Staff disrupted life. With word of the Nanking Incident of 1927, American women and children left. The institution closed in April, but classes continued in the city and examinations were held there. In the fall a new, largely Chinese administration took over and began a relatively peaceful ten years of expansion.

President during this decade was Chung Wing-kwang, former head of the Chinese Department, who had early shown remarkable ability to raise funds among Chinese residents in Southeast Asia, had served as Dean, and had been appointed Associate President with President Henry in 1923. One of three graduates in 1905, Mr. Chung had taken both the first and second literary degrees. Though strongly anti-Christian in his youth, he had become a Christian while in Canton Hospital and remained a strong supporter of religious freedom. He served for a time as Commissioner of Education for the province of Kwangtung and, even after he became president, as a member of the Central Government's Educational Commission.

Among the developments at Lingnan was the Exchange Student Plan, which began with one student from America who spent the year 1933–34 at the university. The next year eleven arrived, and in 1936–37, thirty. In four years, eighty-eight students came from twenty-six American and Canadian colleges.

10

The China Colleges– Central and West China

HUACHUNG COLLEGE

In Central China, the second decade of the twentieth century had ended with one university, one four-year college, and five small "colleges," in reality largely middle schools, attempting to meet the educational needs of that area through the opening of post-secondary courses. In 1922, however, the American Episcopal, Reformed Church (U.S.), Wesleyan Methodist, London, United Evangelical, Yale, and, unofficially, Lutheran Missions came to the unanimous decision that "an attempt should be made to organize a Central China University possibly in Wuchang." The hope of establishing a first-class institution was encouraged by the fact that the two strongest units complemented each other, Yale being strong in science and Boone in the training of church leaders, librarians, teachers, and businessmen.

However, obvious difficulties stood in the way. The five missions, three American and two British, had their vested interests and peculiar goals, backed by home boards with even greater fear and less vision. And there were articulate groups of alumni fearful of losing identity. Nor was the question of site a simple one. In Changsha, where land was cheap, Yale had the newest plant, and its medical school would have to remain there because of an agreement with the provincial government. In Wuchang, the Boone buildings were old, the campus small, and land costly. However, the Wuhan area, the "Chicago" of China, was more accessible to the graduates of the middle schools looked to as feeders. General feeling favored Wuhan.

Four missions quickly approved an overall plan. Most of the institutions of the area agreed to merge their college work in a new university in Wuchang, though Yale-in-China was not prepared to leave Changsha. A Provisional Board quickly approved plans to start in the fall of 1923, with a college of arts and sciences to be located on part of the

Boone campus, the cooperating units setting up residential colleges or hostels, and all alumni to be recognized as alumni of the university. The new institution opened in September 1924 for a three-year trial period, with the Reverend (later Bishop) Alfred A. Gilman as Acting President of Huachung University and the Reverend Arthur M. Sherman as President of Boone University. Boone retained its corporate entity in order to provide for the granting of degrees.

Under this dual control, the university opened with eighty-nine students, of whom thirty-four were freshmen. A surprisingly successful first year was terminated by anti-foreign demonstrations in May 1925. Although the second year saw a lower enrolment, it proceeded smoothly and plans were drawn up for permanent union to follow the trial period. In the summer of 1926, however, interruption came again with the defeat of the local warlord by the Northern Expedition of the Nationalists and the siege of Wuchang, during which Huachung campus became a refugee camp. The third year saw more and more frequent interruptions as anti-foreign demonstrations increased. Yale-in-China in Changsha was forced to close and, at the end of the first semester of 1926–27, its college of science, under Dr. Paul C.T. Kwei, moved to Wuchang with a few students and some equipment. Thus was initiated the first real cooperation between Yale-in-China and Huachung. Following the Nanking Incident of March 1927, most of the Westerners were forced to leave, but the Chinese faculty carried on under the leadership of Dean Francis Wei until, his life being threatened, he too found it advisable to seek safety in Shanghai. Shortly thereafter, the university was forced to close. Thus ended what has been called the First Huachung.

By September the political situation had improved sufficiently to permit the opening of a junior middle school in Boone and the carrying on of Boone Library School under its original name. The university, however, remained inactive for two years and might well have been abandoned had it not been for Bishop Gilman, who argued successfully for an early reopening on a broader basis. A college in that area would be the only Christian institution of higher learning in four provinces with more than one hundred million people. Gilman was the dominant Western figure in the life of Huachung. Succeeding Dr. James Jackson as President of Boone University, he brought it to an enrolment of five hundred, of whom one hundred were in college. He then became the first president of Huachung University. Through the dark days of 1927–29 he never lost sight of the vision, caught many years before, of a university supported by all the missions of Central China.

The Second Huachung opened in September 1929 with Dr. Francis C.M. Wei as president. Five missions pledged support for a total of twenty-five faculty members and Yale-in-China promised an annual grant for the College of Science equipment. Because the program to be offered was comparable to that of an American liberal arts college, the English name was changed to Huachung College. Opening was on a small scale, with seventeen teachers and thirty-one students. Initially the strongest unit in the consolidation had been Boone Library School. With the return in 1928 of its founder, Miss Mary Elizabeth Wood, that school proved the most reluctant to yield autonomy. The fact that, as a result of Miss Wood's help in securing passage of the bill returning to China the last part of the American Boxer Indemnity, the China Foundation made the school an annual grant strengthened an already powerful feeling of independence. Unwilling to become an integral part of the college, Boone Library School chose to go it alone even though on the same campus. Efforts looking toward reunion failed in 1937 and again in 1947–50, and Huachung developed without assistance from Boone other than the granting of degrees, a service no longer required after its registration in 1931. Eleven degrees were granted in 1930.

Leader and molder of the Second Huachung, Francis Wei was one of the towering figures of Christian higher education in China, one of the great Chinese Christian educators. Son of a Cantonese tea merchant, he had established a brilliant scholastic record as a member of Boone University's first graduating class in 1911. He had also become a Christian. He was eventually to serve as representative from China at the International Missionary Conference in Jerusalem (1928) and a delegate of the Chinese Church to the Edinburgh Conference on Faith and Order (1937). He earned a doctor's degree from the London School of Economics in 1929. Combining vision, scholarship, and administrative skill, Dr. Wei gave Huachung and, later, Christian higher education, high ideals and wise guidance.

With him were associated some very able men, American, British, and Chinese. Dr. Paul C.T. Kwei, who came to Huachung from Yale-in-China, built up the College of Science and contributed much to the university as a whole before leaving to join National Wuhan University early in the war. Dr. P'u Hwang, who was a member of the first class to graduate from Yale-in-China and had been Principal of the Yali Union Middle School, filled the post of Dean of Education for twenty years and served as Acting President more than once.

Though Huachung was thought of as a foreign institution, it had no foreign charter or overseas governing body prior to registration in China, when a Board of Founders was set up in New York. With registration, Huachung once again became a "university," with three colleges: Arts, Science, and Education. The last of these was a unique feature, for government policy prevented any other Christian institution from establishing a college of education. As time went on, work in science grew in importance and in quality, and by 1935 more than half of Huachung's students were majoring in that field.

The next few years brought only modest growth but did see improvement of facilities and strengthening of the academic program. There was no seeking after numbers, and not until after the war, when pressures became too great to resist, did Huachung's enrolment exceed 250. The perennial question of a permanent site seemed about to be answered in 1937 with acquisition of additional land and receipt of substantial gifts for Huachung's first complete campus. With growth in academic strength, prospects in the spring of 1937 were brighter than ever before. President Wei left on sabbatical leave in a more optimistic frame of mind than he had been able to enjoy in years. Caught by the war, he was not to see Huachung again for nearly a decade.

YALE-IN-CHINA

The year 1921 brought a serious threat to Yali's future. Among the recommendations of the Burton Commission, those for Central China proposed turning over the academic plant at Changsha to the Hunan Missions for a middle school and Yali's uniting with other organizations in college work in Wuhan. A later tempering to permit non-duplicating senior-college work at both Wuhan and Changsha met a generally favorable reaction from the Governing Board at Changsha but strong opposition among the Trustees in New Haven. Yali continued its college work until Communist troubles in 1927 forced it to close, following which the Trustees approved union with Central China (Huachung) University in Wuhan.

The last years of non-medical college work at Changsha were marred by disorders resulting from the anti-foreign and anti-Christian movements, Yali barely escaping destruction in 1925. A brief interval of quiet ended with the arrival of left-wing members of the Kuomintang organizing laborers, farmers, and students. Outrageous demands led to strikes against Middle School, College, and Nursing School, and pressures on the Medical College. Academic departments closed before the end of the year, and all Westerners had left by April 1927.

As conditions improved, consideration was given to reopening. In August 1928 the Middle School joined a cooperative union with other Christian missions, with Yali furnishing facilities and teachers and the missions meeting expenses. Meanwhile, a start had been made on reopening the various schools and strengthening the hospital, which had continued to operate. The property had fortunately been well protected by the courage and skill of Chinese custodians, but the former Chinese staff had widely scattered.

Dr. Hume had already resigned to make way for a Chinese leader. Dr. K.Y. Wang became superintendent of the hospital and then Dean of the Medical College, which reopened with forty-five students in September 1929. The School of Nursing resumed classes at the same time. The years to 1937 saw both schools raise their standards and reach enrolments of over one hundred. The hospital too provided ever increasing service, most notably in the area of public health.

Late in 1928 the Trustees voted in favor of joining Huachung University, and the following year Yale-in-China transferred to Wuchang its School of Science, which it undertook to support as "The Yale-in-China School of Science in Hua Chung College." Dr. Paul C.T. Kwei, Yale '17 and holder of a doctorate in physics from Princeton, went with the school to serve as its dean.

At the same time that the new Huachung College was uniting the efforts of half a dozen ambitious colleges and middle schools, a new college was coming into being in Central China. At Iyang, in the heart of Hunan Province and not far from Yali, the Church of Sweden Mission in cooperation with the Lutheran Church of China was developing what was to be known as Lutheran College. Emphasizing European languages and philosophy, it opened college courses in 1923. Three years later, when troubles forced it to close temporarily, it had thirty-one students. Though refusing to apply for registration, it reopened but finally gave up college work in 1931, five students then transferring to Huachung.

WEST CHINA UNION UNIVERSITY

The years between 1920 and 1937 were a time of material and academic growth for West China Union University. Chengtu, a thousand miles from the sea, continued somewhat remote from the economic and social developments of the more accessible north, south, east, and even center, but ultimately shared, without great delay or dilution, in the political and intellectual turmoil of the period. Increasingly in touch with the rest of Protestant higher education, West China kept pace, in its own way, with its sister institutions.

The question of incorporation had been given early consideration. Attempts to affiliate the university with the University of Chicago or with Oxford University had failed. In May 1922 West China received a provisional charter from the University of the State of New York, but this, requiring that examination results be sent to New York for inspection, was less than satisfactory. An absolute charter was finally granted twelve years later.

The second decade of the university's life opened with bright prospects and great hopes, but the 1920s were not without trouble. Student unrest affected West China as it did other parts of the country. Anti-foreign and anti-Christian movements quickly penetrated Szechwan, and Communist activity soon reached it. Lawlessness grew under warlords, and no part of China suffered more from brigandage and civil war. Chengtu went through several sieges and a boycott of foreigners and their goods. In 1927 almost all foreigners were forced to leave.

Also at this time the university was struggling with the frustrating and protracted process of registration. Pressure came not only from local groups but from abroad. In 1925 the Board of Governors approved the idea of registration and urged an increase in Chinese leadership. Many Westerners feared that registration would mean loss of Christian character, but the University Senate came to realize that there was no alternative. The Senate was reorganized to include a majority of Chinese, with Dr. Lincoln Dsang as vice-president to handle negotiations. Registration with the Provincial Board of Education was completed by the end of 1927, but negotiations with the National Government dragged on for several years. In 1932 the Senate gave way to a Board of Directors, Dr. Dsang succeeded Dr. Joseph Beech, and, after further political maneuvering, registration was completed in 1933.

Through these disturbances, interruptions, and negotiations, West China Union University continued to grow in size and in variety and quality of program. By the time of registration, the campus covered 160 acres and students numbered some 350. The university consisted of Colleges of Arts, Science, and Medicine and Dentistry, a Woman's College, and a School of Religion. The Colleges of Medicine and Dentistry, united in 1927, had become the institution's most distinctive

feature. A Department of Pharmacy established in 1932 was contributing to pharmaceutical research and the training of pharmacists. In ten
years it reached an enrolment of two hundred, more than one-third of
whom were women.

The question of higher education for women had been raised at the
start, but no action had resulted until 1920, when the founding of a
woman's college was proposed. By 1924 the university was open to
women, and two years later the Woman's College became a separate
unit. Ten years later women students made up to one-third of the total.

Another field in which the university contributed leadership was
agriculture. One of the richest agricultural regions in China, the area
around Chengtu offered both opportunity and challenge. Courses in
agriculture early became part of the curriculum of the Faculty of Education, but a separate Department of Agriculture did not start until 1934.

Other academic developments included a library and museum.
Starting with few books, little money, and no building, the library
achieved by 1933–34 the then respectable total of ninety-five thousand
volumes. Major help had come through a gift of twenty-five thousand
volumes from a prominent Chengtu family. An adequate building rose in
1926. This was shared with an anthropological, archaeological,
ethnological museum. With West China a fertile source in these fields,
the museum became not only outstanding in the area but, in some
respects, of international significance.

In October 1936 West China Union University celebrated its
twenty-fifth anniversary with considerable pride and great hope. Less
than a year later, war broke out and West China became a haven for less
fortunately situated institutions.

Part
4

The China Colleges, An Overall View

11
Foreign or Chinese?

A major handicap facing the Christian colleges as they entered the third decade of the century was their foreign coloring. That this was due largely to unavoidable circumstances rather than to imperialistic intention, did not alter the fact or weaken the criticism which swelled with increasing nationalism. They were obviously foreign institutions in spite of their locations and no matter how earnestly and well they might be serving China.

This was so for a number of reasons. They had been started by foreign missionaries who were under the protection of foreign governments; and they were chartered under foreign laws. They had been staffed largely by foreigners—even in 1920 more than half of the staff members were non-Chinese—and were being run mainly by foreigners. The fact that they were supported by gifts from abroad, while meeting a need the Chinese Church could not itself answer, carried implications, however unfounded, of dollar imperialism. Their religious character was a less irritating factor, objected to on nationalistic rather than specifically religious grounds.

The Christian colleges were also dominantly a foreign type of institution. In the absence of a modern Chinese system of higher education, anything new was inevitably foreign. A modern college was clearly a foreign importation, strikingly different from the classical education of China. The introducers were Western and the pattern they provided was basically Anglo-American, the curriculum that of British and American universities. That was what the Chinese desired, identifying it with the "modern" education they sought. The earliest government college, the T'ung Wen Kuan, had emphasized European languages—English, French, Russian, German—and scientific subjects. The Christian colleges provided a similar response, though they added an emphasis on religion and moral science.

Though the early schools had suffered from being part of the

Western invasion of China, they had not been singled out for attack. Their educational contribution during a time when purely Chinese facilities were largely lacking served to outweigh their foreignness. But with the intensely nationalistic trends of the 1920s, the naturalization which was desirable on any account became imperative.

Probably most obvious among the factors determining the popular concept of the Christian college as a foreign institution was the preponderance of foreign staff in the early years of their development and the continued presence of a considerable foreign minority during their later years. From the point of view of staff, the Christian colleges were clearly more foreign than government and other private institutions, which had no such overseas ties, though many of the latter would have welcomed them. An important exception was Tsinghua, the Boxer Indemnity College in Peking, which, because of its purpose, in its first years relied heavily on American instructors.

At the beginning this foreignness was unavoidable. There simply were too few Chinese with a modern education. The later presence of Chinese with knowledge of and experience in modern education was due in no small measure to the work of the Christian colleges. These institutions themselves tended to be staffed by their own graduates, especially "returned students," those who had studied abroad and come back. In 1892 the Arts faculty of Peking University consisted of four Americans and two Chinese, the latter teaching only Chinese studies; that of the North China College, of eight Americans and two Chinese similarly engaged. By 1909 Peking University had five Chinese teaching non-Chinese subjects. In the late 1880s, St. John's had on its staff, in addition to three teachers of Chinese studies, five Chinese who had been sent by the government in 1872 to study in America, but these were involved chiefly in the preparatory department. Even in 1906, when St. John's actually became a university, there was, except for three in the Chinese department, only one Chinese with thirteen Westerners. That one, W.W. Yen, later became Prime Minister.

Following the Revolution, there came a steady growth in numbers of Chinese faculty members, a process which accelerated as more and more qualified Chinese were available and as nationalistic pressures increased. All institutions followed much the same pattern except that those which developed late had a greater pool of talent to draw on and could move more quickly toward the goal of a predominantly national faculty. By 1923–24, the total numbers of Chinese and of Westerners on the staffs of the fourteen Christian colleges were almost exactly equal, though percentages of Chinese faculty in individual institutions ranged from twenty to seventy. By 1932, full-time Chinese teachers outnumbered Westerners two to one, and by 1936, four to one. Before the end, as the result of increases in institutional size coinciding with decreases in missionary personnel, the ratio was more nearly nine to one.

The shoe was now on the other foot and the pressure was for more Westerners. Though due in part to the fact that mission boards rarely offered cash in place of person and so every missionary helped the budget, this also reflected a real appreciation of the value of the internationalism to which the Westerner contributed and which constituted a distinctive and important feature of the Christian college. However, there was a growing emphasis on quality, an insistence that the Westerner be as well trained as his Chinese colleagues and have some distinctive contribution to offer. The preference was for scientists, Chinese scientists being in high demand everywhere, and for teachers of English, a field in which foreignness was something of an asset. Missionaries no longer automatically qualified as university professors or were acceptable simply because they came without cost. No institution was aiming at an all-Chinese staff, though in a few instances an increase in the percentage of Chinese was still being sought, but all were seeking the highest quality of Westerner. Academically this usually meant possession of a doctorate as more and more of the Chinese faculty were themselves achieving this goal. In the mid-twenties, a sixth of the teaching faculties of the Protestant colleges possessed the Ph.D. or its equivalent, with more than a third holding the master's degree, figures which would have been higher had it not been that the bachelor's degree or less was usually considered adequate in the field of Chinese language and literature. By the thirties the respective figures were more nearly a quarter and a half.

Fully as critical as the percentage of Chinese on the staff was the issue of the positions held. All Christian colleges started with Western administrators and department heads. Only relatively late in the history of the China Colleges did nationals take over leadership. The first presidents were of necessity Western, and in most cases the top leadership continued to be Western until registration required a Chinese president. This was not due entirely to Western reluctance. In 1910 President Bowen of Nanking argued that Chinese should be pressed into leadership "just as rapidly as, and possibly a little more rapidly than, many think wise," a point of view shared by others in spite of problems of implementation. There was also a factor of Chinese hesitation. A reversal of role, especially as it involved dealing with remote founders and trustees, carried with it unknowns. Nor was there yet an adequate supply of presidential timber. In some instances, election of a Chinese president had been considered earlier, but no Chinese president took office before 1927, when five institutions installed national leadership. Three followed in 1928, three in 1929, one in 1932, and one not until 1937. In the case of Yenching, a compromise resulted in continuing Leighton Stuart in the presidency, which he held until 1946 when he became American Ambassador, and electing a Chinese to the Chancellorship, a technically higher post. Though this arrangement functioned with reasonable smoothness under a succession of Chinese chancellors—for the last dozen years with Dr. H.H. Kung, one of the top leaders of the Nationalist government—it would hardly have worked in all cases. No other institution tried it.

In some cases Westerners continued to serve as deans, but the trend was toward a predominantly national administration. By 1928 the great majority of deans were Chinese. Where Westerners retained such posts, the cause was usually lack of an available Chinese replacement. At least race was no longer an issue.

Initially, local governing bodies, as distinguished from overseas boards of trustees, had been, as Boards of Control, of Directors, or of Managers, or even as University Councils, in most cases entirely Western in membership. Two exceptions were Lingnan, which had functioned without a local board except for its College of Agriculture, which was under Chinese control, and Yale-in-China, whose medical work was under a predominantly Chinese Board of Managers. Beginning in the second decade, Chinese were slowly added to boards until, with registration, they constituted a two-thirds majority. By the late 1920s, therefore, most of the Christian colleges had become sufficiently Chinese in leadership to silence some of the criticism leveled against them as foreign institutions. However, the continuation of overseas boards of trustees and continued financial dependence on overseas sources still provided grounds for suspicion as to the degree of nationalism and independence achieved. In reality the boards of trustees had no power not tied to the strings of overseas purses or dependent on the waning significance of Western degrees. The power of the purse could have seriously jeopardized institutional independence and made a mockery of claims of nationalism had it been unwisely used. Actually it was rarely exerted, the degree of support being almost always affected not by disagreement as to policy but by ability to provide what was needed, and the use of money being almost completely planned and determined in

China. There was very little actual financial imperialism. With the ignoring in China of the American degree and the growing acceptance of the Chinese degree, overseas charters also came to have less and less significance.

With the growing nationalism of the twenties, a major issue confronting all the Christian colleges in China was that of official recognition by the Chinese government. In the absence of any chartering body in China, Protestant colleges and universities sought charters abroad. They were foreign institutions generally welcomed for their contribution to the inadequate total of higher education but not an official part of that education. The issue of government recognition as an essential for domestication had been raised by the colleges themselves early in the century, but government response had been largely lacking. Regulations issued in 1917 and in 1920 sought to integrate mission institutions more closely into the main body of Chinese higher education but involved no government control. The Ministry of Education took the position that "educational institutions established by funds contributed by foreigners ... should receive the same treatment as other private institutions in this country" and therefore had merely to report to the Ministry.

An opportunity to become officially a part of the national system of education first came in 1925 when the Ministry of Education stated the conditions on which "institutions established by funds contributed by foreigners" might register with the government. In addition to requiring that the institution be known as private by having the term *szu-li* (privately established) prefixed to its name, the conditions demanded four important changes:

1. The president or principal must be a Chinese. If a foreigner was head of the institution, a Chinese vice-president could be appointed to apply for recognition.
2. More than half of the board of managers must be Chinese.
3. The institution should not "have as its purpose the propagation of religion."
4. The curriculum should conform to standards set by the Ministry of Education and "shall not include religious courses among required subjects."

Only the two regulations affecting religious purpose and practice caused serious difficulty. These were not solely anti-Christian, being directed also against a move to make Confucianism the state religion and the use of religion as a means of international aggression, especially by the Japanese. On the positive side they represented a conviction, not wholly absent from the Christian educational forces, that the primary aim of education should be education. This belief lay behind the restriction of new colleges of education to government institutions.

Response to this document varied widely. Some institutions acted quickly and positively. In April 1926 the Trustees of Yenching University approved application for registration, having concluded on the basis of a clarification secured from the Ministry that the restrictions were not at variance with the object of a university "founded and conducted on strictly Christian and evangelical, but not sectarian principles." The necessary changes were made and, in February 1927, Yenching momentarily registered on the basis of the 1925 regulations. Following the same interpretation of the Ministry's statement to mean that "Government registration would not compromise the Christian purpose of the University," the Administrative Council of Shantung Christian University authorized registration. Despite opposition from some missionaries and Chinese leaders, the University of Shanghai, which had already made religious courses and exercises voluntary, also applied. At Lingnan University, where religious courses and exercises had also already been made optional, the problem was solved early in 1927 by turning control over to a Chinese Board of Directors which leased the institution from the American Foundation and assumed financial responsibility for all expenses except those for Western personnel. The Hangchow Directors, who had sought recognition as early as 1917, made the necessary changes, but the Trustees disapproved unless the Christian character and purpose of the college could be maintained. Since this was interpreted to mean that worship and religious instruction would be required of all students, registration could not be immediately effected. At St. John's University, President Pott, fearful of the elimination of active Christian teaching and conscious of the revolution then in progress, advised his board to "wait on the course of events." Other institutions explored the problem both on the field and at home but took no action in the early stages of government pressure.

Before any of the Christian colleges except Yenching had been accepted on the basis of the 1925 regulations, a new government with stronger feelings of nationalism had come into being. In 1927 the Nanking Ministry of Education, while calling more forcefully for registration, stiffened the requirements. For one thing, a Chinese vice-president would not suffice; there must be a Chinese president. For another, two-thirds of the members of the Board of Directors, and not merely a majority, must be Chinese. Again, any institution aspiring to be a university must have at least three colleges.

Registration required that attendance at religious services be voluntary and that courses in religion be elective. Reaction to these requirements varied from fear to relief, the first more common among home boards and Western staff than among Chinese. Among the latter, including graduates of the colleges, there was severe criticism, not only of the religious emphasis as encouraging superstition and furthering denationalization but of religious courses because of the often voluntary and untrained instruction associated with them. Some institutions had already made the change: Shantung and Yenching as early as 1923; Lingnan and Soochow in 1925-26. Others took the necessary steps in the process of applying for registration.

The chief issue continued to be the religious one related to the purpose of the institution. This issue was usually met by restatements which emphasized the educational purpose while retaining the essence of Christian concern. Sometimes these were without reference to the religious motivation. An early statement gave Nanking's aim as promoting higher education in China "for young men of all classes, under the best intellectual, moral, and physical influences." Yenching later gave as its purpose: "To give that type of higher education which develops intellectual, moral and physical strength and equips for leadership, in order to meet the national and social needs of the Republic of China." In other cases an effort was made to retain the essence of Christian concern. At Fukien the new catalog issued in Chinese stated that "Fukien University offers education to the young men of China on a collegiate level in a spirit of love, service and sacrifice." Hangchow and Shantung borrowed this language but added references to moral qualifications and intellectual training in "meeting the needs of society." Other institutions made similar changes but usually retained specific references to Christian principles. Ginling spoke of conforming to the highest educational standards, promoting social welfare and high ideals of citizenship, and developing the highest type of character "in accordance with the original purpose of the five Christian Mission Boards which were its founders." Huachung referred to the purpose of the separate colleges which preceded Huachung as "developing men of talent through higher education on the foundation of the power of love and sacrifice of the Christian religion, with the hope of bringing in the Kingdom of God and perpetual peace among men." Shanghai, after speaking of educational efficiency and citizenship, offered "education which is consciously directed to the promotion of religious ends consonant with the original purpose of the founders to promote evangelical Christianity in China and America."

For most of the Protestant colleges, the added requirements in regard to presidents and boards represented delays rather than insuperable obstacles. With one or two exceptions, the institutions set about the task of reorganization, electing Chinese presidents where these did not already exist, and establishing predominantly Chinese governing boards. Academic reorganization was usually a problem only where university status was sought, since that was not essential for registration.

Fukien could at once meet the first two requirements, but action on its application was delayed by unfriendly elements in Nanking for three years. Hangchow proceeded with the necessary changes but met with obstruction in the provincial Bureau of Education and also waited three years. Ginling was granted registration after making changes in its constitution. Hwa Nan had to go through the same process and was granted temporary registration in 1933 on the understanding that it would make changes in its equipment, staff, and budget. Huachung, which had just been reborn, delayed application pending preparation of a constitution satisfactory to its five home boards and five missions. It was granted recognition late in 1931. Under its first Chinese president, Nanking applied almost at once and was registered within a year. Shanghai was unable to act prior to appointment of a Chinese president, which came a year later, but then had no difficulty. Shantung was able to meet the requirements but was held up by political agitation and was not registered until 1931. West China quickly elected a Chinese president and set up a Chinese board of control, but negotiations with the government in Nanking dragged on for five years before recognition was obtained. Yenching, faced with the need for rather drastic changes in administration, control, and organization, consumed some time in reacquiring the earlier recognition it had enjoyed for so short a time. By 1933, all institutions had registered with the exceptions of St. John's University, and of Lutheran College which, up to its closing in 1931, steadfastly refused to apply.

In the case of St. John's University, fears on the part of the home board blocked registration for a considerable length of time. In 1928 the university wrote to parents to say that it had not registered and might not do so unless the government accepted it as a Christian mission institution openly teaching Christianity. This situation did not appear to affect seriously its popularity, for enrolment continued to increase. However, in the spring of 1931 notice arrived that no non-registered schools would be permitted to take in new students. Since the power of decision was in the hands of absent bishops, the Board of Directors had to reply that it could take no action. Though initial steps were taken later, St. John's continued in this anomalous state, unregistered but accepting students, for fourteen years, until it was finally registered in 1948, shortly before its disappearance.

The necessary changes met in some cases with resistance from home boards. Approval often carried such phrases as "provided Christian character of institution is safeguarded." Since such assurance could only be a matter of opinion and must remain a hope until proved or disproved by events, the question remained an issue in many minds even after registration had been granted. In the course of time it became clearer that whether or not the Christian character of an institution was preserved depended not on any statement of purpose but on the character and convictions of those who guided, administered, and taught. These varied from place to place and from time to time. Likewise, standards of evaluation could not be the same in all places and at all times. In the light of future developments, it does not appear that compliance with the rules regarding religion had any serious ill effects. Such changes in Christian character as took place are better ascribed to alterations in political, economic, intellectual, and moral conditions.

Except for periods of extreme nationalism when the foreign connections of the colleges became sources of irritation, relations with the national government were generally happy and constructive. The colleges conformed to the prescribed curricula, were accepted on an equal basis with government and other private institutions, suffered much the same bureaucratic controls, and benefited from occasional government grants. This feeling of relative ease did not, however, extend equally to the Kuomintang Party, which maintained a careful watch over both students and teachers in all educational institutions. The former were encouraged, albeit largely unsuccessfully, to join the Party's Youth Corps. There was pressure, though not usually compulsion, for faculty to join the Party, but only a small minority did. Few of the Christian college presidents were members, and then only nominally so.

Active demonstration of support of the government was limited to participation in three kinds of activity: a regular memorial service, courses in Kuomintang ideology, and military training, all very much under the direction of the Party. After establishment of the Nationalist government in 1927, a regular Monday morning Memorial Service was required of all registered schools. This consisted of reciting Dr. Sun Yat-sen's will, bowing before his portrait and the National flag, singing the National song, and a brief period of silence. Considered by some to be idolatry, and by others a meaningless bore, it was generally accepted as a serious if often ineffective expression of patriotism.

Courses in the principles of the Party, based on Dr. Sun Yat-sen's *San Min Chu I* (the Three Principles of the People), were required of all college students. They were under direction of an "Indoctrination Officer," whose responsibility was both to instruct and to check deviation. Unfortunately for their purpose, they were rarely so conducted as to hold interest, and constituted one element in the failure of the Kuomintang to gain the support of China's youth.

Military training, which also became a requirement in 1928, was under a Director of Military Drill appointed by the institution but approved by the Party. Held three days a week, it constituted a form of required exercise whether or not it proved of great military value. For some, requiring a Christian college to give military training constituted an unhappy infringement of academic and religious liberty.

Supervision of dormitory life also became a responsibility of the military officer. More serious and ultimately damaging were the attempts at thought control which resulted in the posting of Party representatives in the faculties of all institutions and even the placing of spies in classes. The result was an absence of public discussion of political and other controversial subjects and increasing alienation of students and faculty from the Party.

12
Academic Programs

What sort of institutions were the China Colleges as measured by their academic programs? Whatever other qualities might be read into the term "education," formal learning necessarily constituted a basic goal—indeed a *sine qua non* without which they neither should nor could have existed. This fundamental academic concern was almost universal even when special emphasis was placed on the social, moral, and religious aspects of education. The colleges were educational institutions which fully recognized their academic responsibilities.

As might be expected, the China Colleges met these responsibilities with varying degrees of success: some very well, some perhaps less than adequately, and in all cases with a wide range of achievement within the institution itself. Evaluation of academic quality itself varies with the yardstick used: Chinese or Western, university or college, the top ten or the bottom hundred. No scientific study was ever made; only a rough judgment can now be offered.

First, it is clear that not even the best of the colleges should be compared in sweep of offerings, extent and quality of facilities, or luminosity of scholarly galaxies, with the Harvards and Oxfords of the Western world or the Todais (Tokyo National) of Asia. Comparison with the top government universities of China is also of doubtful validity. Except on the Chinese scale in which three departments constituted a college and three colleges earned the title of university, even the largest of the Protestant institutions, with eight hundred to a thousand students and not reaching beyond an occasional M.A., were not universities in the Western sense and but small versions in the Chinese. Even the most ambitious was hardly more than a college with a professional school attached. As such they can more fairly be compared to American colleges—especially church-related colleges—though the programs attempted were often more varied and more ambitious.

From the start the China Colleges were basically undergraduate institutions, granting the B.A. and B.S. degrees for the completion of four years of a post-secondary education roughly comparable to that provided by American colleges of the same era. (With registration and the prescribing of curricula by the Ministry of Education, the matching of details becomes difficult, but the comparison remains fundamentally valid, the chief difference being a higher degree of specialization in China.) At first, limits were set by practical considerations or by chartering bodies abroad; later, restraints were imposed by the government, which was soundly cautious in authorizing graduate courses.

There is some uncertainty as to the date of the first bachelor's degree offered by a Christian college. Yenching University, through its predecessor Peking University, would appear to hold a clear lead since it granted five B.A. degrees in 1892, but its claim is clouded by the fact that it had assumed degree-granting power not actually specified in its charter, a fact which was not recognized until 1918 and not rectified until 1929. In 1907 St. John's, on the basis of very liberal Articles of Incorporation granted two years earlier by the District of Columbia, bestowed what is claimed to be the first B.A. degree.

An evaluation for the year 1925–26 made by the Council of Higher Education, using standards somewhat lower than those usually applied in the United States, rated two institutions as "A", five as "B", and four as "C", a "dubious condition." Five fell below even that unflattering level. But there was as yet in China little first-class higher education of any sort. A study published in 1928 pointed out in detail many weaknesses in staffing, in student-faculty ratios, in teaching loads, in curricular offerings, in research. Though many of these problems, resulting usually from inadequate resources, continued to plague the colleges, the next ten years saw substantial improvement. By 1937 all the China Colleges had some degree of academic respectability, while several ranked high in the Chinese academic world. It is probably safe to say that the strongest of the China Colleges compared not unfavorably with some of the better American church colleges, while most were more nearly on a par with the average.

THE ENGLISH LANGUAGE

Very early there arose the issue of the language of instruction. Should it be Chinese or English? The question received widely differing answers and, in some instances, continued acute to the end. The World

Missionary Conference of 1910 gave it serious consideration, finding that "on no question of educational policy are missionary educators more sharply divided." At that time, Boone, Canton, St. John's, and Soochow made large use of English; Hangchow, Peking, Shanghai, and Shantung depended on Chinese while teaching English as a subject; and North China used only Chinese except in teaching a few advanced courses.

From the start, Shantung undertook to teach in Chinese. The proposal sent to the Presbyterian Board in 1881 for establishment of a college at Tengchow stated specifically, "That the Chinese language be the medium of instruction throughout the course, English being taught only as an extra in special cases." And the medical school which developed a generation later undertook to provide a first-class medical education using the Chinese language. This emphasis was the result in part of a conviction that education should be in one's native language and in part of the institution's provincial setting and its concern for rural Shantung. This policy was gradually modified, largely at the insistence of Chinese who felt that at that stage in China's development such limitations were too rigid. English was first introduced, tentatively, in 1908, with only six percent of the students taking it. It was not until 1922 that the restrictions, further relaxed, permitted alternative sections, Chinese and English, in the Arts, though requiring English of medical students.

At the other extreme, St. John's University gave all instruction, except in Chinese subjects, in English. Although early emphasis had been on Chinese and there had been strong opposition to teaching English at all, English was soon not only accepted as a necessary subject but given a place of pre-eminence. So much so that St. John's graduates were often criticized for being "illiterate" in their own language and culture. On the other hand, they were in great demand in government and business circles where a ready command of English was a distinct asset.

North China College, near Peking, also used Chinese exclusively. Concentration on Chinese was for "the most cogent reasons. Chiefly because the teaching of English would open to the young men a possible and most tempting future, wholly alien to the objective of the special service of the church. . . . There is another reason—in spite of its manifest defects, every year sees the Chinese language become a more worthy medium for the teaching of even the most advanced lines of science, and to be content to teach the sciences from English textbooks is to admit defeat before the battle has well begun, and to retreat in advance from the efforts to build up a system of education along the lines of national self-respect as in the end shall inevitably win the day." While unnecessarily restrictive, this point of view was both forward-looking and prophetic.

In contrast, Peking University insisted on English. Its argument ran as follows: "It will be our aim to give the student a critical and practical knowledge of the English language such as will open up to him all the treasures of Theology, of Science and Philosophy, and enable him, by the aid of current literature, to keep abreast of the times and render him fit to be a leader among the millions of his people to whom all this is a sealed book."

For most institutions there was a gradual shift from an early emphasis on English, which had been the result partly of popular demand, partly of the preponderance of Western teachers, and partly of the lack of textbooks in Chinese, to a recognition of the need for both Chinese and English. As early as 1880, Dr. Andrew P. Happer, in his dreams of the future Lingnan, stated that "with Mandarin and English the graduates will be citizens of the world." Educators generally agreed that a knowledge of his mother tongue and its culture was an essential part of a college student's education, and that the English language was needed as a supplementary tool. The trend was toward combining both points of view, with most institutions becoming fundamentally bilingual, varying only in the relative emphasis on English. Especially where the proportion of Western faculty, most of them unable to teach in Chinese, was large, English held equal rank with Chinese. Most of the Christian colleges were distinguished from other institutions by the addition of English to Chinese rather than by its replacing the mother tongue.

In the case of English, many of the Christian colleges were superior to their secular peers, and a few achieved real distinction. In the teaching of the English language as a tool, they had the advantages of a large proportion of native speakers, even though these were all too often amateurs—wives and other part-time teachers—and usually too few for the heavy load of required courses. Gradually, however, academically qualified and professionally trained personnel, both Western and Chinese, formed increasingly effective nuclei of language-training programs. Programs such as those at Lingnan, Nanking, St. John's, and Yenching were well regarded, achieving recognition and at times providing significant national leadership.

In the programs offered English majors, the Christian colleges had a similar natural advantage over most wholly Chinese institutions;

courses in literature and advanced courses in language were taught almost exclusively by Americans and British. A disadvantage, however, lay in the frequent absence of scholarship; at first few of these Westerners had had significant graduate training in the field. Yet the presence of such teachers not only gave the Christian colleges a favorable reputation but in many cases produced a course of study which was clearly superior to that provided in most other institutions. As time went on, an occasional scholar in the field, Chinese as well as Western, brought distinction and strength. Several of the Christian universities were recognized for instruction in the field of English. With the acquiring by Chinese scholars in other institutions of British and American graduate degrees in Western literature, this advantage tended to disappear.

In summary it can be said that the Christian colleges played an important part in the introduction of the English language into education, contributed largely to meeting a sudden widespread need for that language, set respectable standards of achievement, and trained many men and women whose command of English was an important factor in their service to society. Their work in literature contributed greatly to the understanding of Western culture.

CHINESE LANGUAGE AND CULTURE

In the field of Chinese language and culture, the Christian colleges started with no advantage except a relative freedom from the shackles of the classical tradition. Only with time were they generally able to recruit true scholars in the field. Here their foreignness constituted a disadvantage. In only a few cases were they recognized as good; in most instances, public opinion was far from flattering.

Through the nineteenth century and well into the twentieth, the work in Chinese continued to center on the Chinese Classics and to be taught according to traditional methods. Such classics as the Book of Odes (*Shih Ching*), the Book of History (*Shu Ching*), the Book of Rites (*Li Chi*), the Commentary of Tso (*Tso Chuan*), and the Book of Changes (*I Ching*) had to be memorized; the Analects of Confucius (*Lun Yü*), Mencius (*Mengtzu*), the Great Learning (*Ta Hsüeh*), and the Doctrine of the Mean (*Chung Yung*) were critically studied. Composition followed the pattern of the literary essays required in the government examinations and the writing of poetry according to rule. The Christian colleges had had no great trouble following this basic pattern, since it had been easy to recruit old-style scholars if one ignored absence of method and modern outlook. The results, however, were without distinction and made the colleges more and more vulnerable to criticism.

This situation did not greatly change until the Literary Renaissance of 1917. The reforms of 1898 had proved short-lived. The educational reforms of the early twentieth century had dealt with organization and with curriculum in general and had left the content of Chinese courses largely untouched. But with the declaration by Hu Shih and Ch'en Tu-hsiu that the classical language had outlived its usefulness, the door opened for a complete revision of the curriculum and the substitution of the spoken language, a form of Mandarin colloquial, for the ancient classical style (*wen li*). Lectures on classical philology or on esthetics did not constitute a meaningful approach to the effective use of modern Chinese in the social and natural sciences.

The Christian colleges were not wholly unprepared for this change. Well before the end of the century, Calvin Mateer at Tengchow College, ahead of his times, had required his students to write essays in Mandarin as well as in the classical style. Other institutions had also taken some liberties with the traditional pattern. By and large, however, they had done their pioneering in other areas. From the time of the Chinese Renaissance on, the problem was one of developing and maintaining departments of Chinese which would command the respect of secular institutions and scholars. In this, most institutions were only moderately successful. Though there were exceptions such as Professor Chung Wing-kwang of Lingnan, who had taken both the first and second classical degrees and was a Christian, and Wu Lei-ch'üan, a Christian Hanlin scholar who came to Yenching in 1929, the colleges found it difficult, almost impossible, to attract Confucian scholars of first rank. This problem was sometimes met by part-time employment of scholars of standing from government universities even though these might lack any distinction as teachers.

However, after the distribution of the Hall estate and the establishment of the Harvard-Yenching Institute in 1928, several institutions were in position to finance the more effective teaching of Chinese studies. The Hall estate provided a million dollars for Yenching, seven hundred thousand dollars for Lingnan, three hundred thousand dollars for Nanking, two hundred thousand dollars for West China, one hundred and fifty thousand dollars for Shantung, and fifty thousand dollars for Fukien. The Harvard-Yenching Institute, from part of its share of the Hall estate, continued to encourage and support Chinese studies in these institutions. (The primary purpose of the Institute in relation to the six institutions in China was "to provide . . . facilities for research in the field of Chinese culture and in other aspects of Chinese studies.") The result was a small number of relatively strong departments of Chinese and considerable significant research and publication, greatly improving the public image of the Christian colleges as Chinese rather than foreign institutions.

The China Colleges were not at first noted for their production in the field of Chinese studies, but, especially after help came from the Harvard-Yenching Institute, not a little research of value appeared, largely in the institutional journals and monographs at such places as Nanking and Yenching. Much of this was of a methodological character, but some was of more general interest and usefulness. Chen Kuang-lu of Nanking produced several very solid histories which were widely used as textbooks: *China in the Last One Hundred Years; History of Japan;* and *General History of China* (2 vols). Professor Chan Wing-tsit, who was for some years professor and dean at Lingnan before going to Dartmouth College as Professor of Chinese Culture, was to become one of the great introducers of Chinese thought to the Western world. Two major Chinese philosophers were introduced to the West in *The Ethical and Political Works of Motse* (1929) and *Motse, the Neglected Rival of Confucius* (1934) by Professor Y.P. Mei of Yenching; and *The Complete Works of Han Fei Tzu* (2 vols., 1939) by Professor Liao Wen-k'uei of Nanking. A monumental work was the *Index to Chinese Classical Literature* of Professor William Hung of Yenching, which comprised seventy-seven volumes in 1950.

A considerable amount of sound scholarship was also represented in works in English by Westerners, particularly British. Such production began early. James Legge, teacher in the pre-treaty-port Anglo-Chinese College of Malacca and Hong Kong, produced his monumental *Chinese Classics* before moving to the Professorship of Chinese at Oxford. His successor in that chair, W.E. Soothill, founder of a "college" and President (1911–14) of the proposed Central China Union University, made a notable English translation of the *Analects of Confucius* (1910). From the pens of other early scholars associated with the colleges came such works as Calvin Mateer's *Mandarin Lessons* (1892), Chauncey Goodrich's *Pocket Dictionary and English Syllabary* (1891), and Courtenay H. Fenn's *Five Thousand Dictionary* (1926).

China's history, ancient and modern, was also the object of considerable research and interpretation. James M. Menzies of Shantung dealt with *Prehistoric China* (1917); Cheng Te-k'un of West China, with

Archaeology in China, published in 1956 after he had gone to Cambridge University. Harley F. MacNair, at St. John's from 1912 to 1927 and then at the University of Chicago, wrote on *The Chinese Abroad and China in Revolution* and co-authored with Hosea Ballou Morse *Far Eastern International Relations* (1928). The translation of Dr. Sun Yat-sen's *San Min Chu I (Three People's Principles)* by Frank W. Price, at that time at Hangchow, was long a useful document.

With the growing recognition of the political, social, and economic problems besetting China, there came increased interest in the social sciences on the part of students, a more adequate response in the curriculum to that interest, and a closer relation of institution to society through research on those problems and practical attempts at their solution. Almost all institutions developed departments of economics, political science, and sociology, and many of these moved from the theoretical to varying degrees of practical concern with public affairs. When the North China Council for Rural Reconstruction was set up in 1933, two Protestant universities, Nanking and Yenching, were among the eight cooperating organizations. Sidney D. Gamble, then on a visit to Peking, and Professor John Stewart Burgess of Yenching pioneered in their *Peking: A Social Survey* (1921), the first such study of an Asian city, which remains a classic. The latter's *The Guilds of Peking* (1928) was a valuable in-depth study of a basic element in traditional Chinese life.

In the thirties, Professor Lewis S.C. Smythe of Nanking carried out useful social surveys; then and later assisted in the development of Chinese industrial cooperatives. Professor Ma Wen-huan of Nanking's Department of Political Science engaged throughout the thirties and forties in research and practical training in local government.

A number of the faculty members of the Christian colleges served at one time or another on various governmental agencies concerned with economic, political, or social problems. Dean Hsü Shu-hsi of Yenching's College of Public Affairs left the university to join the Ministry of Foreign Affairs. Dean T.T. Lew of the School of Religion served as member of the Legislative Yuan, or Parliament, while on leave from Yenching. Professor Leonard (Shih-lien) Hsü, who wrote widely in the field of the social sciences, served, while on extended leave, on the Rural Rehabilitation Commission of the Executive Yuan, on two commissions of the National Economic Council, and on the Economic Commission of the League of Nations.

Much of the research carried on in these fields found its outlet in a number of journals of varied nature published by the China Colleges, some of which achieved, in limited areas, a degree of national acclaim and even some international recognition. Most of these made their start in the period from 1927 to 1935. The *Yenching Journal of Chinese Studies* (1927) gained a reputation for scholarship in Chinese culture. The *Nanking Journal* (1931) covered a wider area but contained much valuable material. The *Journal* of the West China Border Research Society, sponsored mainly by West China Union University faculty though unrelated to the university, published information on that little known part of China. Occasional monographs issued by several institutions added to knowledge in various fields.

FINE ARTS, MUSIC, AND LETTERS

The Fine Arts had no official place in most of the China Colleges. There was little demand for them and few qualified instructors, and they were generally considered luxuries. Beyond an occasional elective course in appreciation, usually of Western Art, and extracurricular exploration of the techniques of painting and occasionally of modeling, no college attempted to provide either instruction or training in the visual arts.

However, scholars associated with the colleges did produce some noteworthy contributions in the field of Art History. *Outlines of Chinese Art* (1919) and *Chinese Painting* (1927) by John C. Ferguson of Nanking were scholarly introductions to their subjects. A six-volume *Index to Recorded Paintings*, published in Nanking, was also of value to scholars. Had it not been for the Communist victory in 1949, Dr. Ferguson's impressive collection of Chinese art would have been housed at the University of Nanking, giving that institution unique status among the China Colleges if not among all Chinese universities. Recorded too should be the unusual work entitled *A Grammar of Lattice*, by Daniel S. Dye of West China, which was published by the Harvard University Press.

Music, probably because of its association with worship and the practical need of the Church for men and women with some musical competence, almost immediately won a place for itself in education at all levels. In the 1850s, Mrs. Nevius in Ningpo had "a good choir, capable of carrying all four parts, soprano, alto, tenor, and bass; and the accuracy with which they sang, considering, of course, all circumstances, was remarkable." Curricular and extracurricular programs of music soon came to have an important place in almost every college. Five institutions—Fukien, Huachung, Ginling, Hwa Nan, and Yenching—developed departments of music. The first two offered only minors, though Huachung was planning a full-fledged School of Music when World War II intervened.

All institutions had glee clubs, student choirs, or oratorio societies, and everywhere music was an important extracurricular activity. One future university president played the organ at chapel during his undergraduate days. Performances of such oratorios as Handel's "Messiah" and Stainer's "Crucifixion" were given in many places and many times, sometimes by combined choirs. A Music Week at Hwa Nan included recitals by outside artists as well as by very competent members of the staff. Even in wartime, song went on, whether in the camphor groves hiding Lingnan or in Shanghai's Roxy Theater, where Hangchow's sixty voices presented a sacred concert to an overflow crowd.

Though the colleges produced few virtuosi, a field in which they made no attempt to compete with rapidly developing secular schools of music, they did much at first to stimulate an interest in Western music and then to continue to meet the need for teachers, organists, and choir leaders. Some contribution was also made in the field of Chinese music through use of Chinese tunes in the Protestant Church's *Hymns of Universal Praise*, for which Professor Bliss Wiant of Yenching was music editor and Francis Jones of Nanking a member of the editorial board, and in such collections as "Min River Boat Songs" by Stella Marie Graves of Ginling and Malcolm Farley of Fukien, and "Songs of Chinese Children" by Maryette Lum of Yenching Women's College.

In the field of letters, the outstanding name is that of Pearl S. Buck, whose *The Good Earth* was largely responsible for her winning the Nobel Prize. Her translation of the *Shui Hu Chuan*, a famous thirteenth-century Chinese novel, under the title *All Men Are Brothers* (1933) also appeared while she was with the University of Nanking. Writing in Chinese, there was Lao She, author of *Ricksha Boy*, which was translated into English, and many other novels and plays. A former Yenching student, he taught Chinese at Shantung Christian University under his real name of Shu She-yü from 1931 to 1934.

SCIENCE

Though the Christian colleges of China rose in response to the need for a trained clergy and an educated laity, the education which they offered was neither narrowly theological nor predominantly humanistic, but surprisingly broad in conception. Very early they acquired a marked degree of scientific orientation, and through the years they made important contributions in the area of science, both pure and applied. In some aspects of science education they were pioneers; occasionally they were outstanding. Along with the Japanese universities which trained so many of China's first scientists, they participated in China's awakening to and entering into the modern Western-oriented world of science and technology. In the process they made important contributions to Chinese society and its leadership.

This scientific concern on the part of missions manifested itself early. The founders and early instructors of the colleges were often ahead of their times in their interest in science and other fields not directly related to evangelization. Before there was anything resembling a college, Mateer was teaching theological students physics and chemistry. In 1881 he secured a ten-inch telescope for the astronomy course that was part of the curriculum of the infant Tengchow College. By the end of the century, the Reverend Junius H. Judson had set up surprisingly up-to-date work in mathematics and physics at Hangchow Presbyterian College, which had just achieved junior-college status. Early in the twentieth, he returned to Hangchow with the latest in wireless and x-ray equipment.

The spirit at work in these early days is well summarized in the words of two pioneers. In 1877 Calvin Mateer of Tengchow told a General Conference of missionaries that "Christianity is truth, and all truth is related. Hence a true philosophy of mind and matter is the best adjunct and support of Christianity." In 1890 the Reverend J.L. Hawks Pott of St. John's reported that "the teaching of Natural Sciences is very important for understanding the unity and revelation of God. . . . Scientific training is the enemy of superstition and the best form of mental training one can give." The certificate of incorporation of Peking University (1890) stated as one purpose, "to aid the youth of the Chinese Empire and of other countries in obtaining a Literary, Scientific or Professional Education."

This belief was not universal, nor did it influence the development of all institutions, but it did result in many cases in the natural sciences early becoming an important part of the curriculum. This somewhat surprising interest in science, encouraged doubtless by the realization of China's need for a share of the bases of the technological civilization of the West, helped insure the development of relatively balanced institutions of higher education. The pre-1900 institutions all included in their curricula courses in science; those which started in the twentieth century began with either separate colleges of science or combined colleges of arts and sciences.

Such early emphasis on the natural sciences did not automatically assure superior achievement. The cost of such courses proved an impossible handicap. In the majority of institutions, however, very respectable levels of undergraduate science education were reached, with colleges of science often the strongest unit in their respective institutions. In some cases these ranked with the best in the country. Such results usually occurred where there were special sources of income, such as the RockefellerFoundation, the China Medical Board, and Yale-in-China.

Fully as important as money, however, was the notable group of scientists, first foreign and then Chinese, who staffed the major departments. In their formative years the Christian colleges somehow drew outstanding scholar-teachers in the natural sciences, well trained by contemporary standards and unusually committed to the tasks they had undertaken. At the very start of the twentieth century, Nathaniel Gist Gee, M.A., biologist from Vanderbilt University, joined the newly established Soochow University; a few years later, Arthur W. March, biologist from Wooster College, went to Hangchow College; in 1907, George Weidman Groff, horticulturist from Pennsylvania State College, started his outstanding work at Lingnan; in 1911, Charles K. Edmunds, Johns Hopkins Ph.D., started work at Lingnan, and Dr. Clifford Stubbs, chemist from Manchester, England, at West China Union University; and in 1915, William H. Adolph, Pennsylvania Ph.D. and Yale biologist, arrived at Shantung. By the early 1920s, some fifty Western scientists with advanced degrees were teaching in the China Colleges.

By the mid-1920s, however, these were more than matched by their Chinese colleagues, who soon outnumbered them in doctorates in science. Some of these were outstanding. Dr. Chinfu Wu, student of Gee at Soochow, succeeded him as head of the Biology Department and then held a similar post at Yenching. Dr. Yü-ting Chu of St. John's received recognition for his research in ichthyology. Dr. H.R. Wei, graduate of the University of Nanking, returned with a Ph.D. in physics to serve as Dean of the College of Science, after 1950 becoming delegate from the Republic of China on the Atomic Energy Commission of the United Nations. Drs. Lucy Wang and Wu Yi-fang, with doctorates in chemistry and biology respectively, were drafted by Hwa Nan and Ginling Colleges as their institutions' first Chinese presidents. In the twenties Hwa Nan's three major science departments were all headed by Hwa Nan graduates with doctorates. At Huachung, Dr. Paul C.T. Kwei, Princeton Ph.D., head of physics and dean of science, participated in the Carnegie Institution's world-wide magnetic and ionospheric research. These scientists were no better trained than others in secular institutions, probably fairly representative of China's returned scientists in this respect, but they were in most cases so motivated that they preferred the opportunity for service in a Christian institution to the greater prestige and financial reward of other posts. The Laymen's Missionary Inquiry of 1931–32, which was noted for its critical attitude, expressed the opinion that "some of the strongest men we found in the faculties are in the field of the natural sciences, and we are informed that in the teaching of science some of the Christian colleges are conspicuously successful."

A unique and far-reaching service in the field of science was the Biological Supply Service of Soochow University. This developed out of efforts to meet the need for specialized materials not then available in China. Middle schools as well as colleges had been depending on supply houses abroad, especially in parasitology materials. In addition local artisans were encouraged to produce basic science equipment of metal and glass.

Though handicapped by inadequate equipment and insufficient funds, the scientists of the Christian colleges, both Western and Chinese, were not without productive research. This covered such fields as nutrition, ceramics, fertilizers, genetics, geography and geomorphology, and entomology. Several outstanding collections were created: Groff's twelve thousand specimens, representing five thousand species of plants; and his notes on ten thousand plants which earned the comment from American scientists that "we look upon it as pioneering in a very important field just as Asa Gray in the United States"; the collections of thirty thousand economic tree specimens, sixty thousand insects, and forty-five thousand specimens of West China flora at the University of Nanking; and C.F. Wu's monumental catalog of nineteen thousand Chinese insects at Yenching. Though not limited to science, the Tsinan Institute at Shantung contributed to the education of the public through a museum drawing some two hundred thousand visitors in one year.

The work of science departments found expression in a number of noteworthy publications such as the *Fukien University Science Journal*, the *Lingnan Science Journal*, and the *Nanking Journal*. Much research also appeared in other technical journals, not only in China but in America and Europe. Among the programs of research, three definitive studies in the field of botany were so outstanding as to attract international attention. At Nanking, Professor Chen Yung of the College of Agriculture and Forestry published in Chinese a monumental *Classification of Chinese Trees* (*Chung-kuo shu-mu-fen-lei-hsueh*, 1937). Professor Albert N. Steward's *Manual of Vascular Plants of the Lower Yangtze Valley, China* was a product of the same period though not published by Oregon State College until 1958. A *Report on the G. Weidman Groff Collection* (notes compiled while he was at Lingnan University) was published for the Penn State-in-China Committee by the Pennsylvania State University in 1961.

Not the least important contribution of the Christian colleges in the field of science was the men and women whom they trained. Not only were the institutions themselves ultimately staffed by these graduates, who had returned with advanced degrees from abroad; they gave many qualified scientists to other institutions, government service, and business. And in so doing they in many cases contributed much more than scientific knowledge and skill. The 1955 edition of *American Men of Science* contained the biographies of fifty-five Chinese graduates of the Christian colleges of China, twenty-seven in the physical sciences and twenty-eight in the biological. The transfer, chiefly post-1948, of these men and women to an American setting constituted a serious brain drain for China, but the status accorded them in the West indicates the quality of some of the graduates of the China Colleges. In addition to these, American institutions were also enriched by other members of the faculties of these institutions who left China in the post-war years.

It is impossible to avoid the conclusion that, in spite of weaknesses, the Christian colleges contributed significantly, and clearly out of proportion to their numbers, to the awakening of China to the modern world and to its ability to grapple with its technological problems. Their relative eclipse by more adequately financed government institutions does not deny their earlier achievements. Nor need it obscure the relatively more modest but still important contribution in science education which many made to the very end. In this field, they were markedly successful and made one of their major contributions.

GRADUATE EDUCATION

Graduate education did not begin until well into the twentieth century. By 1915, Peking University was offering graduate work even though its master's degree was on a somewhat questionable basis. St. John's granted two master's degrees in 1920 and continued to offer graduate courses in both arts and sciences. From 1922–23 on, the University of Nanking was giving master's degrees in both science and agriculture; Shanghai, in education. By 1927–28 Yenching University was providing graduate work in seven fields, and in 1934 it added five more. Though the Ministry of Education recognized only four of the twelve, Yenching continued the others under the handicap of their earning only American degrees. In 1935 the Ministry authorized graduate study at Nanking in history, chemistry, and agricultural economics. In the 1930s graduate degrees were also being offered by Lingnan in science and by Soochow in law.

The obvious difficulties in the way of any graduate work of quality and the practical impossibility of developing it in all the institutions tempted to do so led very early to suggestions of a truly united effort in this area. As early as 1906 Dr. Pott of St. John's advocated organization of an International Christian University for postgraduate and professional studies. But no action followed and twenty years later five institutions were offering graduate courses hopefully leading to the master's degree with a combined total of less than fifty students in twenty fields (exclusive of theology), thus averaging between two and three students per field.

Troubled by the danger of competition and dissipation of resources inherent in such a situation, the China Christian Education Association in 1926 urged development of a single strong graduate school either in Peking or in Shanghai. Two years later the Correlated Program recommended two strong correlated centers, one in North China, with Yenching responsible for religion, social service, Chinese studies, and modern languages, and Shantung for medicine; and one in East China, with agriculture at Nanking and the natural sciences in Shanghai. The door was left open for graduate work in education at some unspecified location. These proposals had little effect and graduate work continued to depend on the ambitions and resources of individual institutions.

13

Vocational and Professional Emphases

Prior to 1900, the Christian colleges consisted almost exclusively of colleges of arts or combined colleges of arts and sciences. Curricular emphasis lay heavily on the side of the humanities and the pure sciences. To some extent this situation reflected the continued power of the Chinese classical tradition, but there were other reasons. The humanitites were where preparation for clerical and other educational service to the Church was best provided; the sciences were the areas in which the sought-after modern knowledge lay. The new century brought even greater response to the search for knowledge: expansion of the standard offerings in both areas and limited addition of the social sciences. Prior to 1920, two-thirds of all students concentrated in the arts colleges alone.

This situation was such as to evoke criticism, both in China and abroad, of the colleges as being too largely academic in their emphasis and too little concerned with the vocational needs of China's youth. Response to growing pressures was slow but eventually resulted in a very considerable emphasis on the vocational and professional. As students came to seek such preparation and as the institutions themselves laid the more general foundations which were essential for more specialized training, it is probable that vocational courses and professional schools failed to receive earlier and more proportionate emphasis not only because of the staggering costs of all those related to science but because of the traditional Chinese prejudice against work with the hands. In spite of this fact, in 1937 schools and departments with professional and vocational goals numbered about thirty. There were six colleges of medicine (four among the China Colleges), two colleges and one department of agriculture, and one college and four departments of engineering. There were also one college and one school of commerce and/or business administration, one college of education, one college of law, and some dozen schools of theology, as well as one college and one institute of rural reconstruction, the former becoming a college of agriculture during the war. By 1937, students in the arts constituted only one-fifth of the total in the colleges.

MEDICAL EDUCATION

One of the most far-reaching contributions of the Protestant colleges of China lay in medical education. Missionaries had built the first clinics and hospitals and started the first medical-training programs. Some of these became medical schools, usually associated with Christian universities. Such schools did much to disseminate the procedures of Western medicine and give direction and strength to the country's medical profession.

Medical missions, like educational missions, began shortly after the first Protestant penetration of China. Peter Parker had started an ophthalmic clinic in Canton as early as 1835, but medical missions got fully under way with the opening of the country by the treaties of 1842–44. Hospitals soon started in such cities as Canton, Shanghai, and Peking. Development was rapid. By 1876 the number of hospitals had risen to sixteen, with over forty thousand patients; by 1889 to sixty-one, with nearly 350,000 patients. Medical practice without hospitals, carried on in many places, added untold thousands to these totals.

Almost from the beginning, medical missions undertook the training of Chinese assistants. At first this was on a very elementary and apprentice basis, but in 1870 Dr. J.G. Kerr, Parker's successor in Canton, organized the first class of young men to study medicine. Nine years later he accepted two women destined to be the "first Chinese lady physicians to begin the practice of Western medicine in the Empire." Similar instruction soon developed in connection with hospitals in other cities. By 1893, a half century after the first Christian hospital, a total of 151 men and twenty-eight women medical students were participating in Christian programs of medical education. To what extent any of these training programs deserved the name of medical college is a question. Not only did they consist of mere handfuls of students but their standards were definitely lower than those of most nineteenth-century medical education in the United States and Europe. Their equipment was generally inadequate, their staffs small and usually without specialized training. Prerequisites for admission were minimal and uncertain. Yet in these beginnings modern medical education in China was taking shape.

The story of Christian medical education in China is one of many beginnings, closings, and consolidations, and the final emergence of a few extraordinarily successful institutions. In 1910 it would have been possible to count thirteen colleges in ten centers. Ten years later the number had fallen to seven colleges in seven centers, two of which, West China and Hsiang-Ya, were new. All were private institutions except Hsiang-Ya, which was a joint government-mission undertaking. Of the seven, five were of full medical-school standard; two were of somewhat lower grade. Three of the seven were parts of larger institutions; the other four were independent. In this process of concentration the foundations had been contributed for an institution no longer church-controlled though continuing a Christian concern, the Peking Union Medical College, without doubt the outstanding medical college in China, if not in all of Asia. Within the next decade one independent college merged with a university, and a new independent medical school started. In the thirties still another independent school united with a university, leaving the final total at six, of which four were parts of Christian universities, one was independent, and one was government-related.

One of the first medical training programs deserving serious consideration was that which Dr. William J. Boone initiated in Shanghai in 1880. This was actually the "Medical Department" of St. John's School, which at that time was offering a few post-secondary courses. However, a better date for the beginning of modern medical education is 1896, when the department became a "Medical School" requiring graduation from the college-preparatory department and offering a four-year course. The first class was graduated in 1900. Seven years later its graduates, bearing the B.A. degree under a District of Columbia charter, were accepted by such American medical schools as Pennsylvania and Yale. The first M.D. degrees were not awarded until 1920.

An almost equally early beginning was made in 1886 when Dr. Walter L. Lambuth, moving from Central China with two students, set up the Department of Medicine of Peking University in connection with the Methodist T'ung Jen Hospital. Beset by problems of finance and staffing, the department struggled on until 1905, when it united with the Lockhart Union Medical College, recently opened by the London Missionary Society in connection with the hospital started by Dr. Lockhart in 1866, to form the first (Peking) Union Medical College. This new college received a warm official welcome, with the government providing recognition and the right to grant degrees and the Empress Dowager making a financial contribution. It was the only mission medical college whose graduates were entitled to enter government examinations and to receive government degrees and ranks.

The new century saw the start of a number of projects in medical education. In Central China two British missionary societies joined in 1902 in a Union Medical College in Hankow. This was unrelated to any university until it moved to Tsinan in 1917. Across the Yangtze River in Wuchang, the Boone College of Medicine got under way in 1906–7, but continued for only a few years.

Farther to the south, at Changsha in Hunan Province, where Yale-in-China had started medical work in 1908, an unusual development took place when an agreement between mission and provincial government, accepted in 1912 and made permanent in 1914, provided for government financing and Yale-in-China staffing of a medical college. The Mission was to build and equip a hospital and recruit and pay graduates of Western medical schools serving as physicians and teachers; the government was to provide a site and money for buildings for the medical college and to cover expenses of medical school, nursing school, and hospital. The Hunan-Yale (Hsiang-Ya) Medical School admitted its first class in 1916.

The new center grew out of the hospital started by Dr. Edward H. Hume in 1908. Though not officially church-related, the school had Christian origins and continued Christian motivation on the part of many of its staff. It was not to be affiliated with any university in China. Son of missionary parents, Dr. Hume had been working with his father in India when recruited for Yali. He continued direction of the medical work at Changsha until 1927, serving during the last three years as Yali's first president.

With the Hsiang-Ya Agreement, a Nursing School opened in the fall of 1913. The foundations had been laid by Nina D. Gage, R.N., sister of Brownell Gage, one of the founders of Yali. She was a pioneer in the development of modern nursing, helping to establish the Nurse's Association of China. Out of 520 applicants—four hundred men and 120 women—fifty became the first students, forming two divisions, one for men and one for women. For some years the former was the larger, but eventually the school accepted only women.

In East China, a medical school started by Dr. W.H. Park in 1904 became the Medical Department of Soochow University. With the promotion of an East China Union Medical College, this closed in

1912 and Soochow concentrated on premedical training. The previous year seven American missions had cooperated in a Union Medical College, which, in 1913, became the Medical Department of the University of Nanking, soon joined by the Hangchow Medical College of the Church Missionary Society which had developed out of the hospital started there thirty years before. The new department did not, however, long continue in Nanking, for, disliking the largely premedical rank assigned to it in the ultimately abortive plans for an area-wide East China Union Medical College, it accepted in 1916 an invitation to move to Tsinan, where it helped strengthen the Medical College of Shantung Christian University. Meanwhile, in 1912, a "Harvard" Medical School had started in Shanghai on a five-year experimental basis. Though this school had no more official connection with missions than it did with Harvard University, its founders were men with missionary interest and it began in a cooperative arrangement with St. John's. This soon collapsed, Harvard then turning to the Shanghai Red Cross Hospital, and finally winding up its operations in 1916 in connection with plans of the China Medical Board. Also in Shanghai, four women's missionary societies opened in 1924 the Woman's Christian Medical College. Rarely enroling more than thirty students, this was unusually well equipped and maintained high standards. More than two-thirds of its faculty were women. While cooperating with St. John's, it remained independent.

In South China, early in the century, the South China Medical College was carrying on in connection with the Canton Hospital of the China Medical Missionary Association, an offshoot of Peter Parker's work. In 1909 it was joined by Hackett Medical College for Women, which Dr. Mary Fulton had established in 1901 when Dr. Kerr had resigned from the Canton Hospital, taking all male students with him to a new enterprise. Canton Christian College also had a medical department, started in 1907 in affiliation with the Christian Association of the University of Pennsylvania. This, however, ceased to function in 1914, when the Association transferred its interest to Shanghai and its representative, Dr. Josiah C. McCracken, to what became known as the Pennsylvania Medical College of St. John's University. Later, seeking to revive the teaching of medicine, Lingnan accepted in 1928 responsibility for Canton Hospital and negotiated with Hackett Medical College for a joint enterprise. The union was speeded by the surprising gift from the Nanking government of a suitable building on a site next to the Canton Hospital. Lingnan's medical college opened in 1935 as the Dr. Sun Yat-sen Medical College, named after the father of the Republic, who had been a student fifty years before in the newly opened College of Medicine in nearby Hong Kong.

North of Canton in the port city of Foochow a Union Medical College initiated in 1910 survived for only a decade. Fukien Christian University never succeeded in developing medical education and had to be content with premedical training. In 1948 Foochow was for a few months the temporary home of the Medical College of Shantung University, then a refugee after its home campus had fallen to the Communists.

In North China, one of the strongest centers of medical education developed at Tsinan. This had started in 1910 with a plant provided by the English Baptists and with Dr. James Boyd Neal of the Presbyterian Mission, who had long been engaged in peripatetic medical training in Shantung, as Dean. By 1914 it was offering a five-year course with a four-year college prerequisite and numbered twenty-five students. In 1915 the Rockefeller Foundation recommended that it be the one medical school of high quality using Chinese for instruction, in contrast to the Peking Union Medical College, which used English; and the China Medical Board contributed fifty thousand dollars in return for its taking over three classes while the new PUMC was being built, and promised an additional hundred thousand dollars over five years. During the next two years Shantung welcomed medical schools from Nanking, with fourteen students, and Hankow, with twelve students. Finally, in 1924, the North China Union Medical College for Women, finding itself superfluous with the PUMC becoming co-educational, transferred to Tsinan and became part of the Medical College of Shantung Christian University.

Still farther north, in Manchuria, Moukden Medical College was opened in 1912 by the Scottish and Irish Missions. This was built on the medical work begun in 1892 by Dr. Dugald Christie, one of the outstanding figures of medical missions, who served as its first principal. Though approved by the home boards, the school was dependent financially on fund-raising by Dr. Christie himself and on local Chinese support, which was fortunately generous, with regular government grants and significant private gifts. Further support came a few years later with contribution by the Danish Lutheran Mission of the services of Drs. Ellerbek and Pedersen. The former served as principal from 1924 to 1939 and was succeeded briefly by the latter.

The college began with a five-year course based on college graduation and sought from the first to maintain standards acceptable in

Scotland. Diplomas were presented in the name of the Provincial Governor. Demand for places was great, and graduates were much sought after. Women students were admitted from 1924 on. In 1940, the student body numbered ninety-eight men and thirty-one women. The college maintained an independent existence until the late thirties, though voluntary affiliation with North-Eastern University was prevented only by the destruction of that institution during the Japanese seizure of Manchuria in 1931. Increasing government pressure, however, brought a change in name, to The Christie Memorial Medical College, Moukden in English, and to Moukden Medical University in Chinese, and concentration of the course into four years instead of five. With World War II the college was taken over by the Japanese; in 1949, by the Communists.

One of the last, but also one of the most successful, medical schools to be developed was that at Chengtu. A basic reason for establishing a university in West China had been the desire to train Chinese doctors for the area. In 1914, four years after the start of West China Union University, a Medical Department was opened in a small two-story building, with a faculty of five American and Canadian doctors and a class of seven middle-school graduates. The moving spirit behind this development was Dr. Omar L. Kilborn of the Canadian Methodist Mission, whose son, Dr. Leslie G. Kilborn, was to lead the future college through its most productive as well as difficult years. Initial difficulties were so great that West China considered sending medical students to Peking Medical College for the last two years of training. But by 1917 the decision had been reached to provide four years in Chengtu, and construction had started on a more adequate center. Meanwhile, Dr. Ashley W. Lindsay, perhaps the first dental missionary, had opened a dental clinic. In 1917 the dental courses he was teaching took the form of a Department of Dentistry. By 1912 this had evolved into a college, a pioneer development which was for some time unique in China and which was to train many of the leading dentists and dental educators of the country.

In 1927–28 the College of Dentistry joined with the College of Medicine in a College of Medicine and Dentistry. In its curriculum this institution followed the pattern of Grade A medical and dental schools in the United States. It granted M.D. and D.D.S. degrees under charter from the Board of Regents of the University of the State of New York. By 1948, enrolment totaled 376 in medicine and seventy-six in dentistry, nearly half of all being women.

During the war, medical and dental staffs from Shantung Christian University, Peking Union Medical College, and National Central University cooperated with those of West China Union University. In 1937 work began on one of the most extensive hospital centers in China. This was completed in 1944, shortly before the end of the war.

The record of the Christian medical colleges is one of notable growth in quality. Never free from financial worries or able to compete in the race for new equipment, these colleges all ranked high in medical education in China. Their graduates had little difficulty, except occasionally in the matter of language, in pursuing postgraduate training abroad. This was due in part to the quality of their missionary personnel but also, especially in the later stages, to that of the Chinese staff, largely graduates of these same institutions who had completed specialization abroad. The concern of these same instructors for the individual student, an attitude toward the healing art which made it a matter of more than technical training, and a refusal to be seduced by the lure of numbers also contributed to the reputation these schools had and deserved.

It is difficult to overemphasize the contributions made by Christian medical education. Protestant missions were responsible for the first hospitals and dispensaries. They initiated the first medical schools. Until well into the twentieth century the majority of Western-oriented hospitals and medical schools were those started by missionaries. After the war, four colleges of medicine (one of them of dentistry as well), all parts of Christian universities, a fifth college carrying on without such affiliation, and a sixth functioning under joint government-mission control were among the leading medical colleges of China.

Not only had Protestant medical schools been pioneers and stimulators, introducing the concepts of modern medicine and setting worthy examples. They had introduced basic techniques and provided essential tools. Among these latter were standard medical books in translation. The early efforts at medical education had faced the complete absence of textbooks in Chinese in all areas of Western medicine. For the Peking Union Medical College and St. John's, which depended on English for instruction, though knowledge of Chinese terminology was essential, this was no great problem; but for Shantung, West China, Moukden, and the increasing total of medical schools under purely Chinese auspices, the lack of textbooks was critical.

Pioneer medical missionaries made efforts to meet the need. As early as 1850, Dr. Benjamin Hobson of the London Missionary Society undertook preparation of five works on medicine. Two decades later,

Dr. J.G. Kerr of Canton, a pioneer in the training of Chinese in medicine, produced the first of fifteen medical texts. Well before 1900, an English-Chinese Dictionary of fifteen thousand medical and scientific terms, a *Materia Medica*, and a translation of Gray's *Anatomy* had appeared. Useful as these books were, they were inadequate and needed updating, and there were many gaps to be filled. After 1900, more advanced textbooks, such as the volumes on Ophthalmology (1910) and on Skin Diseases (1911) by Dr. James B. Neal of Shantung, and *The Diseases of China* (1914) by Drs. W.H. Jefferys of Formosa and J.L. Maxwell of Shanghai, began to meet the need.

A major attack on the problem came with the establishment of a Translation Bureau at Shantung Christian University under the auspices of the Publication Committee of the China Medical Missionary Association and the direction of Dr. Thomas Gillison, who had come to Tsinan with the Hankow Medical College in 1917. The work of this bureau in translating and revising medical texts was a major achievement. It included creation of new terminology where Chinese medicine did not provide usable terms. It produced textbooks in Anatomy, Surgery, Histology, Embryology, Obstetrics, Pathology, Physiology, Orthopedics, Dermatology, Venereal Diseases, General and Diagnostic Medicine, Internal Medicine, and Gynecology. These were adopted by almost all medical schools using Chinese as the medium of instruction.

Most importantly, a modern medical profession in China was very largely the creation of Protestant missions, and especially of their medical schools. In the course of the years, they gave China many hundreds of well-trained, often highly motivated, and frequently outstanding practitioners of the healing art. They contributed disproportionately to the staffing of government and private colleges of medicine and dentistry. Their contribution was especially distinctive in the case of dentistry. For a considerable period West China Union University was the only institution in China preparing qualified dentists. As a result, the other dental institutions which later developed were almost entirely initiated and largely staffed by West China graduates. This was also true, though to a lesser degree, of the departments of pharmacy at Shantung and West China.

Prior to 1910 modern doctors trained in China, men and women, were almost exclusively the product of Christian medical schools. As government and other secular schools developed, this situation changed, but the contribution of such personnel, especially of doctors with Christian motivation, remained highly significant. In 1930, six Chinese

144

colleges (not including Hunan-Yale, temporarily in eclipse) had 355 students in addition to having graduated 737. Addition of graduates of schools no longer in existence would raise the latter number to at least a thousand. At that time the colleges were contributing some ten percent of all the medical graduates of the country. During the next two decades, it is probable that they were providing an annual average of seventy to eighty graduates.

Another contribution of medical missions in which the medical colleges played a part, though not always at the full four-year post-secondary level, was in the field of nursing education. Mission hospitals helped to raise nursing service from a menial to a dignified status; mission training schools were important factors in the education of women as nurses; and missionary and mission-trained nurses were key figures in the founding of the nursing profession in China. In all these developments the Christian colleges played a part through the Schools of Nursing connected with hospitals affiliated with their medical schools. Only in the case of Hsiang-Ya did the course of training lead beyond a certificate; there, in 1926, postgraduate courses led to a B.S. degree.

AGRICULTURAL EDUCATION

In yet another area of obvious and vital public service the China Colleges were pioneers, leaders, and outstanding contributors. This was agriculture in its varied aspects of education, research, and extension. In its effect, both direct and indirect, on the lives and welfare of the Chinese people, what was achieved in this area ranks in importance with the contributions made in medicine.

The first genuine college of agriculture did not make its appearance until the middle of the second decade of the twentieth century, but the first stirrings in agricultural education had come considerably earlier. A concern for the economic welfare of China's peasantry had developed in mission work well before the end of the nineteenth century, aroused in large part by the disastrous famines of the seventies, eighties, and nineties. Practical response had taken such forms as the introduction, by John L. Nevius, of better fruits, for which eastern Shantung Province soon became noted, and of improved peanuts by Charles R. Mills which, by the mid-1920s, had resulted in crops of ten million tons in Shantung alone. Such attempts to deal with fundamental causes, together with long-fruitless efforts to stimulate government grappling with such problems as that of Yellow River control, reflected a growing recognition of the place of practical service in the work of missions. Though early in the twentieth century this concern found expression in elementary agricultural education, it was not shared by all. Even as late as 1920–21, the China Educational Commission encountered arguments that agriculture was a public function, too costly for missions, and that technical education was not a logical function of Christian colleges.

No university-grade program existed until the Department of Agriculture of the University of Nanking was established in 1914. This was the second such institution in the country, the first being a German College of Forestry in Tsingtao, Shantung, which quickly turned over its students to Nanking. The initial impetus for the department came from Joseph Bailie, Professor of Mathematics in the university, who had become involved in relief work as a result of a devastating flood in the lower Yangtze River Valley and had started reforestation work near Nanking and colonization projects in Kiangsu and Anhui Provinces. In these undertakings he had been handicapped by lack of personnel trained in farm work. To the college he started, several provincial governments sent students.

Though this was a very modest undertaking, with only two full-time teachers and twelve students, it soon became a solid educational enterprise and one of the strongest units of the university. To the Department of Agriculture started in 1914, was added in 1915 a School of Forestry. Under Dean John H. Reisner, later to become Director of Agricultural Missions Foundation in New York, the College of Agriculture and Forestry rapidly developed into the leading institution of its nature in China.

By this time there were two other Christian colleges—Canton Christian College and Yenching University—offering college-grade instruction in agriculture. Yale-in-China began giving courses in forestry in connection with biology in 1920 but soon discontinued them. Interest in agricultural education had been stimulated at Canton by the starting of a citrus introduction station in 1916, work in sericulture two years later. By 1921–22 a Department of Agriculture was offering a full-fledged, four-year, B.S. degree course as well as a one-year course for farm managers, extension workers, and teachers in lower schools. But registration remained low and even a subcollegiate course failed to increase numbers greatly. Lingnan's greatest effectiveness in the area of agriculture was probably in research, where it made a number of contributions.

At Yenching University, work in animal husbandry resulted in 1919 from a request by a Chinese businessman that the university operate an experiment station on some twelve hundred acres he controlled. The university was finally offering courses in agronomy, poultry, dairying, horticulture, and agriculture in addition to animal husbandry. In spite of receiving a share of the income from unspent famine funds, Yenching soon found that it would not have the additional funds required and came to the conclusion that the University of Nanking was a more logical place for the development of work in agriculture.

At much the same time came beginnings in agricultural education in Shantung which were to affect the development of Shantung Christian University. In 1923 Wen Hua Middle School in Weihsien started a Department of Agriculture, offering courses in agriculture and in rural sociology, and sending some of its best students for further work to the University of Nanking. The agricultural fairs which it initiated proved very popular and set a pattern which spread widely. It served, as did the Shantung Agricultural and Industrial School at Yihsien in Southern Shantung, as a regional center for the Cornell-Nanking Improvement Program. A Rural Institute at a nearby village, with a small demonstration center on the edge of the Tsinan campus, was the work of the College of Theology of Shantung Christian University.

On the foundation of such activities the university had hoped to develop a department, and hopefully a college, of agriculture, but had been discouraged from doing so by the Correlated Program of 1928, which proposed a vocationalized curriculum with a rural emphasis. It recommended further development of the Rural Institute into four departments: agriculture and economics, education, health, and homemaking. So strengthened, the Institute made significant contributions in both research and extension. A notable example was *The Christian Farmer* started in 1934 by T.H. Sun and H.Y. Chang. Using a limited vocabulary suited to new literates, this publication almost at once had a paid-up circulation of five thousand and soon reached a peak of thirty thousand.

The Correlated Program which restricted Shantung had also ruled out an agricultural college at Fukien in spite of the argument that that province presented unique conditions and an unmet need. Since 1919 the college had been informally engaged in research in silkworms, rice, and reforestation, to which, in 1935, the provincial government turned over the neighboring rural experiment station. But it had to be content with a Department of Rural Service. In 1936 this became a College of Rural

Reconstruction and finally, during the war, the long-sought College of Agriculture.

Agricultural work in West China started in the 1920s when Dr. Frank Dickinson imported a pedigreed Holstein-Friesian bull to improve the native stock. His success in building up a substantial herd in spite of epidemic diseases resulted in a Szechwan Dairy Improvement Association and the wide distribution of improved stock. Dairy goat and poultry improvement were important later developments. At the same time research began in fruit, vegetables, and corn, with the development of improved and new varieties. Courses in agriculture for teachers and students in theology came early, but a Department of Agriculture had to wait until 1934. A two-year extension course began in 1937; in 1941 an Institute of Agricultural Research with four divisions: Plant Pathology and Entomology, Foods and Nutrition, Animal Husbandry and Veterinary Science, and Horticulture.

At the end of the war, the participation of the China Colleges in agricultural education and service consisted of colleges of agricultural at Fukien, Lingnan, and Nanking Universities, an Institute of Agricultural Research at West China, and that part of Shantung's Rural Institute that had survived the war years.

What had been the contribution of this work in agriculture? First, the China Colleges had helped to stimulate and set a pattern for education, extension, and research for the government and private colleges of agriculture which ultimately followed Nanking's initial effort. Second, they had contributed overwhelmingly to the initially non-existent supply of critically needed personnel. This was especially true in the case of Nanking. At one time in the thirties Nanking graduates headed seven government agricultural colleges, five of seven technical departments, and three of five national research institutes of the Ministry of Agriculture and Forestry. Altogether many hundreds of graduates of the Christian colleges must have taken part in the improvement of the rural life and agricultural productivity of China.

Third, the Christian colleges led the way in research in agriculture. With China's population rapidly outstripping the growth of productive acreage, which was increasingly vulnerable to flood and drought and pestilence, there was critical need for greater and more assured productivity. Crop improvement of all kinds, development of tools and techniques and social and economic studies contributed outstandingly to meeting that need.

The famine prevention program launched by the University of Nanking in the early 1920s resulted in important and highly successful improvement programs for such crops as wheat, rice, corn, soybean, millet, and cotton. These were carried on in cooperation with church and other organizations throughout Central and North China. By 1937 twenty-seven new strains were being distributed, those of wheat bringing a twenty percent increase in yield. Lingnan, Nanking, and West China all contributed to the improvement of citrus and vegetable crops through selection and disease control.

At the University of Nanking, social and economic studies were pioneer and far-reaching approaches to an understanding of rural China. J. Lossing Buck's *Chinese Farm Economy* (1930) was widely used as a textbook in other colleges. His *Land Utilization in China* (1937), covering the entire country, was a monumental work providing a unique picture of China's agricultural life. Both have continued to be standard sources and have been reprinted. Other research activities included the collecting and organizing of old Chinese literature on agriculture and the publication of an *Agricultural Index* of all literature on agriculture in China published in all languages since the middle of the nineteenth century.

Both Lingnan and Nanking carried on research in sericulture, contributing to improvement through distribution of disease-free eggs. At Lingnan, Weidman Groff was responsible for a plant exchange program with the United States which introduced many new species into that country. On a minor scale, the Rural Institute at Shantung demonstrated disease-control methods and distributed improved seeds and fruit stock. World War II interrupted a potentially revolutionary technique for so composting the fecal material that had for centuries been the chief source of fertilizers for China's farmers that the heat of fermentation would kill the sources of fecal-borne diseases. In matters of economics, nutrition, and health, the Institute also made numerous contributions to the Shantung rural areas. Fukien carried on useful studies in rice-breeding and in improved strains of wheat and soybean, in the development of fruit, and in reforestation. West China made important advances in livestock and fruit trees.

A fourth contribution of the Christian colleges in the field of agriculture was in the extension work that related scientific knowledge to actual practice. A major effort lay in the distribution of improved seeds and seedlings. It is estimated that in a period of thirty years the University of Nanking distributed some two thousand tons of wheat seed and fifteen hundred tons of cotton seed exclusive of seed produced in farmers' fields under its supervision. Similarly important distributions of silkworm eggs came from Lingnan and Nanking. In Szechwan the distribution of improved breeds of cows, goats, and chickens by West China and of improved fruit and vegetable stock had a significant impact on the rural life of that great province.

An important part of Nanking's outreach consisted of the training of farmers themselves. This took place through the preparation, within the limits of a thousand characters, of "job-sheets" on practical problems and of simple textbooks on rice, cotton, and oranges, and through short courses and institutes.

Many of the Christian colleges participated actively in rural development, a movement which swept China in the twenties and thirties and for which Dr. James Y.C. Yen's Chinese Mass Education Project at Tinghsien in 1926, an attempt to transform a single community, constituted something of a pilot project. By 1937 there were some three hundred rural development centers, many sponsored by Christian institutions and church bodies. Nanking and Shantung Universities had particularly active community development centers, social laboratories seeking to improve rural life by coordinated attacks on social, economic, educational, and health problems. The Mass Education Movement and many other reconstruction programs drew personnel, technical skills, and knowledge from the colleges. In the mid-thirties, Nanking and Yenching Universities joined the Peking Union Medical College, one government and one private university, and the Mass Education Movement in organizing the North China Council for Rural Reconstruction. With Rockefeller Foundation support and government cooperation, this project sought to reconstruct an entire country and then to use it for demonstration and training. In 1937 a very successful beginning was cut short by the war.

During the war, several institutions carried on service to rural communities in their refugee locations. After the war, the colleges contributed personnel to the new Joint Commission on Rural Reconstruction financed with American aid funds, which, had it been started in time, might have affected the history of China but had barely gotten under way when forced to move to Taiwan, where it established a remarkable record. To this organization, Yenching contributed its Comptroller, Mr. Stephen Tsai; the University of Nanking, a Commissioner, and several department heads. Both before and during the war, Christian college personnel were active in development of the Chinese Industrial Cooperatives.

RELIGION AND THEOLOGY

One of the features which distinguished the Christian colleges from others was the emphasis on religion as a vital part of education. Throughout their history, they always provided undergraduate courses in religion, at first required and then elective.

In the first colleges, courses in religion bulked large, provided either by departments of religion or by the beginnings of schools of theology. Considerable totals of credits in religion were required of all students, whether given in the form of weekday curricular courses or as Bible classes on Sundays. How effective these may have been as tools of evangelism, it is difficult to say. However, at their best they were an important part of the education offered by the colleges. The quality of instruction varied widely, especially after the increase in enrolments made it necessary to call upon the volunteer services of individuals with little specialized preparation in the field and often preoccupied with other duties. However, many of the courses were of high academic quality.

With registration, courses in religion could no longer be required. Several institutions, recognizing the need for change, had already made them elective. St. John's, though unregistered, in 1931 made such courses obligatory for Christians only, and in 1941 completely voluntary. In most cases, departments of religion gave way to courses in religion placed under departments of philosophy or of philosophy and religion. Or aspects of religion were dealt with under appropriate departments such as history, philosophy, psychology, and sociology. Nanking, registering early, was able to retain a Department of Religion, with courses made elective and providing neither major nor minor.

With the change to a voluntary basis, enrolments naturally slumped. Though election of courses in religion remained surprisingly high, governmental "reform" of the university curriculum in 1940 left practically no room for electives of any sort.

The founders of the first colleges laid great stress on the raising up of leaders for the Church and some at once instituted courses in theology for the training of pastors. Presbyterian classes in theology and the English Baptist Theological Institute were synchronous with the be-

ginning of Tengchow College. As early as 1869 Hangchow College, then
no more than a boys' school, instituted a course in theology. The North
China College originally had no other purpose than the training of men to
"give their services to the Church." A Theological School was part of St.
John's College before that achieved full college status.

After 1900 there was a renewed and extensive development of
theological education. The beginnings in and near Peking grew into the
North China Union Theological College (1905). Ten years later this
combined with the Wiley College of Theology to form a part of the new
Peking University. In Shantung, Presbyterians and Baptists joined in
Gotch-Robinson Union Theological College (1904), which in turn
became part of Shantung Christian University. In Shanghai, St. John's
Theological School continued as a department of the College of Arts. In
1906 a College of Theology was the first unit of the new Shanghai
College. In West China, a Faculty of Religion was a part of the new
Union University. A Divinity School was part of the new Boone College. No Protestant college established before 1910 lacked a theological
course, department, or even "college," most of their programs little if at
all above the middle-school level.

As the colleges and universities developed, however, other more
general educational objectives assumed greater importance, and specifically theological departments were no longer the major or central
concern. Some became non-vocational departments of religion; others
simply did not survive; still others were absorbed into new institutions,
as in the case of the theological department of the early Nanking University, which became part of the new Nanking Theological Seminary.
By 1927, there were theological units in only six of the Christian colleges
and universities: Huachung, St. John's, Shanghai, Shantung, West
China, and Yenching.

With registration, under which religion was not recognized, the
status of these schools underwent change. In Central China, the problem
at Huachung disappeared when Boone Divinity School moved to
Shanghai, joining St. John's. St. John's, remaining unregistered, carried
on its theological school without change until that merged with the
Central Theological School in Nanking. The seminaries at Shanghai and
Shantung continued on their campuses as unofficial units of their universities. At West China, the Faculty of Religion became an independent
School and then College of Religion. Yenching's Theological Seminary,
renamed the Yenching School of Religion, formally separated from the
university while continuing to be an integral part of its life.

In addition to these units of larger institutions, independent theological programs and schools were developing in many centers. Some of these started early in the nineteenth century. Many began and continued at a largely secondary level, but several became at least in part post-secondary, and some ultimately offered post-collegiate training. By the mid-twenties there were four with post-secondary programs: Nanking Theological Seminary, Union Theological Seminary (Foochow), Union Theological College (Canton), and Lutheran Theological Seminary (near Hankow). The presence of these institutions undoubtedly contributed to the fact that the Protestant universities, at least in Nanking, Foochow, and Canton, did not feel it necessary to develop their own colleges and departments of theology.

The first Protestant colleges, like their sisters in the United States, had had definite vocational goals in relation to the Church. Theological training had been one purpose, and they had, especially in the early days, prepared a not inconsiderable number of men for the ministry. Following the 1910 revival stirred by Pastor Ting Li-mei, there had been a sudden flood of volunteers, with hundreds of young men at least beginning theological studies. But this had subsided rather rapidly, and by the early twenties the dearth of applicants for all theological schools was causing serious concern. The causes were not entirely clear but undoubtedly included the Anti-Christian Movement and its after-effects, the attraction of various new forms of service, and the fact that the Church had, educationally, fallen behind its schools and neither demanded nor could afford a highly trained and therefore costly ministry. Moreover, with the expansion of the colleges into other fields and the development of separate theological institutions, the latter came to carry the major responsibility for training a ministry. The former were playing a numerically minor role, their students constituting, in the mid-thirties, fewer than twenty percent of the total number training for the Protestant ministry at the collegiate or post-collegiate level.

By the mid-thirties, the pattern of theological education had settled down to eleven institutions requiring at least middle-school graduation, five of these being parts of or associated with colleges or universities, the other six being entirely independent. In 1934 the so-called Weigle Report, *Education for Service in China—The Report of a Survey Commission*, recommended that these and a dozen other institutions with lesser requirements be consolidated into four theological colleges functioning in four centers under the overall name of Nanking Theological Seminary, three union theological training schools, and two graduate schools of theology. Its recommendations were never carried out.

Contribution by the China Colleges of students to graduate schools of theology was not great, since only two, Yenching School of Religion and Nanking Theological Seminary, with a total of only twenty students in 1933–34, maintained departments requiring college graduation for entrance. This situation, with the China Colleges playing a minor role in supplying pastors for the Protestant Church, continued without fundamental change through the war and after.

The China Colleges, however, indirectly played an important role in the programs of many of these theological institutions through contributions to their staffs. This was true not only for college-related schools but, where distance did not forbid, for separate schools as well. This participation of faculty members in both theological and non-theological programs was often to the mutual advantage of both. The Yenching School of Religion offers an especially striking example. The Dean of the School, Dr. T.T. Lew, was simultaneously Chairman of the Departments of Religion, Psychology, and Philosophy in the Arts College. University Chancellor Wu Lei-ch'üan taught the History and Philosophy of Religion. Professors of History William Hung and Philippe de Vargas taught Church History; Professor of Sociology John Stewart Burgess, Christian Ethics and Sociology; and Professor of Music Bliss Wiant, Sacred Music. In Nanking, there was a less extensive but similar sharing by the university with the physically and organically separate Seminary, which maintained a Rural Church Center at Shun Hua Chen, a nearby village.

Throughout their history, the China Colleges made other important contributions, especially to the leadership of the Church and its organizations, and in the field of Christian scholarship. The great evangelist Ting Li-mei was a member of one of Tengchow College's first classes and a product of the peripatetic theological training that preceded Shantung's College of Theology. Episcopal Bishops Kimber Den, Shen Tzu-kao, and Y.Y. Tsu were graduates of St. John's; Methodist Bishop Z.T. Kaung, of Soochow. T.C. Bau, a leader of the Baptist Church in China and a vice-president of the Baptist World Alliance, was a Shanghai alumnus. Leaders in the National Christian Council and the Church of Christ in China came from a number of institutions: C.S. (Chester) Miao, Secretary of Religious Education and briefly General Secretary of the National Christian Council, from Shanghai; K.T. Chung, General Secretary, from St. John's. T.Z. Koo, St. John's alumnus, became internationally known as a Secretary of the World Student Christian Federation. Personnel from the colleges represented the Church in China at the Jerusalem (1928), Madras (1939), and Amsterdam (1948) meetings of the World Council of Churches. Dr. T.C. Chao of Yenching and President Wu Yi-fang of Ginling were at various times vice-presidents of that body.

The contribution of the colleges to the leadership of the YMCA and YWCA was also notable. Among city secretaries of the YMCA were Fei Ch'i-hao (Peking) of North China Union College and Lee Ying-lam (Canton) of Lingnan University. David Z.T. Yui of St. John's was National General Secretary for many years. Miss Ting Shu-ching of North China Woman's College and Miss Ts'ai K'uei of Ginling College between them held the General Secretaryship of the YWCA for some thirty years. President Wu Yi-fang was at one time Chairman of the National Committee.

From members of the faculties of the China Colleges came a number of important scholarly works in the field of religion. Among those scholars producing works in English, most notable was Harold Henry Rowley of Shantung, who became one of the world's foremost Old Testament scholars and Professor of Chinese in the University of London. Before leaving Shantung, he had done much of the work on two books: *Submission in Suffering and Other Essays on Eastern Thought*, and *Prophecy and Religion in Ancient China and Israel*, both published by British university presses. The *Concordance of the Revised Mandarin Bible* (1909, 1922) by Dr. Courtenay H. Fenn of the North China Union Theological College (later Yenching School of Religion) provided the Church with a basic tool. Professor Soothill, while still in China, translated *The Analects of Confucius. Religious Liberty* (1945), by Professor M. Searle Bates of the University of Nanking, is a definitive study of the subject. Dr. T.C. Chao of Yenching's School of Religion, one of the most thoughtful of Chinese writers on religion, was known for such books in Chinese as *Christian Philosophy and Present-Day Religious Thought and Life in China* and *Our Cultural Heritage*.

OTHER FIELDS

The impatient quest for technology which marked the awakening at the turn of the century stimulated the Christian colleges to early efforts to develop courses in engineering. At St. John's, the subject was introduced before 1920, and a School of Engineering soon developed, though that never went beyond the civil engineering with which it started. In the early 1920s, Hangchow's Construction Department evolved into a Department of Engineering. This grew in strength and was the only such development among the China Colleges to achieve the status of a college of engineering. At Lingnan, a college of civil engineering alone was set up in 1930, but this was soon merged as a department into a College of Science and Engineering. In the early thirties, Nanking developed majors in electrical engineering and industrial chemistry within the program of its College of Science.

The preparation of teachers, particularly with a view to staffing the rapidly multiplying primary and middle schools, was one of the earliest objectives of the Protestant colleges but rarely took the form of extensive professional training. Departments of education were slow in developing, but by 1920 more than half of the institutions had such departments, all relatively strong units of their respective schools. Several might well have expanded into teacher's colleges had the Ministry of Education not ruled that colleges of education could be established only in connection with government institutions. The only Christian university to have a college-grade school of education was Huachung, which had acted early and was permitted to carry on. But twelve of thirteen institutions offered majors in education, with a total enrolment of 272 in 1933–34. The two women's colleges laid special emphasis on teacher-training, Ginling being noted for its work in physical education. A large number of graduates of all Christian colleges turned to teaching at all levels. In 1925, some thirty percent were reported as teachers, three-fourths of them in Christian schools. A dozen years later, the figure had risen to thirty-eight percent, with a somewhat higher proportion employed in non-Christian schools.

Law received professional emphasis at only one institution, Soochow University. Others had departments of economics and political science, which elsewhere were often major units of what were known as colleges of law in the sense of "government" or "political sciences," but in their cases were usually parts of colleges of arts. In the case of Yenching, they constituted (with momentary help from courses in "Jurisprudence") its College of Public Affairs. In Shanghai, Soochow University's Comparative Law School of China, which required study of three legal systems—Civil, Anglo-American, Chinese—developed into one of the leading law schools of the country. In 1936, ninety-five graduates had taken advanced studies abroad, seventy-two were teaching law, and four were presidents of law schools; thirty-one were serving as judges; seven of nine advocates of the Municipal Council of Shanghai's International Settlement were Soochow alumni.

Courses in economics, to meet the needs of China's developing economy, appeared in the colleges of arts at an early date, and departments quickly followed. The emphasis was often practical rather than theoretical, preparing graduates for life in the expanding business world. Even before 1920 some departments were offering courses in "business," and soon thereafter several were experimenting with departments of business or commerce. Hangchow developed a college of commerce which later changed its name to College of Business Administration. Lingnan's Department of Business Administration became a college and then its College of Commerce. St. John's Department of Business Administration was, after a short time, merged into its Department of Economics. About 1930, Shanghai developed the Downtown School of Commerce which became its most popular unit.

With or without specialized vocational or professional preparation, graduates of the Christian colleges were to be found in almost all vocations and professions. At the same time, they appear to have contributed with more than normal strength to certain fields. By 1900, the colleges could claim some 250 graduates. Of these, ten percent entered the ministry, twenty-five percent other forms of social and religious work, and twenty-five percent teaching, mostly in Christian schools. Twenty years later, nearly fifty percent of the total of more than two thousand graduates were still engaged in these three areas of service, but with only five percent and fifteen percent respectively in the first two categories.

By 1937, when war with Japan interrupted their development, the colleges had contributed to Chinese society some ten thousand graduates. Of these, more than thirty-five hundred had taken up teaching, two-thirds of them in Christian schools; more than five hundred were in social and religious service; and over a hundred had entered the ministry. Nearly seven hundred were engaged in the practice of medicine—a most impressive figure—nearly four hundred in agriculture and forestry, over a hundred in engineering, and over three hundred in law. Public life had claimed nearly nine hundred, but business only a few more; approximately the same percentages of the total as in 1920. One astounding figure is that in 1936–37 more than eleven hundred graduates had engaged in further study, some three hundred of them abroad.

By 1950, another sixteen thousand graduates had been added, making a total of some twenty-six thousand graduates of the China Colleges during their less than seventy years of life. It is probable that another thirty-five to forty thousand students had been in attendance but had not completed the course, making a total of some sixty to sixty-five thousand men and women who had had some experience of the Christian colleges.

14
The Tools of Education

How well equipped were the Protestant colleges and universities for what they were attempting to do? How did their facilities compare with those of other institutions, public and private? No formal appraisal was ever made, but the impressions of informed individuals and some suggestive data permit a rough evaluation of the adequacy of the tools with which the China Colleges had to work.

The early years of any institution saw it facing serious problems of site, buildings, and equipment. Some solved these problems more adequately than did others. But in 1937, when war forced most from their homes and substituted survival for growth, the fourteen China Colleges were, from the point of view of size of campus and number and quality of buildings, on the whole not only adequately housed but, in comparison with most secular rivals, well provided for. The problem lay rather in the area of libraries and laboratories. All were having to struggle to acquire and keep sharp the increasingly numerous and costly tools of education. In the matter of physical facilities, the China Colleges were both relatively well off and in want, adequately housed but often in-adequately equipped.

In their campuses the Christian colleges of China exhibited both striking similarities and wide-ranging differences. They were, with the exception only of those with separate downtown centers, unified campuses, residential in nature, in or near large cities. On the other hand, they varied widely in setting, size, and architecture.

Six of the colleges—Ginling, Nanking, St. John's, Moukden, Soochow, and Woman's Medical—were in metropolitan areas though, in the case of the first two, their sites were in a part of the city of Nanking that was, at the start, largely rural in character. Six—Hwa Nan, Huachung, Shanghai, Shantung, West China, and Yali—were situated on the edge of populous areas. Four—Fukien, Hangchow, Lingnan, and Yenching—found quieter and often ampler sites a few miles from large cities. But all were in close touch with the great concentrations of population—sixteen institutions in or near eleven great cities. Of the dozen largest population centers of China in 1937, ten were occupied by Christian colleges or universities.

Campuses ranged in size from the purposefully compact and the necessarily restricted to the amply extensive. One or two managed on a score of acres, others enjoyed the freedom of hundreds. But all consisted of unified groupings of academic and residential buildings. Divided campuses existed only where there were "downtown" schools for such subjects as commerce, law, and medicine, as in the cases of St. John's, Shanghai, and Soochow. Most distinctive probably was their residential character, in which all shared to some extent. Whether in close proximity to the academic buildings or in separate groupings, hostels and faculty residences were integral parts of each main campus.

Campuses also varied widely in their settings. Those in or near the hearts of cities could rarely boast of the beauty of environment, though they could themselves be beautiful, as in the case of Ginling, or impressive, in the case of Nanking. Those at some distance from cities could enjoy the advantages of pleasing natural settings. Fukien, on hills overlooking the Min River, had what one admiring visitor described as one of the ten best college locations in the world; while Hangchow, on the Ch'ien T'ang River, boasted that its campus had been rated one of the most beautiful in the world. Allowing for local enthusiasm and vagueness of criteria, the beauty of both sites cannot be denied. Far from any river but blessed with lakes and gardens, Yenching had advantages of its own which it fully exploited by careful planning and construction.

The buildings erected on these sites ran the gamut from the unsightly to the delightful, from the work of untrained and uninspired builders to that of creative architects, from the most tasteless of then contemporary Western to highly pleasing adaptation of the Chinese. Where there was competent and creative planning, the results not only were good but also contributed to the architecture of modern China. The China Colleges were, in their use of Chinese elements, innovators and stimulators at a time when, in its institutional architecture, China was unhappily aping the West.

Several of the colleges attempted to combine East and West in their architecture, both in style of construction and in layout of buildings. The first school buildings in mission institutions had been uninspired and unattractive combinations of four plain walls and roof, the latter occasionally "Chinese" in its use of the tiles and eaves familiar to local workmen. St. John's was the first consciously to attempt "to preserve certain features of Chinese architecture, especially the graceful curved roof, so that the building would not look like a foreign importation." This was in 1893, and future buildings, with the exception of the Chapel, perhaps intentionally preserved from contamination by "non-Christian" traditions, followed this principle. Unfortunately, such features were rarely more than unassimilated decorations. A far more successful building was the Social Hall completed in 1929. Modest attempts were made elsewhere in the early years of the twentieth century, and by the middle of the second decade all but two of the colleges—Shanghai and Soochow, which preferred a less expensive conventional style or pseudo collegiate Gothic—were giving some Chinese features to buildings.

Hwa Nan was the first educational institution in Foochow to add the Chinese roof to otherwise Western buildings. Though this step created something of a sensation in 1914, Hwa Nan never went further.

At Chengtu, West China Union University was one of the first institutions to experiment in applying Chinese architecture to academic needs. Some of its major buildings, designed by Fred Rowntree and Son, of London, probably went further than even Ginling and Yenching in the use of native features, especially those characteristic of the architecture of that area as distinct from that of Peking. Experimenting with styles resulted in some unfortunate results, as did the insistence of a Western donor on a clock tower amid Chinese settings, but West China made a significant contribution to the development of architecture in the area.

Early buildings at Lingnan paid little attention to Chinese features and were largely reflections of the common Western-influenced utilitarian style of the South China region. Later buildings added the usual Chinese touches with the usual questionable results until, in the thirties, a high degree of sinicization was achieved with perhaps too great copying of the Peking palace style.

Nanking was the first Christian university to adopt a uniform, even if not wholly indigenous, Chinese architecture for its campus. Mr. Fellows of Perkins, Fellows, and Hamilton of Chicago produced for the new campus a restrained but impressive modified Chinese style in grey brick, using no color. The use of the magnificent large bricks from the Nanking city wall, then in the process of partial demolition, contributed to the stateliness of the structures. This basic style was adhered to thereafter with modifications in the interest of efficiency, notably in the case of the Library completed just before the war, where concrete replaced the no-longer-available bricks.

Fellows was also responsible for the new buildings at Shantung, where the results were somewhat less successful, the Chinese roofs tending again to be awkward appendages, the Chapel a slightly sinicized Gothic. Perhaps most successful were the dormitories, which, being low and grouped around courts, resembled Chinese dwellings.

Huachung was so long cramped for space and dependent on existing structures that it never had an opportunity to develop its own style, though the Middle School Gymnasium was an interesting attempt to use Chinese features. Plans drawn in 1936 proposed buildings in a modified Chinese style and included a copy of the famous "Yellow Crane Tower," a local landmark, but were delayed by the war and finally made meaningless by the Communists.

Not even such plans were made at two East China institutions. The University of Shanghai remained loyal to a certain conception of collegiate Gothic which provided needed space and, in the later buildings, increased efficiency. The result was structures not inappropriate for a setting such as that provided by Westernized Shanghai but alien to the broader environment. Soochow University erected a succession of nondescript buildings with little recognition of Chinese or any other architectural style. A "Pavilion of Benevolent Longevity" celebrating the eightieth birthdays of Drs. Cline and Nance was a lovely but incongruous wholly Chinese decoration on a drab and alien campus.

A major impetus came from Henry Killam Murphy of the New York firm of Murphy and Dana. Murphy made his first visit to China in 1914 in connection with planning for Yale-in-China's new Changsha campus. After visiting Peking, he wrote: "When I first entered the Forbidden City, I was completely swept off my feet by its majesty, beauty, and dignity, and I felt then—as I still feel—that the Forbidden City in Peking is the finest thing, architecturally, in the world. Then and there was born my resolve to develop an adaptation of this magnificent old architecture of China, which should preserve the aesthetic qualities of the original, but should be carried out in modern construction." He was to attempt expression of this resolve in several campuses, culminating in Yenching. He also stimulated the revival of the old style in construction for other purposes, notably the Murphy-designed pagoda on Purple Mountain near Nanking and the Chinese-designed memorial to Dr. Sun Yat-sen in the same area.

After experimenting with only moderate success at Yale-in-China, he developed a more elaborate and colorful style at Fukien and Ginling. At Fukien the dormitories employed the acute uptilt of South China roofs, the academic buildings the more restrained curves of the Forbidden City. The latter was superior to anything yet attempted in the palace style but, because of their multi-story height, which had no precedent in Peking, fell somewhat short of a successful combining of utilitarian body and Chinese roof. At Ginling, the quadrangle completed in 1923 was one of the finest examples up to that time of Chinese architecture adapted to modern needs. To the curving roofs and orderly grouping of buildings he added that other feature of Chinese architecture, the rich coloring of columns and cornices. Though suffering some utilitarian weaknesses, it was a beautiful and effective use of Chinese principles in the grouping of buildings and of Chinese line and color in their design.

It was at Yenching, however, that a few years later Murphy produced the most extensive and probably most successful modern educational plant in a Chinese style. From the palaces of the Forbidden City, "matchless in stateliness and grandeur," he borrowed their pillars, overhanging roofs, proportions, and use of color. The result was buildings of impressive beauty but with an unfortunate appearance of luxury. The use of a pagoda to house the water tower was a startling but ornamental feature of the campus.

While considerable success had been achieved in the use of the external features of Chinese architecture, the buildings rarely achieved internally the utility and efficiency which were also sought. Unlighted, unventilated attics beneath unbroken Chinese roofs often constituted expensive waste space, and close copying of external features tended to restrict internal flexibility and use of space. A leading American librarian described one of the most beautiful libraries as "an architect's dream and a librarian's nightmare."

Introduction of the new though old architecture might have been carried still further in the postwar Yali campus planned for Changsha, which hoped "to achieve and organize growth from China's own tradition which will represent and express the best in art and science of both the Orient and the Occident," had the end not come too soon to all of the China Colleges. Such a goal, sought by all the colleges which made experiments, was never fully achieved, but the efforts made constituted an important and influential step in domesticating institutions which were obviously foreign in many other ways. They were also factors in the adaptation of China to the modern world in one significant aspect of life. The Christian colleges had a powerful effect on the architecture of educational institutions, government buildings, and other public edifices of the first half of the twentieth century. The main building of the Greater Shanghai Municipal Center was an enlarged adaptation of the Administration Building at Yenching. In Nanking, the buildings for the Ministries of Railways and of Communications, and, in Peiping, the National Library were striking examples of the revival of Chinese architecture. Probably only the war with Japan prevented much wider development.

Splendid sites and impressive buildings did not necessarily mean adequate equipment. It was easier to secure the space for education than to find the tools. Donors preferred to give buildings. Even in their strongest years, the China Colleges were only moderately supplied with the basic tools of libraries and laboratories and were constantly hard put to it to keep up with growing needs. They were in danger of falling behind the best of their secular rivals.

In the first stages, any institution which had any books at all could be viewed as relatively adequately supplied with a library. For reasons of tradition, which concentrated on a few classics, and of language, which provided few modern books in Chinese, reliance had to be placed almost wholly on textbooks and lectures. It is to be noted that in 1914, the four-year-old University of Nanking had just over five thousand volumes, only eight hundred of which were in Chinese. Five years later this total had tripled. In 1916, the ten-year-old Shanghai College had slightly less than five thousand almost equally divided between English and Chinese. Low as these figures are, the minimum standard for American colleges a few years later was only eight thousand volumes, and even as late as 1918 a number of fairly well known Protestant colleges in the U.S. reported collections of from five thousand to fifteen thousand volumes.

There is no way of appraising the quality of these collections, but the probability is that they consisted largely of unwinnowed donations. The Protestant colleges had hardly begun to realize the necessity of strong libraries. However relatively strong collections might appear, none constituted more than the beginning of a college or university library.

The first census of Protestant college libraries, giving figures for 1925–26, reported collections ranging from 2,950 in the case of the almost defunct Lutheran College to just under sixty-four thousand in the case of Lingnan and Nanking. Five institutions listed collections of twenty-five thousand to thirty-one thousand; four, between ten thousand and twenty thousand; and four, from five thousand to nine thousand. The proportion of Chinese books was growing, now roughly equal to that of Western books except in the cases of Lingnan and Nanking, where Chinese collections were two or three times the size of Western.

Comparison with government and private institutions for the same date indicates that some of the Protestant colleges were not in an unfavorable position, at least so far as numbers of books were concerned. Only one institution, Peking National University, had a larger total than Lingnan or Nanking—166,000, or which 140,000 were Chinese. Four other institutions had collections which, while smaller than those of Lingnan and Nanking, were larger than those of other Protestant colleges.

Eight years later, in 1933, there had been substantial growth in the libraries of all Protestant institutions. Collections now ranged from twenty thousand to 250,000, with books in Chinese constituting from fifty to eighty percent of each figure. In 1934, Yenching, which had had no library in 1918, had one of the four largest university libraries in China, the others being Tsinghua, Sun Yat Sen, and Peita (Peiping). Subsequent growth kept its standing high. No other Protestant institution came near it, though the University of Nanking had nearly 120,000 volumes, and most compared well with neighboring institutions. Among the latter, the library of the Jesuit center at Zikawei (Shanghai), with its two hundred thousand volumes, ranked high. Several Protestant colleges, however, still had wholly inadequate libraries. For all, a basic problem continued to be the lack of funds either to provide essential current acquisitions or to correct long-standing inadequacies. In the early thirties one of the major government universities was alone spending as much annually as all the China Colleges combined.

The problem was compounded by the necessity of maintaining collections in other languages than Chinese, especially in English. The Protestant colleges often ranked well in the matter of books in English but less favorably, except in a few instances, in that of books in Chinese. In the case of the institutions benefiting from Harvard-Yenching Institute support, however, very respectable, even outstanding, Chinese collections were built up. The Chinese collection at Yenching in the mid-thirties compared favorably with those at such institutions as Tsinghua, Peita, and Sun Yat Sen. Occasional local gifts contributed to the adequacy of some collections. In 1933 a former Grand Tutor to the last Emperor of the Manchu Dynasty presented Fukien with his rare personal collection. In 1919, the grandson of Marquis Tseng Kuo-fan, the famous scholar-statesman, donated to Hangchow several thousand volumes on political and historical subjects. West China at one time received twenty-five thousand volumes from a prominent Chengtu family. In 1948 a venerable Chinese scholar gave Huachung almost his entire library of some twenty thousand volumes.

After World War II and just prior to the Communist take-over, several of the China Colleges were able to report very sizeable collections: Yenching University, four hundred thousand volumes; University of Nanking, 250,000; St. John's University, 150,000.

In regard to laboratories, both instructional and research, the colleges faced situations similar to those that prevailed in their libraries and which ranged from the sometimes inadequate to the occasionally very good. In the early stages, equipment was largely hit-and-miss, depending often on the special interests of the instructor or on the chance acquisition of bits of apparatus. But science was still relatively simple and requirements were not great. Until the second decade of the twentieth century, the Christian colleges did not suffer too greatly from comparison with general standards then obtaining. With the increasing emphasis on and growing complexity of science and technology, however, the colleges entered on a continual struggle to keep pace with the demands made on them. In this they were only partially successful.

In the decades before the war, undergraduate work in science, technology, and such professions as medicine, with only an occasional exception—as in the case of the Second Huachung, where for a while Yali found itself contributing scientists to almost empty laboratories—had sufficient basic equipment. In 1935–36, the University of Nanking was reported as being first in equipment and apparatus among all private universities in China, Christian or non-Christian, though only seventh in size of student body. Except in a few cases, more sophisticated and modern equipment was lacking. Work in professional fields such as engineering, agriculture, and medicine was more adequately provided for, as were such graduate courses as were offered at places like Nanking and Yenching. However, there was little that was not essential simply to meet minimum requirements. Perhaps the chief weakness, even in cases where some research was being carried on, was the usual lack of any but the simplest research facilities. This situation was almost always compounded by discouragingly heavy teaching loads. Minor exceptions to this lack of equipment were several institutions which were enabled by generous grants from the China Medical Board and the Rockefeller Foundation to develop well-equipped laboratories in certain limited fields.

The war years naturally brought added problems, causing the loss of much equipment and placing excessive strains on that which survived. Institutions in Shanghai and Chengtu shared or pooled their resources; those in isolated refuges made shift as best they could. There was an unavoidable decrease in amount and quality of laboratory courses. After the war, a considerable portion of the rehabilitation funds available went into the re-equipping of laboratories. Much had been accomplished in this respect, and the prewar situation was being fully restored and perhaps improved upon, when the political changes in China and the closing of channels of aid from America brought the effort to an end.

15
The Spirit of Education

A common characteristic of the Christian colleges was their emphasis on campus life, the belief that what happened outside the classroom was an important factor in the education of the student, particularly in the shaping of his character. As a way of life, Christianity must find expression in all aspects of the educational community. Social life and extracurricular activities—group and individual—constituted an important part of college life, one in which the faculty played a vital role. These were made easier by the dormitory life. The distinctive and positive college spirit which usually developed was generally a constructive force until its subversion and collapse in the late 1940s.

On their main campuses the Christian colleges were residential, almost completely so in theory and expectation, practically so within limits imposed by finances. This was true from the beginning, and the provision of dormitories usually had priority in building plans. It was a pattern followed by Tsinghua College, which was similarly of American origin, but by few others. When in 1916–17 Shantung set up its new campus in Tsinan, dormitories took precedence over classrooms. In 1921 Ginling College opened its new campus in Nanking with six buildings—three academic buildings and three dormitories.

In the early stages, because of the small numbers involved, residential facilities tended to be adequate, but with the often rapid expansion of enrolments, additional dormitories became a growing need. Student numbers were often limited by the availability of dormitory space. In later years, especially under the refugee and rehabilitation conditions of 1937–50, the problem became acute and had to be met in less than ideal ways.

During the war, makeshift quarters were somehow provided, whether by rental of old buildings or erection of temporary new, but these were both crowded and lacking in many comforts. At Chengtu, Ginling girls lived four in a ten-foot-square room. In Nanping, Hwa

Nan girls lived twelve in a somewhat larger room, sharing one common table. In Shanghai, Hangchow was unable to provide housing and both students and faculty members had to fend for themselves.

Following the war, the return to home campuses brought further problems. Dormitories, when still standing, were bedless and students had to sleep on floors. This situation was aggravated by increased enrolments. In most cases it was proving impossible to hold to former standards of residence. Such dormitories as could be provided became overcrowded and the gates were opened to day students in increasing numbers. These were not an entirely new feature but had previously been restricted almost entirely to downtown colleges, where residence was impracticable.

In most cases dormitories were the sole responsibility of the institutions themselves. In others, however, especially those in which British influence was strong, this responsibility was shared, if not wholly taken over, by missions and churches. At Huachung the American Episcopal Mission opened a hostel for men while the London Missionary Society and the Reformed Church in the United States sponsored jointly a Church of Christ hostel. At West China, the Canadian Methodist (later United Church of Canada), American Methodist, American Baptist, Anglican, and Friends Missions all erected and managed hostels.

Associated with residential facilities but of growing importance as day students increased in numbers, were provisions for the physical and social welfare of students. These took the form of athletic fields, clinics, and social halls. Their effectiveness was strengthened by the extracurricular contributions of faculty members.

Christian education played a large part in the introduction into China of physical education and sports. Chinese life was not without its games and its competitions, whether kite-flying or dragon-boat races, but the Confucian scholar was expected to be grave in his demeanor and unhurried in his actions. Physical exercise other than such dignified activity as shadow-boxing was not part of the training or life of intellectuals. From the start it was an element in the education provided by Christian colleges, first through the example of "undignified" Western professors and then through student participation as the desire to become modern, as Japan had, brought about a new willingness to engage in previously scorned activity.

When North China Union College reopened after 1900, its campus included tennis courts, a football field, and a track. In 1908 St. John's alumni raised five thousand dollars for an athletic field for their alma mater. No institution was without facilities for sports. Gymnasiums were a goal which not every college achieved, but St. John's had built one by 1916 and Hangchow one by 1926. Some gymnasiums were non-descript temporary structures, often no more than a roof without walls, but the Boyd and Warner Gymnasiums at Yenching were among the finest in the country.

Informal sports soon developed into organized athletics. Intramural competition led to intercollegiate. Regional athletic associations grew up and sponsored area competitions. Occasional athletes participated in national meets and even in the Far Eastern Olympics. By 1905 a St. John's student set a college pole vault record of "nine feet plus" before going on to greater heights as a well-known bishop. A student of the Academy left in Tunghsien when North China Union College moved to Peking, won the five-mile run at the Far East Games in 1915. A future president of St. John's served for twenty years as Director of Physical Education. The Director at Yenching, an Overseas Chinese, was a five-letter man from Ohio Wesleyan. The East China Intercollegiate Field and Track Meet of 1918 and the National Athletic Meet of 1931 were both held at Hangchow College.

The Christian colleges thus were pioneers in the introduction of physical exercise into the life of the intellectual and in pioneering intercollegiate athletic contests. The process was not always simple. Fear of loss of face prevented many an underdog team from showing up, and for many years defeat could not be accepted with good grace. As one of China's foreign ministers pointed out, this was one of the most valuable lessons China's youth had to learn. Unexpected complications also arose, as when a hammer-thrower was jerked off the ground by his queue. The sports engaged in were varied. Archery and gymnastics soon gave way to group games. Soccer football, where childhood games with the feet had laid a foundation, was perhaps most popular, though basketball eventually came to rival it. Volleyball, tennis, swimming, and track were the chief other sports. Hangchow at one time even had a crew using racing shells borrowed from a defunct rowing club, but could find no competition. By the 1920s, athletics had become a part of college life in China. Even during the war years, when undernourishment took its toll, sports, both formal and informal, were an important part of the program of all institutions.

Student health was an early and continuing concern. Athletics, rousing students from the traditional sedentary life, helped to reduce crippling by tuberculosis and other diseases. Annual physical examinations caught and led to correction of physical defects. Clinics of various kinds met simple troubles or prescribed for more serious. For institutions related to or near mission hospitals, care of the sick was simplified. Others might have infirmaries. Altogether the China Colleges set unusually high standards of care for student health.

Social life took the form of most of the common extracurricular activities—non-athletic competitions and associations. An early and steadily popular type of contest was debating in both Chinese and English. At first entirely intramural, it soon became intercollegiate. Before 1920 annual debates were being held among institutions in the Shanghai area. Early topics included such modern questions as franchise for women and the wrongness of war. Oratory, in both Chinese and English, was also popular. Literary societies were common features of the first colleges, as early as the 1890s, and continued in the mature institutions of the 1920s, though their popularity tended to fade. In the 1930s the University of Nanking reported sixteen clubs related to academic disciplines, and this was probably representative of the situation elsewhere. Dramatic Clubs, Glee Clubs, and a few orchestras provided outlets for performing talents. Such activities furnished what had been a largely lacking side of student life.

More important, however, than these physical and social provisions was the distinctive concern for the student as an individual which was shared by many members of the faculties and staffs and found expression in contacts both within and outside the classroom. These did much to shape the character and direct the life of successive generations of graduates. This was perhaps to be expected of the early missionary personnel and of their often more highly trained Western successors, who were drawn to these institutions by somewhat broader missionary motives. It was also true of the first Chinese faculty and staff members, many of whom had personally experienced this concern.

The emphasis on the development of the whole personality which is a fundamental part of the Christian concept of education naturally found expression in a concern for the spiritual needs of the individual student. Religion, in the sense of the development of the individual's spiritual resources and the satisfaction of his spiritual needs, was a recognized and logical part of the educational program. At first this concern found much of its expression in required worship and courses in religion. With the growth of student unrest and patriotism, this requirement began to lose such effectiveness as it may once have had; with the extreme national consciousness of the 1920s, it had to be abandoned.

Worship became voluntary, courses were made elective, and greater reliance was placed on the words and examples of faculty and staff. The change met with greater resistance in some cases than in others, but in all it ultimately resulted in a more natural and possibly more fruitful pattern of religious influence.

One result of this concern for the individual was the emphasis on guidance. At first this was wholly informal, but with larger student bodies came the need for organization. The Christian colleges were by far the earliest institutions in China to introduce systems of faculty advisers. And throughout, the emphasis was on positive guidance rather than negative punishment. Though a natural expression of the Christian respect for personality, this constituted a new concept of discipline in the Chinese setting.

This broader education, social and spiritual as well as academic, was possible only because of the devotion and commitment of many members of the faculty and staff in whom academic qualifications were supplemented by religious faith and concern. Only such men and women could be counted on for the time and effort required by the contacts outside the classroom—whether on campus or in homes— which were essential to influencing the individual. This relationship was facilitated by the fact that faculties were largely in residence. Institutions were in a very real sense communities in which the devotion of the faculty had opportunity for expression. The fact that families and homes were involved gave to many of the contacts an added richness hard to match in any other way. The Christian colleges were also fortunate in having an unusually high proportion of full-time faculty undistracted by outside demands and undivided in their loyalties. This was in distinct contrast to the common Chinese practice of taking on additional part-time jobs or even of combining two "full-time" jobs. This concentration facilitated attendance at meetings, participation in activities, entertainment in homes, and the informal contacts which often bore such rich fruit.

In their concern for the extracurricular life of their students, the Protestant colleges and universities were importations from America and the British Empire rather than from the European continent or Japan, the influence of both of which was much greater in government and private institutions. They set patterns and standards which were rarely copied and almost never matched. This feature, perhaps more than any other, elicited favorable comment and won for them public approval. It is possible that the rapid increase in numbers and the growing pressures of academic life may have contributed to a diminution and dilution of this concern, but it remained a significant and distinctive feature of the Christian college until the end.

16
Cooperation and Concentration

From the beginning, cooperation, coordination, and union were live issues in Protestant higher education in China and important factors in the development of institutions. None of the China colleges was unaffected by plans for concentration and unity, and four of the final fourteen were the result of mergers. In these four, earlier institutions found new life. Though the total of four-year collegiate institutions never exceeded seventeen at any one time and reached that figure only briefly during the early 1920s, the over-extension of Protestant forces in the field of higher education was a constant cause of concern both in China and abroad.

Strengthening through consolidation started early in the twentieth century and continued for two decades. In 1904, three institutions emphasizing respectively arts and sciences, theology, and medicine united to form Shantung Christian University. In 1910 two "colleges," both of which had only recently undertaken post-secondary work, joined to form the University of Nanking. In 1915 the North China Union College in Tungchow, the Peking University, and the North China Union Women's College made up the new Peking University which was to become Yenching. Finally in 1924, the first Huachung University rose out of the cooperation of British and American missions in Central China and on the academic foundation of Boone University. Four years later, Yale-in-China joined the union.

A beginning of cooperation in education had been made as early as 1877, when a missionary General Conference set up a Schools and Textbook Series Committee. Though this produced little textbook material, it spawned in 1890 the Education Association of China (later the China Christian Educational Association) dedicated to "the promotion of educational interests in China and the fraternal cooperation of all those engaged in teaching." Like the several regional associations which developed later, it was chiefly concerned with primary and secondary

174

education. An Association of Christian Colleges and Universities which came into existence in 1919 pressed the cause of cooperation and union in higher education.

Coordination and cooperation on a national scale was a theme of the World Missionary Conference held in Edinburgh in 1910. While strongly advocating the founding of a great Union Christian University in China and looking to the establishing of "several such institutions in different parts of the Empire," the conference pointed out that it would be "impracticable to develop institutions simultaneously in all the various divisions of the Empire, and it is the opinion of the Commission, having in view the necessity of maintaining only institutions of real excellence, that at only a very limited number of points should the attempt be made at present to develop work of a distinctly university calibre. It is of the opinion also that, when in any of the great divisions of the Empire the time is ripe for the development of university education, all the Christian forces in that region should unite in the development of one institution of higher learning." The central university to the establishing of which the conference gave most attention did not quickly come into being, finally appearing in 1924 as Huachung College on a much smaller scale than originally envisaged. Meanwhile, the decade 1910–20 saw the birth of a considerable number of institutions, not all of which conformed to the cooperative pattern proposed by the conference.

In November 1921 an Educational Commission sponsored by the mission boards of North America and Great Britain and headed by Professor Ernest D. Burton of the University of Chicago and thus usually referred to as the Burton Commission, visited China, "to study all types and grades of education as carried on in all parts of China, and on the basis of such study to suggest to the Christian forces engaged in educational work in China a policy for the future." In addition to distinguished educators from abroad, the Commission included members from China and two Chinese and two Western presidents of Christian colleges. The Commission found education essential to the church through its building up of a Christian community, and a place in Chinese education for Christian schools that were in sympathy with the ideals of the nation and educationally efficient. It also proposed a program for Christian education that would make it "efficient, Christian, and Chinese." To this end it recommended, among other things, that quality not quantity be a determining factor and that the existing sixteen colleges (according to its count) be federated into not more than six regional universities, one each in six areas: North China, East China, Central

China, South China, West China, and Fukien. In South and West China, it gave support to the one existing institution; elsewhere it proposed the merging of two or more independent institutions. It recommended greater vocational and professional emphasis, with concentration on training for the ministry and teaching, and because of expense, limiting medical schools to four or five. It also urged the development of provincial Boards of Christian Education.

While there was general acceptance of the idea of concentration, specific recommendations met with questioning and resistance. One was the proposed amalgamation in North China of Shantung and Yenching Universities to form a single institution operating in two centers, with schools of education and medicine at Tsinan, of arts and science and of literature at Peking, and of theology at both centers. In spite of the impracticability of such merging of two institutions three hundred miles apart, both schools reluctantly accepted the plan. It was also approved in principle by the Shantung home board, but was turned down by the Trustees of Yenching.

A second recommendation involved two institutions in the same locality, Hwa Nan College on one edge of the city of Foochow and Fukien Christian College ten miles on the other side. An initial proposal that Fukien be reduced to a junior college was changed to read that it be "the only institution (in its area) doing junior and senior college work, and that the senior college offer a single course in arts, education and theology," these being the least expensive subjects. The Woman's College of South China (Hwa Nan) would become "a union college, affiliated with Fukien Christian University." Nothing came of this. Hwa Nan was not interested, and Fukien continued not only the subjects proposed but its work in science, which was being largely supported by the China Medical Board. A third recommendation was both more practical and more productive. It gave support and impetus to long-discussed plans for the establishment of a Christian University in Central China, which finally resulted, in 1924, in Huachung University.

For East China the Burton Commission proposed the establishment of an East China University of which all six existing institutions, together with Nanking Theological Seminary, should become parts. These six were Hangchow, Nanking, St. John's, Shanghai, and Soochow Universities, and Ginling College, in four cities as much as one hundred and fifty miles apart. This was not an entirely new concept, the bringing together of Hangchow, Nanking, Shanghai, and Soochow having been unsuccessfully proposed in 1913. The Commission's proposal resulted in negotiations which dragged on for years without concrete result, frustrated by institutional loyalties and denominational interest, by political developments, and by a high degree of impracticability.

To assist in carrying out the program proposed by the Burton Commission, there was organized in America in 1925 a "Permanent Committee for the Co-ordination and Promotion of Christian Higher Education in China." In July 1926, a Council of Higher Education met in Shanghai with Dr. Earl H. Cressy as secretary. Since the Burton Commission had published no data, the next two years were spent in a survey of the twenty-six Protestant institutions of higher education then in existence: nine universities, seven single colleges, four separate schools of theology, and six colleges of medicine, with a total enrolment of over four thousand students. This was carried out under the direction of Dr. Cressy who, as Secretary of Higher Education of the China Christian Educational Association, for many years sought ways of bringing about a greater degree of cooperation and concentration. On the basis of this survey, an Advisory Committee of Chinese educators drew up a series of recommendations which the Council reviewed and then referred to the institutions concerned. These constituted what was known as The Correlated Program (1928).

The Correlated Program came out strongly for fewer and stronger institutions, the principles of union institutions (while urging consideration of denominational colleges in some situations), training and research on Chinese problems to meet Chinese needs, and a central controlling body for Christian higher education in China. It recommended as the most practical method of reorganization in certain situations a "Centralized-federated University" consisting of "a group of colleges on adjoining campuses, each retaining its essential autonomy and corporate life, but with federation and division of labor through a senate representing all the constituent units." It stressed the need for continued financial help, for international cooperation, and for preservation of the Christian character of institutions. Specific recommendations were for two strong centers of graduate work, one in Peking concentrating on religion, social service, Chinese studies, and possibly modern languages, and one in East China, with agriculture in Nanking and natural sciences in Shanghai. Shantung would have a professional school of medicine, and East China, schools of law and possibly medicine. Graduate work in education was recommended without being located.

In regard to undergraduate work, the recommendation was that in North China that of Yenching and Cheeloo should be correlated as thoroughly as possible, Yenching maintaining a college of arts and sciences as well as work in education, home economics, and possibly jounalism, Shantung emphasizing training for service in rural communities while maintaining a college of medicine, a theological school, and a junior college. In East China, existing institutions should be correlated as a centralized-federated university with a larger center in Shanghai and a secondary one in Nanking. In South China, Fukien and Hwa Nan should be affiliated, ultimately as a centralized-federated university of three hundred students with a vocationalized curriculum and no graduate work; Lingnan, limited to four hundred students, should also have a vocational emphasis, with departments of commerce and education but no graduate work, its agriculture limited and affiliated with Nanking. In Central China, the Christian colleges should be reorganized into a union or centralized-federated university with two hundred students, a vocationalized curriculum, and no graduate work. West China should have a college of arts and science with two hundred students, a vocationalized curriculum, no graduate work, and a school of medicine of not more than a hundred students. The Council of Higher Education would itself serve as the central controlling body.

Response to this program was mixed. Yenching, where the recommendations generally accorded with the actual situation, responded promptly and favorably. At Shantung, though the Board of Governors approved, alumni, students, and faculty were overwhelmingly opposed to the rural emphasis and the University Senate agreed only because of the financial support which was proposed. In East China, the strongest opposition developed. The University of Shanghai refused to have anything to do with the plan, and possible moves by other institutions were balked by the absence of funds. Fukien Christian University, while resenting the restriction against a school of agriculture, was willing to combine with Hwa Nan, and a joint committee of the two boards worked out a scheme of consolidation, but this was turned down at the last minute by Hwa Nan, which feared loss of identity as a woman's college. Lingnan took no action one way or the other. The proposal for a union or federated institution in Central China was in accord with the thinking in that area and encouraged the existing concentration on Huachung University. Similarly the recommendation for West China fitted the mood and plans of that area and was well received.

Even where the plan was accepted or approved, there was no immediate implementation. A powerful factor in winning acceptance had been the lure of a joint financial campaign, with the Committee on Financial Program in America prepared to cooperate. Early in 1929 the future appeared bright, but by autumn the depression had begun and prospects dimmed. The campaign was first postponed and then abandoned. By the fall of 1931 mission boards were making cuts in their support and there was little that could be done. The Council of Higher Education continued in existence, with occasional meetings, but was never effective in implementing coordination or correlation of the programs of the Christian colleges and universities, not to mention effecting union or avoiding duplication and competition.

Ten years after the Burton Commission came another study, this time of foreign missions as a whole. This was the famous "Layman's Foreign Mission Inquiry" conducted by a Commission of Appraisal headed by Dr. William Ernest Hocking, whose summary report appeared as *Re-Thinking Missions*. Reporting favorably on the character and place of the Christian Colleges of China, it also called attention to the failure, except in one instance, to carry out the recommendations of the Burton Commission. It emphasized that, as a result of the inadequacy of resources to support thirteen often-competing institutions, many were "in serious danger of losing the reputation for excellence which they once enjoyed" and some were "not a credit to the Christian cause." It was convinced that the only remedy lay in "the establishment of centralized authority" and treatment of the Christian colleges in the Orient as a single enterprise. The dangers and needs which the report pointed out were clear, as they had been for years, but the report brought little if any change on the field. Such influence as it had was more clearly evident abroad, especially in the United States, where the thirties and forties saw intensification of efforts to provide the support required for excellence, and a centralization, not of authority—which no longer resided abroad—but of activities on behalf of indigenous and independent institutions.

After another ten years, attention again turned, both in China and abroad, to the possibilities of coordination and concentration. In the spring of 1943, with the thought that the end of the war would provide a favorable situation for realignment of the resources and facilities for Christian higher education in China, a Planning Committee under the charimanship of Dr. Henry P. Van Dusen of Union Theological Seminary, then President of the Associated Boards, met in New York "to give thoughtful consideration to the future of the Christian Colleges in postwar China, and to cooperate with a similar group in Great Britain as well as with Boards of Managers in China where the principal decisions will have to be made." A similar Planning Committee under the Reverend T. Cocker Brown had met in London. In China, the Council of Higher Education appointed a Commission on Post-War Planning under the chairmanship of Dr. King Chu, then Vice-Minister of Education.

By the spring of 1946, reports had been issued by all three groups. These were in substantial agreement on basic principles which should guide educational policy, on the need to reduce centers of Christian higher education to nine in number, on limitation of Law, Engineering, and Commerce to one college each, on intimate coordination, if not actual union, of the institutions in Foochow, and of the two in Nanking, and on the union in the Shanghai area of St. John's, Shanghai, Soochow, and Hangchow Universities. London had reservations on several points on which New York and China were in agreement: the need for both small (350–900) undergraduate colleges and larger (800–1500) universities offering graduate degrees and having professional schools; limitation of graduate study to three or four centers; restriction of medicine to five. In China, while there was acceptance of general principles, specific recommendations in some cases brought cries of anguish.

Recommendations of the New York Planning Committee met with varied responses. Yenching, while seeking to add a college of engineering, was generally content with the recommendation that it continue as an institution of the highest academic standards with both undergraduate and graduate courses. Shantung was less than satisfied with a restricted college of science, a college of rural reconstruction in place of one of arts, and a college of medicine. The four Shanghai institutions were for a while prepared to unite, but first the University of Shanghai and then St. John's withdrew, leaving Hangchow and Soochow to continue with moves which political events finally terminated. Ginling College and the University of Nanking, which were to be mutually independent institutions collaborating in staff and facilities, got no further than considering a central library and a joint academic building. Ginling, moreover, wished to become a university by separating Arts and Science and adding a College of Education. Little change was proposed for Huachung, Lingnan, and West China, each of which was the only Christian institution in its area, though Huachung was advised against developments it proposed in commerce and theology. In Fukien, the recommendation for coordination at a single center of the work of Fukien Christian University, Hwa Nan College, and Fukien Theological College, was accepted in principle; but the recommendation that Fukien Christian University limit itself to Colleges of Arts, Science, and Rural Reconstruction was countered by plans for great expansion of both Arts and Science, adding Engineering and substituting Agriculture for Rural Reconstruction.

In medicine, the Committee favored continuation of five institutions—the United Board-related colleges at West China, Shantung, Lingnan, and St. John's (with integration with the Woman's Union Medical College), and the Christie Medical College at Moukden. In theology, which was considered outside the province of the Committee, it expressed the hope that theological colleges would be academically integrated with universities at Peiping, Tsinan, Nanking, Foochow, Shanghai, Canton, and Chengtu.

With the growing uncertainty in regard to the future of the country, all planning tended to lose meaning; with the certainty of imposed change, it was abandoned. The approach of the Communist armies sounded the knell for all such moves.

Largely unsuccessful though they were in efforts at cooperation and consolidation, the China Colleges were, in many cases, impressive examples of interdenominational cooperation. Seven represented the interests of two or more denominations, two were non-denominational. Only five were the care of a single denomination, and in only one case was the participation of other churches categorically declined, denominational status being the result rather of institutional than of church loyalties and of the inadequacy of resources for commitments already undertaken.

They also represented international cooperation, not only in being both Chinese and Western but in having behind them British and Canadians as well as Americans. The story has two references to New York for every one to London or Toronto, but the non-American forces were vital factors in the starting and shaping of several of the China Colleges. British missions participated in seven of the fourteen: the London Missionary Society in Ginling, Huachung, Lingnan, Shantung, and Yenching; the Anglicans in Fukien, Shantung, and West China; the Wesleyan Missionary Society in Huachung, Lingnan, and Shantung; the English Baptists and English Presbyterians in Shantung; the British Friends in West China. British societies were particularly active in the development of Shantung and West China, in both cases being founders as well as continuing partners. Canadians concentrated on the same two institutions, the Canadian Presbyterians on Shantung and the Canadian Methodists (later the United Church of Canada) on West China. Europe was represented through Moukden Medical College, the short-lived Lutheran College in Central China, and limited contacts with Huachung.

While cooperation was being discussed in China, it was being increasingly practiced abroad by mission boards and the institutional boards of trustees related to the Christian colleges of China. As early as 1918–19, joint conferences in New York of North American boards and organizations supporting these institutions led to the setting up in New York in 1923 of a China Union Universities Office representing finally five institutions, Fukien, Nanking, Shantung, West China, and Yenching, each of which had to deal with three or more mission boards. The function of this office was primarily secretarial and accounting service to these institutions and coordination of mutual relationships in the field and among mission boards in North America. Two years later, ten boards of trustees formed, with a somewhat broader charter, a Permanent Committee for the Coordination and Promotion of Christian Higher Education in China, a name changed in 1928 to the less wordy Committee on Christian Colleges in China.

In 1932 the functions of the China Union Universities Office and the Committee on Christian Colleges in China were combined and given greater effectiveness in the Associated Boards for Christian Colleges in China. Starting with ten institutions but eventually including eleven— all except Lingnan, Moukden, Shanghai, Woman's, and Yale-in-China, which chose to remain wholly independent—the membership of the Associated Boards comprised the boards of trustees of the participating institutions together with members-at-large elected by these. Twelve American, two Canadian, and seven British mission boards were represented in this corporation. Though somewhat cumbersome because of the necessity for separate meetings of eleven boards, this structure proved extremely effective, especially during the difficult war years. However, as early as 1936 the idea of a single united board was taking shape, and in 1945, with the union of the boards of Fukien, Hwa Nan, Ginling, Nanking, West China, and Yenching, the United Board for Christian Colleges in China came into being. Later, with the addition of Hangchow, Huachung, St. John's, Shantung, and Soochow, this board included all the institutions formerly making up the Associated Boards.

17
Meeting the Cost

Such issues as those of registration, staffing, administration and governance, and purpose were chiefly problems of relationship to the Chinese setting of the colleges. The problem of academic and physical livelihood more fully involved their relations with each other and with foreign constituencies. And these two relationships overlapped. The existence of adequate facilities and sufficient operating income was not only dependent on overseas sources but affected by the extent of the total need. These two related issues of support and cooperation were to plague the China Colleges for their entire existence.

From the start the Protestant colleges were dependent on support from abroad to meet all expenses not covered by tuition fees, and on foreign gifts for almost all physical development. This continued to be the situation until the end, with annual subsidies reaching the million mark and capital gifts totaling many millions. Support from abroad was a vital factor in their lives. Without it they could neither have come into existence nor have continued to function. Inevitably this relationship distinguished these colleges from others, government and private, and encouraged suspicion. Such aid, however, was not necessarily imperialistic and, indeed, rarely had threatening strings. It was necessary because local support was at first entirely lacking and never adequate.

Support from indigenous sources developed only slowly and was never wholly to replace contributions from abroad. In 1928 delegates from China to the Jerusalem Meeting of the International Missionary Council reported that "the financing of the higher educational institutions is now and will remain for some time to come quite beyond the ability of the Chinese Christian community. The continued generous support of friends from abroad is, therefore, still needed and will be greatly appreciated." This situation persisted until the end and, as a result of war, postwar rehabilitation, and constant inflation, was especially acute during the last decade or so.

Such very limited local support as was received by the early colleges came almost entirely from fees. At best these were nominal and contributed little to the meeting of actual instructional costs. At Hangchow in 1898, tuition, board, and room were twelve dollars a year, an amount that did not even cover the cost of food. St. John's, in the more expensive setting of Shanghai, was charging thirty dollars in 1899 and barely covering cost of board and room. Similar situations existed elsewhere. The answer to such unbalanced budgets lay largely in the almost complete staffing by missionaries, whose salaries came from other sources. Even so, further foreign subsidies were necessary, a fact which tended to create tensions in missionary circles between evangelists and educators.

Fees rose with increased living costs—at Hangchow, doubling between 1912 and 1918—but continued in almost all cases to do little more than pay for board and room. Instruction and overhead had to be met in other ways. In 1925–26 it was estimated that in Protestant colleges the proportion of instructional costs borne by student fees ranged from a high of more than one-half at Nanking to just over one-twentieth at Hwa Nan. The proportion in science and professional schools was considerably lower. Even at Lingnan, where, in 1929, there were complaints that high costs, amounting to three hundred dollars a year, resulted in an "aristocracy," students paid only one-fifth of the cost of their education. St. John's, with its relatively affluent clientele, was something of an exception: by 1927 student fees were covering all expenses except foreign salaries, which of course amounted to a considerable sum.

The reductions often granted church-sponsored students added to the inadequacy of fees. From its start, Hangchow so favored sons of Christian parents. Soochow gave free tuition to all sons of ministers until forced to restrict the favor to Methodists. Up to 1920, students sponsored by the Presbyterian and Baptist missions paid no tuition at Shantung, except in medicine. In addition, in all institutions there was a growing need for scholarships for needy students of all kinds. At first this was met entirely by grants from abroad, which continued to be the chief source, though some support from alumni developed later.

Support from other Chinese sources was slow in developing. Philanthropy of this sort was not in the Chinese tradition. Nor was the Chinese Church in position to help, being largely composed of the poorer members of society and itself dependent, for much of the time, on support from abroad. Far from assisting the colleges, the Chinese Church proved a financial burden. The government too had its hands full with the development of public education.

Perhaps the first instance of private Chinese giving to Protestant colleges was the response to a St. John's appeal in 1893, which brought in three thousand dollars. St. John's also had early success in soliciting capital gifts from alumni: five thousand dollars in 1908 for an athletic field; the same amount later for a gymnasium. In 1908 Lingnan raised some twenty thousand dollars for its first dormitory. The first major campaign came in 1917 when Lingnan, with its strategic contacts with Overseas Chinese, achieved marked success in Southeast Asia. Through the efforts of Chung Wing-kwang, professor and later president, Lingnan raised from Chinese residents in Malaysia the equivalent of $120,000. Eight years later, Mr. Chung helped to secure two hundred thousand dollars from the same source.

At the University of Shanghai, in 1929, the first Chinese president, Herman Liu, succeeded in raising ten thousand dollars for buildings. Two years later, Shanghai's Downtown School of Commerce attracted nearly twenty thousand dollars. Yenching began cultivation of a Chinese constituency about 1924 but found the going slow. A dormitory and a wall around the campus were finally secured, but a "Million Dollar Campaign" (US $330,000) in the thirties achieved less than a third of its goal. In 1935 the University of Nanking raised twenty-five thousand dollars in a twenty-fifth anniversary drive. Most institutions, however, engaged only feebly in fund-raising.

Individual philanthropy was not entirely unknown in China, though likely to be associated with memorial structures, but large individual gifts to Christian education were slow in developing. One of the first contributions of note must have been a gift to Hangchow in the early 'teens of five hundred dollars for science apparatus. Another was a gift to Yenching, by a Chinese general, of ten thousand dollars toward the purchase of land. Yenching was also the recipient of twelve hundred acres of agricultural land, which proved something of a white elephant. About 1928, Huachung benefited from the generosity of a Yen family, which made a grant for a hostel for women. In 1934 the family of Mr. Sze Liang-ts'ai, noted editor of the Shanghai *Shen Pao*, gave some thirteen thousand dollars to Hangchow for an economics building in memory of a student killed by bandits. Notable gifts of personal libraries added greatly to the resources of several college collections.

The Sino-Japanese War brought tremendous needs which, in spite of economic conditions, sometimes resulted in astonishing responses. The University of Shanghai secured sixteen million Chinese dollars for the Chungking School and then fifty million Chinese dollars for use in Shanghai. The success of the university's alumni in the business world contributed to these accomplishments. Yenching did very well in 1945 in raising twelve million five hundred thousand Chinese dollars in a "Ten Million Dollar Campaign." However, the rapid depreciation of Chinese currency deflated all these figures, and when the millions were counted in U.S. dollars, they amounted in the case of Shanghai to about fifty thousand dollars each time, and in the case of Yenching to only twenty-seven thousand five hundred dollars.

For much of their history, with two exceptions the Protestant colleges received little assistance from government sources. This was the result partly of the government's having its hands full with its own program of higher education and partly of a fear of government control on the part of the institutions themselves. The exceptions were the Hsiang-Ya Agreement of 1913 which involved the Hunan Provincial Government in major support of Hunan-Yale Medical School, and the Kwangtung Provincial Government's grant to Lingnan University in 1927 of forty thousand dollars a year, a figure later raised to a hundred thousand dollars. By the early thirties, however, significant National Government aid was being provided several other institutions. In 1933–34, seven of the China Colleges received a total of about a hundred thousand dollars, the Council of Christian Higher Education recording its gratification that the grant had been made "without conditions detrimental to the original policy of the Christian character of the colleges." In addition, by 1935 the University of Nanking had received one hundred thousand dollars which the Government had earlier approved as payment for the damage suffered in the Incident of 1927, for which the University had submitted no claim. This was used for a new Library Building which was completed just as war broke out. After 1926 Boone Library School received annual grants from the China Foundation (Boxer Indemnity Funds).

Over the years, especially in the twenties and thirties, there was a gradual growth in income from all Chinese sources. In 1925 this still constituted only a tenth of the field budgets of the colleges, which in most cases did not include the very substantial cost of Western personnel, but by 1937 this figure had reached a peak of over one-half. Inclusion of mission-supported personnel would probably bring this down to something over one-third. Many local gifts, however, were for special purposes. For the years 1930–36, the University of Nanking reported a total of nearly three hundred thousand dollars from Chinese sources— "but for special, not general budget." For example, in 1934 the Farmers' Bank of Anhui, Kwangsi, Hupeh, and Hunan Provinces gave approximately one hundred thousand dollars for a survey by the College of Agriculture and Forestry of marketing conditions, landlord-tenant relationships, and soil productivity. Though grants from national, provincial, and private sources continued, the war reduced local income and increased dependence on funds from abroad, a dependence which was only beginning to lessen when the end came.

The extent of this overseas aid is difficult to measure with exactness, but into the Christian colleges ultimately went a truly astounding investment of money and lives. It is probably safe to say that over the decades this investment involved a total of something like fifty million dollars in cash and some two thousand individual Western personnel. Without some such assistance the colleges could never have come into existence; or, if they had succeeded in doing so, must have continued on a very small scale and at a much lower level. The trickle which made possible the beginnings gradually became a real stream, always too small to nourish fully all that sought to drink from it, but a truly significant source of support for China's developing education and a magnificent demonstration of sound philanthropy.

The costs of early beginnings were, by modern standards, inconsiderable. In 1877 Bishop Schereschewsky undertook to start St. John's with a promise of thirty thousand dollars from his home board; the first building, a chapel, cost six thousand dollars. Fifteen years later, the original buildings were replaced for twenty thousand dollars. In 1889, the North China College secured a ten-acre site for fifteen thousand dollars and a few years later erected a handsome group of buildings for less than fifty thousand dollars. Even in the first decade of the twentieth century, costs were helpfully low. The buildings for the Shantung campus at Weihsien cost thirty thousand dollars in 1904; the first science building in Tsinan in 1905, five thousand dollars. In 1906 Hangchow spent forty thousand dollars for its new plant, seventy-five hundred dollars of which was for a dormitory. In 1904 St. John's erected a combined assembly hall and library for twenty-two thousand dollars. In 1905 Shanghai set up its new campus for forty thousand dollars. Soochow was unusually favored in being promised $150,000 for its new campus in 1901.

This early support came almost wholly from boards of missions, mainly American, and was largely for land and buildings. Endowments were rare, operational costs being underwritten in some cases by promises of annual contributions of cash and personnel. In the case of union institutions especially, these were often written into agreements in which participating boards assumed specific responsibilities. In 1913, for example, five boards each pledged Ginling ten thousand dollars for buildings and equipment, six hundred dollars annually for current expenses, and one representative on the faculty. For Nanking University in 1907, the pledge was four teachers and forty thousand dollars in land, buildings, or endowment from each of three boards. In 1914, at Yenching, expectations were somewhat higher: a hundred thousand dollars for capital, four thousand dollars annually for operations, and two teachers from each of four boards.

The British missionary societies never constituted a major source of financial support though they played important parts in the setting up of Shantung Christian, West China Union, and Yenching Universities, contributing land, funds, and personnel. Contributions of personnel were, however, excellent in quality and, while not large, constituted a significant factor in the life of several colleges. British giving was seriously affected by the two world wars, and support declined in the forties. British interests were represented not only by mission societies but by the China Christian Universities Association, something of a counterpart to the Associated Boards. While never able to provide large sums of money, the Association made helpful grants and encouraged appointment of British university graduates to university staffs. Significant aid also came from the British Boxer Indemnity Funds, which had been involved as early as the first decade of the century in plans for Central China University. During World War II the British China Relief Foundation provided emergency aid to several colleges. After the war, a benevolent trust in Britain made a gift of forty-five thousand pounds for a library at Huachung, while British firms gave endowment for two academic chairs at the same institution.

Two Canadian missions, those of the Presbyterian Church of Canada and the Canadian Methodist Church, were important participants in the development of Shantung Christian and West China Union Universities respectively. The Library at Shantung was a Presbyterian gift. The Methodists made important contributions of land, buildings, and operating funds to West China. After the formation of the Associated Boards, of which both churches (by this time, Canadian Presbyterian and United Church of Canada) were members, their aid was largely channeled through that organization. Canadian contributions of personnel to both institutions were considerable in number and high in quality.

European churches played almost no part in the China Colleges, support being limited to a brief and tenuous relationship of the Lutheran missions in Central China to Huachung and contribution by the Danish Lutherans of doctors to Moukden Medical School. The Norwegian Lutheran Church of North America assisted Shantung modestly with cash and personnel for a dozen years. A committee of intellectuals in Switzerland financed the service of four young Swiss at Yenching University for three-year terms between 1923 and 1939.

Important contributions also came from other sources, notably individuals. A twenty-five-thousand-dollar gift from an American layman gave the University of Nanking its first building, the science hall of 1912. The Yali Hospital was financed by the generosity of a Yale alumnus, who made gifts in 1913 and 1917. By the end of the second decade of the century, the colleges were receiving individual gifts of fifty thousand dollars; in the twenties there were some of a hundred thousand dollars and more. Especially active in campaigning for its new campus, Yenching was the chief beneficiary, with many of its main buildings gifts, often memorial, from friends. However, all institutions benefited to some extent from such individual generosity, even in cases where mission boards assumed the basic cost of construction.

A distinctive source of support from abroad, important not only for its material aid but for the international relationships it represented, was a number of colleges and universities in the West. Altogether some twenty-five to thirty American educational institutions contributed to the China Colleges through gifts from undergraduates, faculty, and alumni, or by means of fellowships for graduate study. In the last year before the Japanese War, there were fifteen connections of this sort. Some contacts were modest and short-lived. A few, however, were well organized and resulted in substantial assistance.

The earliest such relationship was that of Yale-in-China with the work at Changsha centering in the Medical College, and later with the College of Science at Huachung. This was unique in the degree to which it was responsible for starting and, for a while, maintaining an entire institution. It continued for forty-five years and involved over a hundred regular appointees and some ninety short-term "bachelors," as well as substantial financial aid.

Another early and long-lived relationship was that between Smith and Ginling Colleges, established in 1916, when the Smith College Association for Christian work adopted Ginling as its foreign project. Assistance started with one thousand dollars a year but soon reached four thousand dollars. In 1923, a Smith Alumnae Committee for Ginling gave fifty thousand dollars for a recreation building and became a major supporter, with annual grants of as much as fifty-five hundred dollars. "Smith-Ginling" was active until the Communist take-over.

By 1920 Wellesley College had entered a sister-college relationship with Yenching Woman's College, maintaining a faculty member there and sending visiting professors. Funds came from campus and alumnae drives. For support of a faculty member, there was later substituted an annual grant of from two thousand to four thousand dollars. This was maintained to the end. Special contributions helped out during the war and in the process of rehabilitation.

Yenching also benefited from its relationship, through an alumni- and student-supported project, with Princeton University. In 1924 Princeton-in-Peking, which had carried on a program of English-teaching at the Peking YMCA, agreed to develop the Department of Sociology at Yenching. Six years later it expanded into the Princeton-Yenching Foundation and, with help from the Rockefeller Foundation, undertook support of Yenching's College of Public Affairs. This support continued through 1949.

Other relationships included that between Lingnan University and Pennsylvania State College, the faculty and students of which supported Professor Groff from 1912 to 1942, and that between Hwa Nan College and its seven Methodist sister colleges, each of which adopted a department and contributed from three hundred to two thousand dollars a year. Hangchow was the beneficiary of postwar sympathy at Centre, Davidson, and Hampden-Sydney Colleges, which provided beds for the students and a car for the university. Grinnell-in-China, though intending to supply Western staff for a middle school, ended up in 1920 supporting a professor of theology at Shantung Christian University. In 1946 Syracuse-in-China, which had a history of missionary service in China but had not established a relationship with any college, sent accumulated student-alumni gifts to West China Union University. It contributed the services of teachers on two-year terms in 1947 and again in 1949.

Such relationships were usually unofficial, being between students, faculty, and alumni of the American institution on the one hand, and the university administration in China on the other. The association between Cornell University and the College of Agriculture of the University of Nanking, which brought specialists in plant breeding to China during the years 1924–1930, differed in that Cornell University was officially a partner. Harvard University was officially linked with six of the colleges through representation on the Trustees of the Harvard-Yenching Institute.

While mission boards continued to be a major source of support, especially in the matter of personnel, and individual gifts provided an uncertain though at times substantial assistance, the colleges were having to place ever greater reliance on special fund-raising activities, whether in the form of annual efforts or occasional campaigns. As early as 1914–1917, Mr. Henry W. Luce had raised $305,000 for Shantung. In 1921, a three-million-dollar campaign for "Seven Oriental Colleges for Women" produced six hundred thousand dollars each for Ginling College and Yenching Woman's College, and $350,000 for the North China Union Woman's Medical College, which shortly thereafter became part of Shantung Christian University, bringing that institution welcome strength. The "Famine Funds" unspent in 1922 brought the University of Nanking's College of Agriculture six hundred thousand dollars in 1932. A purely Yenching campaign in 1927–1929 produced four hundred thousand dollars. However, a proposed combined campaign for all the colleges in 1930, totaling $8,250,000, encountered the depression of the thirties. Its failure contributed to the collapse of negotiations looking to greater concentration of Protestant higher education in China.

Following organization of the Associated Boards of Christian Colleges in China in 1932, substantial support came from that source through annual united fund-raising activities and occasional campaigns for specific needs and individual institutions. Such aid was a vital factor in preserving the colleges during the war years and in restoring them afterwards. By 1937, the combined endowments of twelve colleges amounted to nearly seven million dollars. The cost of physical plants was estimated at ten million dollars.

In the 1930s the thirteen institutions related to the Associated Boards were receiving annually from mission boards, endowments, and fund-raising a total of some eight hundred thousand to nine hundred thousand dollars. Of this roughly one-half came from mission boards and one-quarter each from endowments and fund-raising. With the outbreak of hostilities in China, additional aid was needed and a Sustaining Fund was developed which provided another quarter of a million or so. After Pearl Harbor, all support was combined in one fund, largely financed by United China Relief. This support reached totals of $660,000 in 1942–1943 and $1,115,787 in 1943–1944 after the National War Fund had started. In the first years after the war, nearly two million dollars was contributed for rehabilitation, and more than that amount for support of operations.

With the Communist take-over, the United Board and related mission boards sought ways of continuing financial assistance to the China Colleges, but the door was tightly closed to all phases of what was termed "cultural imperialism," bringing to an end a history of altruistic support which had poured many millions of dollars and many hundreds of lives into higher education in China.

Part
5

The Last Chapters
(1937–1950)

18
China at War (1937-1949)

On July 7, 1937, a clash between Chinese and Japanese troops at the Marco Polo Bridge near Peiping started an undeclared war. This quickly engulfed much of North China, with the bombing of two of China's greatest universities, Nankai in Tientsin and Tsinghua near Peiping, resulting in the total destruction of the one and severe damage to the other. After a lull for negotiations made fruitless by the excessive nature of Japanese demands and growing Chinese determination to resist, clashes occurred at Shanghai, with heavy loss of civilian life. In August, war broke out in earnest.

Heavy fighting destroyed large sections of Shanghai and resulted in the decimation of China's best troops. A Japanese landing on Hangchow Bay forced retreat to Nanking, which was in turn occupied by December. Further withdrawal took the government to Hankow, four hundred miles farther inland, and, a year later, when that city was also threatened, to Chungking in Szechwan Province, where it remained throughout the war. The spring of 1938 saw renewed action in the north, with Tsinan quickly brought under Japanese control. In the fall of 1938, the Japanese marched into Canton, and summer brought bombing to West China. Although Foochow was not actually occupied until 1942, it too was from an early stage the object of bombing. Thus, by the spring of 1939, all except the one center of Protestant higher education at Chengtu had either been occupied or seriously threatened.

With the Japanese attack along the coast, began a mass migration that eventually took millions of people into the interior, clogging all lines of communication. Industry and educational institutions joined the exodus. The school year 1936–37 had closed with over a hundred universities, colleges, and technical schools, government and private, in existence. These enrolled some forty-three thousand students, 6,424 of them in the Protestant colleges. Half of all these institutions found refuge in parts of Free China, with Chengtu, Chungking, and Kunming the chief centers, while twenty sought safety in Shanghai's International Settlement.

Over large areas, the years saw the sweep of Japanese armies, never reaching the wartime capital but devastating many cities and huge areas of countryside, and seriously threatening the safety of Free China. Bombing became a regular procedure, and rare was the sizeable city that escaped at least one attack. Much of Chungking was destroyed by bombs and the resulting fires. All land avenues to the outside world were cut except for a narrow-gauge railway and a truck route to Indo-China, and the famous Burma Road had to be carved out of the rugged mountains and dense jungles that lie between Yunnan and India.

The eight years following the Marco Polo Bridge Affair were a period of desperate struggle for military and economic survival. Politically, the war had brought a degree of apparent cooperation between Nationalists and Communists, with the latter's Eighth Route Army in the north engaging in warfare against the Japanese which both benefited national defense and strengthened the party's overall position. The presence of Communist representatives on the People's Political Council, a non-legislative body set up in 1938, added to the appearance of a real United Front. Militarily, the greatest help came after Pearl Harbor, with the arrival, via India and Burma, of the American Air Force. August 14, 1945, brought an end to the war, though actual surrender of Japanese forces in China took until the end of the year.

With the retreat westward, most of the sources of national income had been lost, and the war had to be paid for with paper money, whether imported or printed locally. Inflation gave the American dollar, worth in 1937 roughly three Chinese dollars, an official value in 1945 of thirty-nine and an actual value twenty times that. The cost of living soared and malnutrition was widespread, especially among refugees.

Although the general determination and willingness to sacrifice were impressive, especially during the early years, the war years saw such a growth of incompetence and corruption in all phases of government in Kuomintang-controlled China that both official and public morale slumped badly. There was general support for the concept of a strong central government as contrasted with the warlordism, provincialism, civil war, and helplessness of prewar years, but neither the National Government nor the Party that controlled it any longer inspired confidence or trust. With the passing years, the Kuomintang had become more concerned with protecting its position than with the welfare of the country, and the National Government had clearly lost "the Mandate of Heaven."

On the other hand, the former radical wing of the Kuomintang, now the Communist Party, had begun to recover some of its lost popularity. The excesses of Fukien and Kiangsi days of the early thirties were being forgotten in the romance of the new start in Yenan and in the disgust and despair at the failure of the Nationalists to solve the country's problems. Support of the Communists increased rapidly, especially among students, who flocked to Yenan in ever larger numbers. The way was being prepared for acceptance and even welcome of the Communists when they took over the country in 1949.

Nor was the lot of the so-called Occupied Territories a happy one. Local puppet governments were set up by the Japanese with Chinese at the head and Japanese as advisers. Puppet-in-Chief was Wang Ching-wei, originally a leftist revolutionary, during the thirties ostensibly on good terms with Chiang Kai-shek and even holding office, but by 1939 an advocate of peace with Japan. In 1940 he was installed in Nanking as head of the puppet government. Japanese in large numbers arrived to govern, control business, and make whatever profit was possible.

The war also brought widespread destruction to both urban and rural areas. Bombs wreaked havoc in scores of cities. Transportation came almost to a standstill except for military purposes. Agriculture was hard hit by flooding which devastated thousands of square miles, burying houses, tools, and animals, and by the ebb and flow of military operations. Conditions were so bad that, in 1945–46, Hunan Province, China's "rice bowl," suffered severely from famine.

The end of the war bought hope of a country united in its search for domestic stability and international security. Both Free China and Occupied China looked forward to a new day of peace and progress. But this was not to be. The effects of eight years of war proved more demoralizing and longer lasting than realized, and the country continued a nation divided. The Nationalist government quickly returned to Nanking, to be warmly welcomed by those who had remained behind. The millions of refugees made their way back more slowly, weary but happy to be home again. But quickly Free and Occupied split as both those who had fled and those who had stayed looked upon themselves as patriots and martyrs and upon their opposite numbers as cherishing self-interest. The government started a hunt for suspected collaborators and traitors, while carpetbaggers arrived to take advantage of the unsettled conditions.

The country found itself with several kinds of currency, among them the dollar of the Nanking puppet regime, two hundred of which were declared equal to one Chinese national currency dollar (CNC$). The latter was itself soon worth only one–two thousandth of an American dollar and, by the end of 1947, only one–eighty-two thousandth. Seven months later it was valueless at one–eight millionth. In August 1948 a new currency, the gold yuan, was introduced at an official rate of 1/3.95 but quickly followed the same pattern. By the spring of 1949, the gold yuan itself had reached the meaningless level of something like one–forty millionth. There was economic chaos. With soaring inflation, public morality rapidly deteriorated.

Contributing to the moral and economic disintegration was the fact that the nation was also divided by an all-out struggle between the Nationalists and the Communists. Several small liberal parties composed largely of intellectuals offered momentary hope but had little influence on events. The first year saw a jockeying to avoid responsibility for war, Nanking seizing Japanese materiel in North China; Yenan, with Russian help, doing the same in Manchukuo. By January 1947 General Marshall had failed in his attempt to bring the two sides together, and there was open warfare. The Nationalists scored some initial military successes, but the Communists were soon winning more and more victories. Peiping fell to them in January 1949; Nanking in April; and Shanghai in May. The Nationalists retreated to the island of Taiwan, long nominally part of Imperial China, for fifty years a Japanese colony, and now once again under Chinese control. By the end of 1949 the entire country was in Communist hands.

19
Refugee Years (1937–1945)

For the China Colleges, the war with Japan raised formidable issues and threatened life itself. Sooner or later, all except West China had to choose between trying to carry on in enemy-occupied territory and seeking refuge in "Free China." Where there was fighting, or at least bombing, institutions not only were in danger but in some cases had to move to safer quarters. Those which tried to carry on where they were met with serious problems of space, equipment, and staff. With Pearl Harbor, all lost the relative neutrality derived from their American relationships. For the last three years, all but St. John's, on its own campus in Shanghai, and West China, at home in the far west, were functioning in makeshift refugee quarters.

For most of the war years, there were two major centers and six often floating centers of Christian higher education. The institutions of the Shanghai area—St. John's and Shanghai in the city itself and Hangchow and Soochow from neighboring cities—maintained a difficult and often precarious existence in Shanghai, though parts of the last three set up programs elsewhere. Fukien and Hwa Nan fled to the relatively inaccessible interior of Fukien Province; Lingnan, after a stop in Hong Kong, moved to the interior of Kwangtung Province. Yale-in-China tried to carry on at Changsha but was finally forced to scatter to several places in Kwangsi and Kweichow Provinces. Huachung finally found refuge near the Burma border. Parts of Nanking, Shanghai, and Soochow set up in Chungking, the wartime capital. The major center, however, was Chengtu, where West China was host to Ginling, Nanking, Shantung, and Yenching.

The years were hard ones, filled with constant difficulties and recurring dangers. The incredibly arduous moves, covering as much as two thousand miles, up dangerous rivers and over high mountains, by boat, by truck, and on foot, required no ordinary determination and courage. Makeshift quarters, lack of supplies, undernourishment, and

199

continued danger tested faith and endurance. The mere fact of their survival is moving commentary on the spirit of these institutions.

THE SHANGHAI AREA

The institutions in East China, especially those in and around Shanghai, were the first to feel the full effect of the Japanese invasion. The attack of August 1937 swept across the University of Shanghai campus, which lay between the city and the sea. After some hours in the basement of the science building, over a hundred members of the faculty and staff made their way to the university's Downtown School of Commerce. There, in October, the university reopened with 364 students in the college, 219 in the middle school, and 150 in the school of commerce. Classes continued in spite of daily bombing of the city.

On April 8, 1938, President Herman Liu, who had openly condemned Japanese aggression, was assassinated, almost certainly at the instigation of the Japanese authorities. An Administrative Council carried on until Dean T.K. Van was elected president a year later. A member of the class of 1916, Dr. Van had served the university for ten years as Professor of Education and dean, the first Chinese dean in the institution. He commanded the respect of both Chinese and Western colleagues and was to serve the university well through the very difficult years of the war. With the westward movement of actual fighting, it became possible, first to inspect the campus, which had suffered severe damage and thorough looting, and finally, in the fall of 1939, to reoccupy it. Meanwhile the university had fitted into several buildings in the International Settlement, sharing the library and laboratory facilities of St. John's with three other Christian institutions. Enrolment had risen to over sixteen hundred, nearly half of them in the college.

The Japanese attack on Shanghai found St. John's also in the thick of things even though its campus lay on the other side of the city. It was necessary to move the university to the Continental Emporium on Nanking Road, safely inside the International Settlement. Here the first term of 1937–38 passed amid crowding and confusion and in the absence of laboratories. Fortunately the campus suffered little damage, and for the second term passes permitted access to the university's science building. These facilities and the library were used by all the East China Christian colleges having students in Shanghai. The rest of the campus was crowded with refugees, the continued presence of whom made it necessary to hold many classes in town even after the war had moved west with the surrender of the city late in 1938. Full return was not possible until September 1940, at which time enrolment had reached nearly fourteen hundred, of whom two hundred were girls. Dean William Z.L. Sung had succeeded Dr. Pott as president. Son of China's first Episcopal bishop, Sung had previously served at times as acting vice-president and acting president and had proved a wise, able, and deeply spiritual leader. After the war he was to pay a high price for his service to his alma mater.

The Soochow University campus was not occupied by the Japanese until November 1937, but the university had already made the first of several moves. This was to the middle-school plant at Huchow on the other side of T'ai Hu, the "Great Lake" southwest of Soochow. After only four weeks that location became untenable, forcing a second move still farther south. A breaking-up soon followed, with some faculty members going west but most seeking the International Settlement. There the Law School, whose location north of Soochow Creek had proved dangerous, had found safer quarters and welcomed Arts College students and teachers. The laboratories of an industrialist alumnus provided facilities, and by 1941 enrolment had set a new record for science majors.

The Japanese landing near Hangchow in November 1937 caused panic and the almost complete evacuation of the city. The Hangchow College campus was abandoned by boat and on foot. The faculty tried for a few weeks to carry on in T'ungch'i, 150 miles to the southwest, but soon disbanded. By the next February many had reassembled in Shanghai, working with the other Christian institutions in the International Settlement. At first dependent on the others for books and equipment, Hangchow was later permitted to move its own from the Hangchow campus. Dr. Robert J. McMullen took over while President Lee went to the United States to complete work for his doctorate. With the tremendous demands for places, Hangchow in 1941 enrolled over nine hundred students.

Hangchow, St. John's, Shanghai, and Soochow worked together as "The Associated Christian Colleges," largely in the safety of the International Settlement, sharing such facilities as were available. Headquarters were at the Continental Emporium on Nanking Road. Thus was born of necessity a semblance of the often proposed East China Union. It was not, however, to outlive the circumstances that brought it into being. With the tremendous demand for places created by the closing of many institutions, the associated colleges had more applicants than they could handle. By 1941 their combined enrolments had reached the five thousand mark. Life was difficult but the education provided was superior to much available in occupied China and certainly preferable to none at all. The colleges were filling a void and doing it surprisingly well. The relative peacefulness of this existence was shattered by Pearl Harbor. With the taking over of the International Settlement by the Japanese, the Associated Colleges found it impossible to carry on and gave up the effort.

St. John's suffered least from the change and its work was not seriously interrupted. American members of the faculty had considerable freedom and many carried on until repatriated a year and a half later. However, both Chinese and Western staff suffered from material shortages, overcrowded facilities, and the continued spiritual strain. The fact that St. John's was the only Protestant college in Shanghai running at all normally meant increased enrolments, which reached twenty-two hundred in 1942. Troubled by the fact that it was operating in occupied territory, some of the alumni proposed to start a St. John's in Free China. Though facilities were available, funds were promised, and government approval was assured, the plan never materialized. St. John's was the only Protestant college to function wholly in enemy-controlled territory throughout the war.

Shanghai met the change in another way. With a view to keeping the university alive, it instituted two programs: the Shanghai Institute in Shanghai, and the School of Commerce in Chungking. To avoid Japanese pressure or branding by Chinese as a "traitor school," it entrusted the work in Shanghai to the alumni association under a new name and a new administrative organization even though it consisted of the same courses, teachers, and students as before. The opening of the School of Commerce in Chungking in 1943 followed collapse of initial plans to move to Fukien, plans made impracticable by a renewed Japanese offensive in that area. A 1944 plan to open arts and science divisions in cooperation with Christian institutions in West China lapsed, not only because of the difficulties involved but because of official assurance that such action would not be needed to assure Shanghai's status as a university.

Soochow met the situation in somewhat similar fashion. The Colleges of Arts and Sciences carried on in Shanghai unofficially and largely underground. The Law School set itself up as a new institution with a different name and functioned undisturbed. In the spring of 1942 Soochow cooperated with Hangchow in sending some students to Shaowu in Northern Fukien Province, where Fukien Christian College had refugee quarters. Fearing this too close to the Japanese, these went on to Kukong in northern Kwangtung Province, where they cooperated with Lingnan University until forced by the approach of Japanese in 1944 to break up. Dean Sheng went to Chungking at the invitation of the Ministry of Education and opened a branch of the Law School there in the fall of 1942. Part of the Biological Supply Service carried on in Shanghai while another part moved to Chengtu in response to a request from the Szechwan Provincial Government.

Hangchow University hoped at first to reopen at Kinhwa, two hundred miles southwest of Shanghai, but soon had to move still farther inland. The final stop was at Shaowu in northwestern Fukien, where Fukien Christian University had been in residence since 1938. Hangchow students were at first housed in Fukien dormitories, but increased enrolments soon made this arrangement impracticable and Hangchow erected its own temporary buildings of pounded earth walls without glass or hardware. Nor could Fukien Christian University meet Hangchow's needs for laboratories, and the situation soon became untenable. The College of Engineering moved to Kweiyang in Kweichow Province, seven hundred miles west, where it rented buildings from a refugee private institution. Problems of equipment, staffing, and finance and the rapid approach of the Japanese forced closing in December 1944. In June of that year the rest of the work at Shaowu closed down and the students transferred to other institutions.

While these moves were going on, another temporary East China University had been formed in Shanghai from the faculties of Hangchow and Soochow Universities who had remained behind. This comprised five colleges: Arts, Sciences, Education, Business, Engineering. It carried on until the end of the war.

WEST CHINA (CHENGTU)

Though the institutions in and around Shanghai were the first to feel the effects of the Japanese invasion, it was not long before those in Nanking had to face similar problems. While events brought tension, they did not seriously interrupt academic work until the fall of Shanghai in November 1937. Then the rapidly accelerating threat to the capital, which finally fell on December 13 after severe bombing, forced a hurried evacuation by both Ginling College and the University of Nanking.

In the case of Ginling, freshmen and sophomores were advised to become guest students in other institutions, while centers for juniors and seniors were developed in connection with Christian universities in Shanghai, Wuchang, and Chengtu. At first forty-eight students joined the Shanghai institutions while only a handful found their way west. Faculty dispersed to centers where they were needed or which they could reach. When the Japanese armies overran Nanking, the Ginling campus became a refugee center, with as many as ten thousand women and girls crowded into every possible bit of space. The task of protection, feeding, and education continued until some time after Pearl Harbor, when the Japanese took over the campus.

In the spring of 1938 decision was reached to have but one Ginling, located in Free China. After considering an independent center in a semirural environment, Ginling accepted an invitation to the West China University campus at Chengtu. In the summer a number of faculty and students made a two-month trip of twenty-five hundred miles, going by steamer to Hong Kong, by train to Hankow, by river boat to Chungking, and by bus to Chengtu. A total of thirty-five, including President Wu, finally arrived. West China provided a site and some classrooms, and a grant from the Szechwan Provincial Government made possible erection of a dormitory and a gymnasium. Half a dozen of the Western staff ultimately reached Chengtu; another half-dozen Westerners were recruited during the years there. By the end of the war, enrolment was over three hundred, the highest in Ginling's history to that time.

The University of Nanking also turned its back on Shanghai and sought refuge in West China. In late fall of 1937 large parts of the library and considerable quantities of equipment were hurriedly loaded on steamers going up the Yangtze River. Most of the faculty and students also sought passage by boat, though a number of students set out on foot on the thousand-mile trip to West China. After a brief stop at Hankow, a dangerous ascent of the Yangtze Gorges, and an overland trip from Chungking, they reached Chengtu in the spring of 1938. There the Colleges of Arts and Agriculture were welcomed by West China Union University. The College of Science remained in Chungking, where the greater industrial development provided a more helpful setting for its work in engineering and applied science. In Nanking, members of the staff who remained behind wrestled with the problems of thirty thousand refugees, rendering emergency services through 1941.

At Chengtu Nanking erected its own temporary lath-and-plaster dormitories and some residences, shared some of West China's classrooms and laboratories, rented some as-yet-unoccupied rooms of the great new Medical Center under process of construction, and pooled its books and equipment with those of the host institution. When all faculty and students had arrived, it constituted a major part of a "Down River" community of several thousand who were eventually to spend eight years in exile. The Nanking contingent included half a dozen Westerners and their families as well as President Chen and a large number of Chinese faculty and staff. By 1944–45 enrolment reached 1272, the highest figure in Nanking's history.

The third member of the Chengtu refugee group was Shantung Christian University—especially part of its Medical School. At Tsinan the fall of 1937 saw enrolment cut in half, and by October the rapid Japanese advance had made closing imperative. The Ministry of Education urged a move to the far northwest, but an invitation from West China proved more attractive and feasible. The three upper classes of the Medical School, with fourteen members of the faculty, left for the West. Other students scattered. In Tsinan the hospital remained open with a largely Western staff.

In the fall of 1938, with stabilization of the situation in Tsinan, the reopening of the campus there became a practical issue. A compromise sent the university to join the Medical School in West China but permitted a program at Tsinan which did not duplicate work at Chengtu or include departments registered with the Nationalist government. The College of Theology, the Nursing School, and the Rural Institute reopened and special technician and subfreshmen courses were instituted. Pressure continued, however, for greater reopening and in September 1941 the medical faculty admitted a four-year class. With Pearl Harbor, all classes in Tsinan and even the hospital were shut down.

In Chengtu, Shantung's enrolment soon rose above four hundred. Since relatively few of the Tsinan staff—except in medicine—had made the move, additional staff had to be recruited locally. Westerners numbered only four, one of whom joined the college by way of India. Unfortunately President Liu, whom circumstances forced to serve as president, dean of arts, dean of science, and treasurer, was facing increasing opposition from faculty and alumni. Discontent fed on Shantung's inability to make an impressive showing on the five-institution campus. In February 1943 Dr. Liu was replaced by Dr. Edgar Chih-ho Tang, Professor of Political Science. He lasted only two years and was followed by Wu K'e-ming, a highly admired alumnus who had been associated with "Oberlin in Shansi." President Wu served through the discouraging postwar years until the Communist absorption of the university.

Toward the end of 1942 the four institutions then in Chengtu were joined by Yenching University. When the Japanese took over North China in 1937, Yenching, because of its American and British connections, was largely undisturbed. Though classes opened that fall with only three hundred or so students, the number soon doubled. The faculty stood by the university, some, caught on the other side of the fighting, traveling as much as two thousand miles to cover a straight-line distance of seventy-five. Because Dr. H.H. Kung, then the Chancellor, was a Chinese government official, Dr. Stuart became concurrently President and Chancellor. The Ministry of Education continued its financial support even though the university was in occupied territory. Enrolment climbed rapidly until it reached 1150 in 1941.

On the morning of Pearl Harbor, Japanese forces took over the Yenching campus. Several prominent Chinese members of the faculty were imprisoned and underwent brutal treatment for six months. Dr. Stuart was placed under house arrest in Peking. Two British couples joined the Chinese guerillas in the hills west of the city. Other Westerners were eventually repatriated after considerable periods of time on the campus, in Peiping, and while interned at Weihsien.

With the taking over of the Peiping campus, Yenching alumni determined to reopen the university in Free China, choosing Chengtu as wartime home. There being neither time nor money to build, two Methodist schools, empty because of air raids, and a Confucian temple were rented. Students and faculty, traveling by twos and threes, somehow made their way through and around the Japanese lines, much of the way on foot, covering a thousand miles and more. In October 1942 Yenching reopened in Chengtu with 250 students, 150 of whom had come from Peking, the rest chosen from among some three thousand local candidates. Those faculty members who had succeeded in reaching Chengtu were supplemented by guest professors from government institutions. Only two Western faculty members from Peiping were able to get there, but three American Board missionaries contributed their services, two as successive controllers and one as instructor. Dr. Y.P. Mei, Professor of Philosophy and Director of Studies in Peiping days, served as acting president. With inadequate housing and rapid inflation, life was far from easy, but morale continued high. Though there was some cooperation with the four institutions on the West China campus, the distance between the two sites made Yenching more dependent than the others on its own resources.

For West China Union University the war meant no move either underground or to a new location but did bring striking changes. When Japanese capture of Nanking resulted in establishment of a wartime capital at Chungking, less than two hundred miles away, Chengtu shared the dangers and hardships of the heart of Free China. And within a year, it had become host to two other institutions, and ultimately to four. By the end of the war, spotted with new buildings, mostly "temporary" in intent though proving remarkably permanent in fact, a campus which had held 440 students was serving ten times that number. The enervating effects of uncertainty, undernourishment, crowding, and inflation took their toll of host as well as guest.

The war years were not, however, without progress and achievement. The "downriver" institutions brought new ideas and fresh standards; the presence of colleagues from different economic and intellectual backgrounds stimulated change. The academic program in which West China now shared was richer than that which had been possible with local resources. Both example and sheer necessity resulted in a rapid rise in the number of Chinese in key administrative and teaching positions. Throughout these years research and public service, also stimulated by example and the spirit of the times, received new attention: preparation of needed drugs, help to the sugar industry, extension courses, assistance to the Chinese Industrial Cooperatives, a department of home economics, and further development of agriculture, with an Institute of Agricultural Research set up in 1941. Just before the outbreak of the war, the decision had been reached to establish, in place of the university's School of Religion, an independent theological college, with six missions participating. In 1941 a B.Th. class of six was graduated and courses leading to the B.D. degree had started. By 1943 there were over fifty students. Members of the faculty of the Nanking Theological Seminary who had found refuge in Chengtu joined in what amounted to a united theological institution.

With the arrival of Ginling, Nanking, and Shantung, followed after Pearl Harbor by Yenching, Chengtu, which was also the home of National Szechwan University, became one of the three great educational centers of Free China. The others were Chungking, where two provincial institutions had been joined by National Central University of Nanking and a half-dozen parts and wholes of other institutions, including the College of Science of the University of Nanking; and Kunming, in Yunnan Province, where three great universities—Tsinghua, Peiping National, and Nankai—had formed the Southwest Associated University, and four other institutions had settled in the vicinity. The five Christian institutions at Chengtu constituted the largest and strongest center of such work China was to see and exhibited a degree of cooperation that was not only unprecedented but not to be matched again.

Cooperation among this group of independent institutions forced into close and involuntary propinquity was far from easy but on the whole surprisingly successful. A Joint Presidents' Meeting and a Joint Deans' Meeting helped in administration. In general, courses at the junior and senior levels were open to all qualified students without regard to place of registration, but the fact that the faculties had been selected on different bases or simply by chance prevented as complete coordination as might have been desired. Academic problems increased with the new curriculum instituted by the Ministry of Education in the fall of 1939 which greatly increased both the number of required courses and the degree of specialization. The poor preparation of many candidates also militated against the maintaining of standards, which in most cases fell below both prewar and postwar levels. However, the war years were not without positive and creative developments.

Inflation and the shortage of many essentials made life hard for both faculty and students. Air-raid warnings and bombing raids, even though in later years apparently little more than practice flights, were a disturbing factor until near the end of the war. Fortunately, in the only bombing which involved the campus, that of June 11, 1939, three bombs which might have destroyed the Ginling buildings and the University Library were duds. While the guest institutions were deeply and appreciatively in debt to West China for many facilities as well as for hospitality, this debt was repaid in part by erection from joint funds of a chemistry building which would finally revert to West China. All temporary structures were planned to be removed but actually continued to be used long after the guests had left.

Pearl Harbor made little fundamental difference in conditions except to pose the threat of deeper Japanese penetration and to bring into the area great airfields and as many as ten thousand American air-force personnel. Many of these found their way to the campus and were entertained there. In turn, the university community provided educational lectures at the major bases. The presence of the military broadened, even if it may not always have elevated, the contribution made by the Christian colleges in the area of international understanding and good will. Many alumni and undergraduates, interrupting their studies, had a still closer association through serving American forces throughout Free China as interpreters and in other capacities.

OTHER CENTERS

South China did not feel the direct effects of the war until more than a year after the Marco Polo Bridge Incident. With the Japanese landing in October 1938 at Bias Bay, a hundred miles east of Canton, Lingnan was forced to evacute to Hong Kong. The campus was returned to the Board of Trustees in America and, as American property, served as a relief center for thousands of refugees. Students and faculty turned to the University of Hong Kong, which lent the use of some rooms and of its libraries and laboratories. An apartment house served for biology, physics, and preclinical medicine. Fourth-year medical students joined the clinical classes of the University; fifth- and sixth-year students continued their studies in other places. The College of Agriculture first rented land in the New Territories across the harbor from Hong Kong Island and then moved to Pingshek in the mountains of northern Kwangtung Province.

Some weeks after the Japanese attack on Hong Kong which followed Pearl Harbor, President Lee escaped to reopen Lingnan in the interior. With the fall of the city, fourteen American faculty and staff members were interned, first on the campus and then in the Stanley Camp, finally being repatriated in September 1943. The university reopened in the country near Kukong, a small city 150 miles upriver from Canton and thirty miles south of where the College of Agriculture Had settled. In temporary wooden buildings in a setting of paddy fields and camphor groves, some three hundred students took up work in five departments: Chinese, English, History and Potitical Science, Science, and Commerce and Economics. Here the college was joined by the Canton Union Theological Seminary, which had gone to the far west but had been asked to return. Life continued under difficulties, with a temporary disruption by the threat of invasion in the spring of 1944, until it was permanently interrupted in January 1945 by Japanese capture of Kukong. Many students sought refuge with families or friends;

others, and most of the faculty members, found comparative safety in villages in the hills until forced to seek safer spots. President Lee was preparing to open classes at Minghsien, 174 miles east, when the Japanese surrender came.

In Fukien Province the outbreak of war brought the fear that Foochow would be the next point of attack. Actually, though they early blockaded the port, the Japanese did not attempt to take the city until nearly four years later. But thousands evacuated the city and at the start of 1938 schools and colleges were ordered closed so that students could carry on a program of education among the masses. Both Fukien Christian University and Hwa Nan College chose to seek sanctuary inland rather than run the risk of having to function under enemy control. In May 1938, following the capture of Amoy, Fukien's other great port, 150 miles to the south, Hwa Nan accepted an invitation to Nanping, 120 miles up the turbulent Min River, while Fukien moved to the small town of Shaowu, another 180 miles by road.

Sixty-six girls from the Hwa Nan middle school and forty-four from the college safely made the hazardous voyage up the rapids of the Min and settled into buildings made available by the Methodist Mission. These were barely adequate, students living twelve in a room and President Wang sharing one with two teachers. The biology laboratory was a porch, the chapel a single room in a residence. Two years later nine temporary buildings had somewhat relieved the pressure. Because of the heat and the danger of air raids, classes ran from six to ten in the morning.

In February 1941, Payne Hall, Hwa Nan's first and largest building in Foochow, was destroyed by fire. Two months later Foochow was heavily bombed and then occupied by the Japanese forces. A Chinese faculty member then in the city escaped disguised as a peasant woman; an American member reached Nanping by a circuitous route. Nanping itself faced a Japanese push which met unexpected resistance and collapsed. Foochow fell a second time in October 19, 1944. As the Japanese moved upriver, Nanping became unsafe and a second move further inland was initiated. Advice came for missionaries to leave, and the two remaining American members of the faculty set out for the west. In May 1945, however, the Japanese suddenly abandoned Foochow, and shortly thereafter the war ended.

When it evacuated its dangerously exposed Foochow campus, Fukien Christian University undertook a move the feasibility of which was far from clear. Many things had to be left behind, but most of the Chinese faculty and students and basic equipment reached Shaowu safely. There a number of buildings, mostly residences, of a sixty-year-old mission station of the American Board were available for use. Additional needs were partially met by construction of a combined chapel-classroom. Western faculty had stayed behind to look after the Foochow campus, but within a couple of years fourteen joined the college in its refugee quarters.

Fukien remained in Shaowu six years. During that time there were considerable achievements. Research in agriculture produced practical results, and development of a college of agriculture brought full recognition as a university. For a short time, starting in the fall of 1942, Fukien was host to Hangchow Christian College. In June 1944, in the face of growing danger from a Japanese advance, all Americans were evacuated. That fall the Foochow campus was thoroughly looted, with loss by fire of the Arts Hall.

For Huachung College, deep in the center of the country, nearly a thousand miles from initial points of attack, neither the Marco Polo Bridge Incident nor the attack on Shanghai posed an immediate threat. The opening of college in the fall of 1937 saw a record enrolment of 240 students. Work proceeded normally until the fall of Nanking brought Ginling and Nanking as transient visitors. Many felt that Huachung should join the westward migration, but in spite of bombings the academic year continued without serious interruption. By summer, however, a move had become unavoidable. Since Chengtu, already crowded with refugee institutions, appeared to have no room to spare, the decision was made to move to Kweilin, six hundred miles south, which could normally be reached with comparative ease by water and rail. A chartered steamer towed laden junks to Hengyang but there, since no trains were available, heavy freight had to be stored and people made their way on by truck. The trip from Wuchang to Kweilin took a month and a half. With delays in the arrival of equipment, overcrowding, and frequent bombings, Kweilin proved untenable and, after one semester, Huachung moved farther westward to Kunming, capital of Yunnan Province. Faculty and students traveled by truck to the Indo-China border, then by rail to Hanoi and from Hanoi to Kunming, a fifteen-hundred-mile trip to cover a bird's flight of five hundred. Equipment and heavy baggage had to make the slow and hazardous journey by road.

In Kunming, which proved crowded and expensive, one of the wealthiest families in the province suggested a move to its home town, Hsichow, not far from Tali, an ancient city near the Burma Road 250 miles west of Kunming. With their help accommodations were found: for the people, in family courtyards and ancestral temples in town; for classes and offices, in three temples half a mile away. The Confucian Temple became the Library; a Buddhist Temple, with blue cloth covering the images, chapel and assembly hall. Nearby was a shrine dedicated to Marco Polo, who had visited Hsichow seven centuries earlier.

Many of the key members of the faculty and staff, both Chinese and Western, had made the journey to Hsichow. Life for them was hard. Tribal people and even local Chinese spoke largely foreign languages; space was limited and furniture scanty; other key members had remained behind. Improvisation was a fundamental part of existence. The college bus, run on charcoal gas, provided power for laboratories and light for evenings. Local wine re-distilled provided alcohol for burners. Recruitment of students proved difficult and enrolment dropped below a hundred and remained there until the end of the war. Spirits were buoyed only by the never abandoned hope of return to Wuchang.

President Wei continued the key figure in Huachung's life, but he was supported in his sustaining of morale by a number of others. Chief among these was Dean P'u Hwang, of the School of Education, who had been a tower of strength on the westward trek. In June 1945 President Wei left to become the first Henry W. Luce Visiting Professor of World Christianity at New York's Union Theological Seminary.

Yale-in-China like Huachung did not immediately feel the effects of the Sino-Japanese War. Changsha like Wuchang appeared to be far enough inland to be safe, and Yali opened in September with normal enrolment. However, air raids soon became a problem and the city filled with refugees, taxing the capacity of the hospital. By the spring of 1938 it was evident that the Middle School would have to leave the city, and it moved to Yuanling, two hundred miles west. There it occupied three buildings lent by the Evangelical Mission and others hastily erected, and caves in the neighboring hills. The Yale-in-China College of Science at Huachung was sharing the fortunes of that institution in the successive westward moves which ended near the Burma border.

The Hsiang-Ya Medical College evacuated Changsha in October. At the invitation of Dr. F.C. Yen, then Minister of Public Health, who had been Dr. Hume's colleague and then his successor as Dean of the Medical College, and with government financing, it moved some five hundred miles west to Kweiyang, capital of Kweichow Province. There it cooperated with the Kweiyang National Medical College, first in almost impossible quarters in town and then on a pleasant campus with temporary buildings two miles outside the city. Departure from Hunan had left the college without that province's support and the national government took it over as "National Hsiang-Ya Medical College."

Shortly thereafter the Hsiang-Ya Medical Center was set up to maintain the private nature of the whole medical program and to serve as a clearing house for mission medical work in Central China. During the next four years enrolment in the Medical College increased to over two hundred. By 1944, however, the Japanese threat to Kweiyang became so serious that the college moved to Chungking, 350 miles away, where it carried on until the end of the war. Throughout the war, Director of the Hsiang-Ya Medical College and in charge of the entire medical program was Dr. H.C. Chang, a graduate of the first medical class. The School of Nursing had been forced to shut down at Changsha in 1938 but had reopened at Yuanling the next year. There it remained throughout the war, maintaining its R.N. program and contributing graduates for war work.

Alone of the various units of Yale-in-China, the Hsiang-Ya Hospital remained in Changsha. It survived the great fire of November 1938, which destroyed most of the city, and the Japanese looting of the city in September 1941. A renewed attack in December of that year was repulsed, but not before the Japanese had set fire to both medical and academic plants. Most buildings were destroyed, but the main structure of the hospital remained intact and within a month the Hsiang-Ya Hospital was again functioning. It continued to do so until the spring of 1944 when the Japanese again took the city, this time to stay until the end of the war.

At various times during the war, Chungking provided refuge for parts of four of the China Colleges. The University of Nanking's College of Science was the first to arrive, settling there while the rest of the university made its trek to Chengtu in the spring of 1938. Arriving early, it found adequate accommodations on the outskirts of the city and functioned in relative safety and comfort and with marked success until its return to Nanking in 1946. Soochow University's College of Law and the School of Commerce of the University of Shanghai opened branches in Chungking in the winter of 1942–43. They were called The Associated University of Shanghai and Soochow and shared a building provided by the Ministry of Education, but functioned quite independently under their own boards and administrations. Neither had much difficulty enlisting able faculty, largely part-time, or recruiting all the students it could care for. In January 1945, Hsiang-Ya Medical College arrived under Japanese threat to its previous stopping-place, Kweiyang. Crowding was so great in Chungking that it carried on through the remaining months with most inadequate housing.

20
Twilight (1945-1949)

For all institutions, the end of the war brought fulfilment of long-deferred hopes. Exile which had been expected to last but a year or two had stretched beyond all imagining. It would be nearly eight years before Ginling, Huachung, and Nanking were home again, and nine before Shantung's College of Medicine made its way back to Tsinan. Shanghai-area institutions would have carried on an uncertain and precarious existence in makeshift quarters for like periods of time. They returned largely empty-handed to badly worn and often empty plants, but return and reopening were carried out with joy, and rehabilitation was undertaken with enthusiasm. Both joy and enthusiasm were only slowly dimmed by increasingly acute awareness of clouds on the horizon.

All sought to return as quickly as possible, but the channels of communication were too limited to carry at once all the returning tide. Institutions with long trails home had to wait, sending only small advance parties and relying on those who had never left to take over home campuses, prepare for the homecoming, or even actually to reopen. Lingnan, St. John's, Soochow, and Yali were able to reopen in the fall of 1945; Shantung and Yenching carried on at both home and refugee bases, the latter through 1945–46, the former for still another year; Fukien, Ginling, Huachung, Hwa Nan, Nanking, and Shanghai all made their way home in the spring of 1946; Hangchow had suffered such losses that it did not reopen in Hangchow until that fall.

Restoration of facilities was a tremendous task. Building materials were in short order; books and equipment had to come from abroad. In some cases, campuses were not only bare and broken but inadequate for the larger numbers institutions were having to care for. Fortunately, the United Board, foreseeing the need, had raised and continued to seek, from mission boards, foundations, and other sources, "restoration funds." These were substantial, as much as $750,000 a year and totaling nearly two million in four years. This was in addition to three quarters of a million from Chinese sources, a third of which came from the Nanking Government. The Board also sent a leading American college librarian to survey the libraries and provide guidance for their restoration and strengthening.

The problem was not limited to physical rehabilitation but included academic restoration and planning for renewed and hopefully greater development. Vision soared and hope ran high. But postwar conditions provided a difficult setting for rebuilding and further growth. Returning and newly freed institutions alike encountered economic anarchy, political uncertainty, and finally military conquest and absorption. The years were hard ones, with dwindling optimism adding to the burden of material problems. By 1948 living costs were rising so rapidly that fees paid at the beginning of a term were exhausted within a month or two. Payment in commodities became necessary, with two hundred pounds of third-grade flour needed to meet fees at Shantung in 1948, and 667 pounds of rice required at Hangchow the following year. Survival was possible only because of the so-called "emergency" and "sustaining" funds from New York, which continued at annual levels of from three hundred thousand dollars to $880,000, amounting to a total of well over two million. With economic deterioration and growing evidence of crumbling Nationalist control and increasing Communist power, came deteriorating morale and doubt as to any future. With uncertainty in regard to the future, there was hesitation about proceeding with any but absolutely essential rehabilitation. A North American campaign for fifteen million dollars, under the chairmanship of Mr. Henry R. Luce, was given up. Finally, in 1949, Communist victory brought a variety of new influences, internal and external, and finally absolute control by a new regime.

Among the Christian colleges, the four Shanghai-area institutions faced relatively minor problems of distance, the farthest home campus, that of Hangchow, being only a hundred miles away, but immediate return was not always possible. In two cases damage had been so serious that plants could not be used until the following year.

St. John's faced fewer physical problems than most of its sister institutions, but its task was not easy. Early in 1946 President Sung was jailed on grounds of collaboration, because St. John's had carried on in the open under the puppet regime. He was not released until exonerated nearly two years later. The university functioned under an acting presidency until inauguration late that year of Dr. Y.C. Tu, once

Professor of Physics at the University of Shanghai and currently Associate General Secretary of the National YMCA. Dr. Tu's failure to win the cooperation of the students and constant undermining by leftist faculty members resulted in his lasting only two years. Dean James H. Pott, son of President Emeritus Pott, served as Acting Vice-President until a new Chinese administration took over in 1949. During this period, the long-deferred matter of registration was finally settled. With both the local Board of Directors and the American Board of Trustees concurring, the process was reinstituted and, by the middle of 1947, after twenty years of anomalous but active existence, St. John's was finally recognized by the Ministry of Education.

Student agitation and demands became so serious that the year 1947–48 closed early without graduation exercises. Though work went on the next year without interruption and with an enrolment of thirteen hundred, a new situation developed with the fall of Shanghai to the Communists in May 1949.

The University of Shanghai reopened in the former International Settlement on October 1, 1945, amid some confusion in regard to the presidency. This was resolved a few months later with the resignation of Dr. Van, who had carried on in Shanghai, and the election of Dr. Henry Lin, who had functioned in Chungking. Dr. Lin, one of a very few fourth-generation Christians in China, was a man of great ability, courage, and faith. He had been very successful in business and had been Director of the government's Bureau of Printing and Engraving, but gave up profit and position to serve his alma mater. He led the university with vision and energy in the face of increasing danger until the fall of Shanghai made it wise for him to retire.

A major task facing President Lin was rehabilitation of the campus, which had been left a sorry sight by Japanese occupation and Chinese billeting. With the two home boards contributing a hundred thousand dollars to the cost, enough repairs were quickly carried out to permit return in April 1946 after an absence of eight and a half years. Several new buildings rose during the next two years. Communist pressures, however, were growing and student strikes constantly interrupted university life. By April 1949, when it had become clear that the Communist forces would succeed in taking Shanghai, all students had left the campus and important records had been moved to the city. Most American faculty members and their wives had withdrawn, leaving only six missionary teachers. Shortly after the city fell on May 27, a group of the Chinese faculty denounced the president and took over the university.

Shortly after the Japanese surrender, five members of the Board reopened Soochow University in Shanghai under an Administrative Committee, using part of the plant of the Moore Memorial Church. The Colleges of Arts and Sciences enrolled more than five hundred students, the Law School more than three hundred. When the Soochow campus was reopened late that fall, a freshman class was immediately admitted for work there. Meanwhile refugees had begun returning from West China. President Yang, who was serving abroad with both the Chinese Information Service and the Chinese delegation to the United Nations and could not at once return, kept in touch with the university through frequent visits. Dean Robert Sheng of the Law School served as acting-president.

The university's plants in both Soochow and Shanghai badly needed rehabilitation but funds were not immediately available. The Methodist Board of Missions undertook the raising of $150,000, but rehabilitation progressed slowly. It was never possible for the Science College, which had been using the cooperative laboratories in Shanghai, to return in full to Soochow. Rehabilitation had not been completed or prewar levels of activity reestablished when the Communists took over both Soochow and Shanghai.

Hangchow University too found its campus in distressing condition, grounds broken up by trenches and air-raid shelters, tea plantations, orchards, and groves wiped out, many residences destroyed and academic buildings completely stripped. Substantial funds from the United Board made restoration possible, but it was a slow process. The university reopened in the fall of 1946 with freshmen and sophomores at Hangchow and juniors and seniors continuing in Shanghai. Enrolment totaled nearly nine hundred. Hopes were high, but a general strike was merely the beginning of troubles that ended only with the Communist take-over. In spite of such agitation, academic work went on without serious interruption, and in July 1948 came final recognition of Hangchow as a university with three colleges: Arts, Commerce and Business Administration, and Engineering. In its last year, Hangchow offered sanctuary to Arts and Science students from Shantung who had found Tsinan no longer tenable. The association was terminated by the Communists when Hangchow fell in April 1949.

The four institutions in and near Shanghai all faced common problems of rehabilitation. The size of these problems once again gave urgency to the long-standing question of bringing together the East China universities. Repeatedly urged and considered since 1913, the idea had found temporary expression during the war years. It was again taken up when the costs and difficulties of rehabilitation appeared to give such a move further logic. Early consultations resulted in recommendations for union or federation and a draft constitution unanimously accepted as a basis for discussion. The United Board not only undertook the raising of the required funds but employed Dr. Walter Gropius of Bauhaus fame and his associates in Cambridge to design a new campus. The University of Shanghai bowed out of the union in 1946, but Hangchow, St. John's, and Soochow Universities continued, if somewhat reluctantly, to consider a federation which would bring the three institutions together on a new campus, with St. John's having colleges of arts, science, engineering, and medicine; Hangchow, colleges of commerce and engineering; and Soochow, colleges of science, commerce, and law. By 1948 St. John's had decided not to leave its own campus. Feeling the need for more space, Hangchow and Soochow agreed to go ahead, holding joint commencement exercises and planning to unite in upper-division work in science and engineering. However, no East China University had developed before the Communist take-over.

For the two Nanking institutions, Ginling College and the University of Nanking, the end of the war meant a retracing of journeys taken nearly eight years earlier and a return to damaged, deteriorated, and largely empty campuses. The reverse flood of the emigration which had taken place over years was trying to make its way in months, through overflowing channels, and immediate travel was not possible for either institution. Another school year in Chengtu, although a shortened one, was necessary. In Nanking, every effort concentrated on putting home campuses in order.

Ginling had hoped to return via the Yangtze River, but since no space would have been available before the fall of 1946, an overland route had to serve. This involved traveling by truck three hundred miles to Paochi, Shensi Province, on the other side of the mountains to the north; by train six hundred miles east to Hsüchow, Kiangsu Province; and then by train south to Nanking—the whole journey requiring nearly three weeks. Return started in April 1946.

In Nanking, the Ginling buildings had fortunately suffered no structural damage, but they had lost most of their contents—furnaces and radiators as well as furniture, books, and equipment—and were badly in need of repair. However, the Japanese had left a new wall and gatehouse, various wooden buildings, and considerable non-educational equipment. Freight from Chengtu and supplies from America did not arrive until a year later; so the first year back in Nanking demanded both making shift and doing without.

218

In spite of difficulties, enrolment was 332, and June 1947 saw a graduating class of sixty-eight, both figures the highest in Ginling's history up to that time. The beginning of the second year brought not only happier conditions but still greater enrolment. This encouraging situation was suddenly changed by Communist successes. Collapse of the Nationalist forces in the late fall of 1948 brought almost complete disruption of college work. Enrolment, which had reached nearly five hundred, dropped to fewer than one hundred. Some of the faculty also left. A few students returned for the spring semester and were on the campus when the turnover took place peacefully in April 1949. President Wu remained with her college.

The University of Nanking faced problems similar to those of Ginling College: rehabilitation of its home campus and transportation for the return trip. Initial preparations for reopening in Nanking began in the fall of 1945 with recovery and preliminary restoration of the campus, but the moving of faculty, students, and equipment could not start until the next spring. The return was made by various routes, though chiefly be retracing that of 1938, overland to Chungking and then down the Yangtze River to Nanking.

The next three years passed, first in enthusiastic and hopeful rehabilitation and planning for the future, and then in growing apprehension on the part of many and anticipation on the part of some, and finally in preparation for the turnover. Not only had buildings been put in good condition and largely re-outfitted at very considerable cost; the academic program had been fully revived and even further developed when Nanking fell to the Communists in April 1949. Though a few members had chosen to leave, most of the faculty, Chinese and Westerners, including President Chen, elected to remain.

For the two North China institutions, Shantung and Yenching, rehabilitation posed somewhat similar problems in that both re-established work on home campuses before refugee units could return. At Tsinan, even before formal surrender of Japanese military forces, two Western faculty members returned to find the campus had been used as a military hospital and was still occupied by nearly two thousand officers and men. Buildings were in fair shape and there were some new structures, but most equipment had disappeared. Because of the difficulty and cost of moving back, the university in Chengtu carried on until the summer of 1947, when four teachers and seventy-nine students returned to Tsinan. Meanwhile Arts, Science, and Medicine took in new students in Tsinan and new and returning Western faculty joined the staff there. The university was no sooner once more a united whole on its own campus than the advance of the Communist armies forced a second evacuation. In March 1948, thirty Westerners and 250 Chinese left for Nanking on a special train. As the situation eased, many returned to finish the school year, but the danger again became acute. Accepting an invitation from Foochow, the Medical College moved there by air and sea, with students finding housing in dormitories of a Methodist school and the college using three hospitals for teaching purposes. The Colleges of Arts and Sciences, a group of four hundred, including 280 students, moved to Hangchow by air and rail. For dormitories, space was rented in the Resting Clouds Buddhist Monastery several miles from the Hangchow campus. Beautiful though the surroundings were, life was austere and distances proved too great for effective functioning. Arrangements in both Foochow and Hangchow were terminated by the Communist capture of Hangchow in April 1949 and of Foochow in August. Meanwhile, the nine-day battle for Tsinan in September 1948 had resulted in considerable destruction on the home campus, to which Shantung now had to return.

At Yenching, within a fortnight of the Japanese surrender, the campus had been reclaimed and a committee had started functioning. The university reopened in October though under difficult physical conditions. The campus was in sad condition—the former buildings badly in need of repair, new structures erected by the Japanese often useless and always unsightly, furniture and equipment almost all gone. Repairs were not completed for two years, and a third of a million dollars had to be spent in the process.

With V-J Day, Yenching in Chengtu had considered immediate return to Peiping, but the absence of transportation made that impossible. For the academic year 1945–46, therefore, Yenching University operated in two centers. Even then return proved very difficult: a southern route by bus and boat to Shanghai, by steamer to Tientsin, and by train to Peiping, a total of some three thousand miles; a northern route by bus and train only half that distance but extremely hazardous. All who started out made it, but university records did not arrive for two years. With the return of the Chengtu unit and the gathering of new and old students in North China, the year 1947–48 opened with eighty-one teachers and a student body of 941. For these, life was very hard; for students in particular, nutrition was far below adequate levels.

Meanwhile, in July 1946 President Stuart had been appointed United States Ambassador to China and given leave of absence. His functions were assumed first by an Administrative Committee with

Professor C.W. Luh as Chairman, then by Dr. William Adolph of the Chemistry Department as Acting President, and finally again by an Administrative Committee. Dr. Luh continued to serve after the Communists arrived. When, in 1948, it became clear that a change was coming, the decision was made not to move again. The majority of faculty and students stayed. Since the campus was some miles outside the city, life under the Communists began for Yenching on December 14, six weeks before Peiping actually fell.

For the two Fukien institutions also, the end of the war brought the dual problems of return and rehabilitation. Return did not involve great distances but posed considerable difficulty and some danger. Fukien solved the problem of transportation by buying logs to pay the rivermen who guided the rafts and to provide lumber for building. It returned to Foochow successfully in the fall of 1945, though not without some loss of life and property. Hwa Nan, its campus unusable without extensive repairs, postponed return until the beginning of 1946. Then, using only the larger lower reaches of the Min River, it was able to move by steam launch, completing the move by mid-March.

Both institutions returned to devastated campuses. Hwa Nan was little more than an empty shell, floors and windows largely gone, all valuable equipment and furniture removed. Its largest building, Payne Hall, had been gutted by fire in 1941 and never restored. Though restoration of Payne Hall was not completed before 1948, rehabilitation had proceeded far enough by the time of return so that, with the help of some wooden structures brought down from Nanping, it was possible to reopen in the spring of 1946. The year 1946–47 saw an enrolment of 228 in spite of economic difficulties. The next year natural catastrophes in the form of fire and flood that swept the city of Foochow, and student troubles which included the constant threat of strikes, added to the burden of sky-rocketing inflation. Nevertheless, the year ended peacefully and 1948–49 opened with a record enrolment of over three hundred. In spite of apprehension caused by Communist capture of Nanping, Hwa Nan's wartime home, the year was completed without interruption. Foochow itself was not taken until late summer.

Fukien found it necessary not only to rehabilitate a badly damaged campus but to enlarge one designed for two hundred students to accommodate six hundred. The Arts Building destroyed by fire at the time of the Japanese re-occupation in 1944 was restored, an auditorium was constructed, dormitories were rebuilt and added to, and the university reopened in Foochow on May 1, 1946. The task of rehabilitation, especially of restoring the contents of buildings which had been thoroughly looted, continued for several years.

Return to Foochow found President Lin in poor health, and he left on a health furlough from which he never returned, a tragic loss not only for the university but for Christian higher education as a whole. With the death of President Lin not only did Fukien lose its architect and leader, China lost one of its greatest Christian educators, a man of true vision, abounding faith, and both courage and humility who was greatly loved and admired. His place was taken for a year by Dr. Theodore H.E. Chen of the Department of Asiatic Studies at the University of Southern California, who had been dean and acting-president in the early thirties.

The postwar years were for Fukien a time of forward-looking development hampered by increasing uncertainty and multiplying crises. As the Nationalists tottered and the Communists advanced, and as one student crises followed another, the optimism with which re-establishment had been undertaken yielded to pessimism in regard to the longer future. Through most of this time, Fukien was under the leadership of Dr. Yang Chang-tung, who took Dr. Chen's place when the latter returned to his post in the United States. A Fukien graduate of great strength and courage, Dr. Yang was on leave from Foochow Union Theological College, of which he had been president. On August 16, 1949, the campus was occupied by Communist troops.

With the Japanese surrender, Lingnan faculty and students, who had scattered earlier in the year, quickly reassembled in Canton, where classes resumed in October 1945. Considerable repairs were required and equipment and books had to be replaced and supplemented, but it was possible to carry on an academic program. Enrolment immediately exceeded prewar figures, with nearly eight hundred in 1945–46 and over a thousand the following year. Those Westerners who had been at Kukong returned to the campus at once; others came from abroad as soon as possible. However, personnel supported by the American Foundation, as many as thirty before the war, never again exceeded eighteen. Several other faculty members were provided by other agencies, including Catholic missions.

The postwar years brought substantial growth and marked improvement. Scholars of national and international reputation gathered, academic standards in some fields rose above prewar levels, the Chinese side of the university was strengthened, and the Christian character acquired new sharpness. Even with the advance of the Communist forces in the north, Canton remained for some time a peaceful haven which attracted scholars from less fortunate areas. By June 1949 the situation had become serious and many, Chinese and American, were leaving. The university resumed classes in September with some twelve hundred students, but on October 14 Communist forces entered Canton.

With the end of the war Huachung College, in its refuge on the western borders of China, faced one of the longest and most difficult return journeys. Preparation of transportation from the remote and, with the shift of interest eastward, largely forgotten region, postponed the move for an academic year. By cutting vacations and speeding up classes, it was possible to close the year and start homeward in April 1946. The trip, by road to Kunming, by rail to Chutsin, by road to Changsha, and then by rail or water to Wuchang, a distance of fifteen hundred miles, took some five weeks. Meanwhile, in Wuchang the process of rehabilitation had been going on since the beginning of the year. All buildings but one were standing but had seen little or no repair in seven years. All books and equipment had disappeared. Many of the windows, floors, gutters, and much of the wiring were missing. Since many houses in the city had been destroyed, temporary quarters for faculty had to be found in hotels and other buildings.

That year the English name reverted from Central China University to Huachung University. At the same time it was planned to erect a new plant for Boone Library School and turn the entire Boone compound over to Huachung. The purchase of several pieces of land prepared the way for the final development, after twenty-five years of crowded and inefficient facilities, of an adequate and functional campus. A Ten-Year Plan worked out in Hsichow called for a student body of six hundred to eight hundred as compared with the prewar figure of two hundred or so. Applications for admission were unusually numerous, more than two thousand taking examinations for some 350 places, the highest enrolment in Huachung history. The postwar years also brought increased mission support, both financial and in missionary personnel. There were also successful efforts to raise funds locally. By the fall of 1948 enrolment had reached nearly six hundred. The year 1948–49, which started with high hope, moved into the uncertainty of growing threats and ended with the final "liberation" of May 1949.

With the Japanese surrender, efforts were made to recover the Yali campus at Changsha before it had been stripped by the Japanese or taken over by the Chinese army. Early in September, the first staff members returned, most of them after a six-day hike. They found the buildings in a sad state, largely stripped of doors, windows, and even floors. The hospital, which was badly needed, was quickly put into usable condition, opening a month later. During the next year all Yali units returned to Changsha. That fall the buildings at Yuanling were dismantled and floated down the river to be used for temporary housing. Staff, students, and equipment were passengers. Middle school students, 350 in number, slept on the floor of an upstairs room, eating and attending classes on the earthen floor below. The Medical College and Nursing School returned by truck and launch. The 110 nursing students lived in a ward of the hospital designed for twenty-four patients. The Science College took part in Huachung's fifteen-hundred-mile trip back to Wuchang the next spring.

All units were besieged by more applicants than they could handle, and enrolment climbed rapidly. By 1947 the Middle School had six hundred students, Huachung College over five hundred, the Nursing School over two hundred, and the Medical School was under pressure to double its size to over five hundred. Permanent buildings to replace the temporary structures were soon under way. In six years, thirty-eight new buildings were erected. Those for the medical and nursing schools were financed largely from Chinese sources, national and provincial. For the Yali campus, a campaign in the United States headed by Henry R. Luce, Yale '20, raised over three hundred thousand dollars. Construction was to have started in 1949 but had to be given up because of political conditions and the occupation of Wuchang and Changsha in the summer and fall of 1949.

West China Union University had no need for physical relocation or major rehabilitation but had to go through the physical and spiritual processes of adjusting to independent functioning. Though transportation problems delayed the departure of the refugee institutions, in some cases until near the end of the academic year, the university almost immediately made plans for expansion to fill the void and to meet greatly increased local needs. The Division of Fine Arts became a department, and a Department of Nursing Education was organized. Enrolment continued to grow, reaching 1770 in the spring of 1948. There was the feeling of a new era, of a West China which had come through eight years of war more up-to-date and far stronger than before and with almost unlimited opportunities for service at the heart of China's West, always prosperous and culturally rich but now less remote and aloof. But the spirit of optimism and expansion soon succumbed to rapid economic and political deterioration. With inflation, finance became an almost unsolvable problem. With growing Communist strength, the future became increasingly uncertain. Communist forces occupied Chengtu December 29, 1949.

21

The Night Falls

The first China College campus to be "liberated" was that of Shantung Christian University, the city of Tsinan falling to the Communists in September 1948. Yenching joined her in December. Others followed as Communist forces occupied various parts of the country. Before the end of 1949, all Christian college campuses were under control of the People's Government. There then followed a period of up to three years in some cases when, under varying degrees of control and through various changes, these foreign-related Christian institutions continued with a semblance of autonomy and under their own names. With the general reorganization of educational institutions in the summer of 1952 all the China Colleges had ceased to exist in recognizable form. A seventy-year history had ended.

The life and work of the China Colleges under the Communist regime was complicated and made difficult by a number of factors, material and emotional. One of the first interruptions to normal functioning came from student efforts to take over or at least control the life of the institution. These had become increasingly troublesome even before final take-over. Even when these efforts did not immediately bring about drastic administrative reorganization, they were disruptive; often they resulted in government by representatives of all segments of the academic community—students and workmen as well as faculty and staff. However, as official government involvement increased, the power of such groups was whittled away and these largely faded from the picture. Control became less capricious but more rigid and bureaucratic.

From the start, political indoctrination was another factor, often started by leftist students but quickly directed by the Party. This took the form on the one hand of courses in the principles of the new order and, on the other, of extracurricular discussion groups. Courses bore such titles as "Principles of the New Democracy" and "Historical Materialism and Social Revolution." Discussion groups tended to be times of accusation and confession, all based on the requirement of complete acceptance of the new order. Attendance might in name be voluntary, but pressures made non-attendance almost impossible. Faculty as well as students devoted endless hours to such discussions, the Yenching faculty, for example, spending twelve hours a week for six months in consideration of the problems of self-interest, prejudice, and laissez-faire.

In time official government campaigns began seriously to interfere with the academic program and further to erode the time given to studies. The Three-Anti Movement of 1951–52, a drive against corruption, waste, and bureaucracy, brought many faculty members before public tribunals which required the fullest self-criticism, a severe examination that not all passed. The goal was greater adherence to Party principles; a side result was often a change of responsibility. Students were very active in this movement. The Land Reform Movement also drew both faculty and students away from the campus into extended periods of service in country areas.

Problems of another sort arose in connection with finances. At first these were caused by the continued inflation and by the resort to commodity standards resulting from a confusing mélange of currencies. Funds from New York for a time made survival possible, but government subsidies increasingly became a factor. The former source was threatened by the U.S. Treasury Department's order of December 7, 1950, brought on by Peiping's entry into the Korean War, which made it unlawful to send money to China without a license. The United Board wasted no time in securing such a license, but first public feeling and then government policy in China soon made it impossible for the institutions there to accept American aid.

From the start, the hyper-nationalism of the Communists made the continued presence of Western members on the faculties of the colleges somewhat uncertain. When the colleges were first threatened with a take-over, most Westerners, motivated by a mixture of loyalty and hope, elected to stay with their Chinese colleagues. The first months, with their promises of religious freedom and relative absence of anti-foreign or extremely restrictive measures, appeared to justify the hope. In most instances a degree of optimism survived the first year of Communist control. Gradually, however, controls tightened, "cultural imperialism" was increasingly denounced, and individual foreigners became objects of public criticism. The growing deterioration of Sino-American relations made the tenure of Americans increasingly insecure.

With Chinese entry into the Korean War, the situation became intolerable if not actually dangerous. Even before the institutions were themselves fully absorbed into the new order, the end had come to the internationalism of the China Colleges.

Departure was not always a simple matter even when ordered by the authorities. Exit permits were needed, and there was often considerable delay in securing these. Although usually not required to leave until their passports or visas expired, most Westerners sought permission to do so when it became clear that they could no longer function effectively or that they were becoming a burden to their Chinese colleagues. Except in a few instances, departures started in 1950. In 1951 they had become a mass exodus and by the end of the year almost all Westerners had left. Fukien, Hwa Nan, and Soochow had been vacated by the end of 1950; most other institutions completed the process in 1951; Yenching was finally clear of Americans early in 1952 and of British as well later in the year. The colleges had been purely Chinese in all matters of policy and control since 1949; by 1952 they had become completely non-Western in personnel.

Incorporation into the Communist educational system was to be the certain fate for all the China Colleges but followed varying patterns of procedure and timing. The process was particularly difficult for Shantung Christian University because the take-over found most of the university away from home. With the fall of Hangchow and Foochow, Shantung's refugee colleges faced the problem of returning to a completely new situation. For the College of Arts, the answer was simple; it was not allowed to reopen. The College of Medicine, 135 persons in all, eventually made its way back by river boats, empty army trucks, and rail, arriving home more than a year after the fall of Tsinan. Enrolment for 1949–50 was eight hundred, higher than ever before, but space had been reduced to one-fifth, most of the campus being occupied by the Communist East Asia Institute and the Provincial Education Bureau. Many students had to be housed in basements and bathrooms. By the end of 1950 the new regime had taken over support of Shantung, and in the summer of 1952 it reorganized the whole institution. The College of Medicine was merged with the Shantung Provincial Medical College and the resulting Shantung Medical College was given the entire campus. The College of Science and the College of Theology were moved to Nanking, the former joining the new National University and the latter Nanking Theological Seminary. Seventy years after first recognition as a college, Shantung University had ceased to exist.

For Yenching University, life under the Communists began on December 14, 1948, six weeks before the city of Peiping itself fell. Yenching was quickly designated one of the four universities of Peiping and several of its faculty were named to important educational posts. Enrolment rose to twelve hundred and there was much optimism. But changes soon began to take place. Discussion and accusation meetings became more frequent and leading members of the faculty, including Dr. C.W. Luh, were singled out for attack. Finally, in the spring of 1951, Yenching was nationalized. A year later its campus became part of Peking University. A little more than a sixty-year cycle of Cathay after the starting of higher education in the Peking area and only a quarter of a century after its establishment on its great new campus, the most prestigious and most widely known of the China Colleges had disappeared.

Ginling College came under Communist control with the fall of Nanking on April 24, 1949. The first months under the new regime were busy with changes in curriculum, organization, and student life, but for the next year and a half most aspects of college life went on much as before. It was even possible in 1950 to celebrate Ginling's thirty-fifth anniversary in the usual way. Nor did the University of Nanking immediately feel the impact of the Communist presence. However, interruptions of program, changes of personnel, and introduction of new courses and patterns became more and more frequent. Finally, early in 1951, the University and Ginling College were merged to form National Ginling University, with the former's dean of science as president and the latter's president as vice-president. Christian higher education in Nanking had come to an end.

Hangchow University came under Communist control on May 3, 1949, when, three days after the fall of Hangchow City, troops overran the campus. President Lee was granted leave and a Provisional Council was set up with an Administrative Committee to look after routine functioning. Dr. J. Usang Ly became president on July 1, 1950, but a year later found it best to resign. By the summer of 1951 the Colleges of Arts and Commerce had been dissolved, the College of Engineering had been moved to the National Chekiang University in the city, and the plant had been taken over by the Chekiang Teachers College. Fifty-five years after acquiring collegiate status and three years after achieving university-hood, Hangchow Christian University was no more, its place taken by a teachers college.

Liberation came to Huachung University in May 1949. The col-

lege year 1949–50 saw growing government control and increasing interruptions for political activities and indoctrination. The next year
brought so much interference as to limit if not wholly defeat classroom
teaching. Beginning with 1951–52, Huachung University and the
Government Teachers' College were amalgamated to form the Normal
School in the Wuhan area. Boone became a practice school for that
institution. President Wei was initially vice-president but later simply a
faculty member. Two years after celebrating its twenty-fifth anniversary and five years after becoming a university, Huachung disappeared
into a government normal school.

The city of Soochow fell to the Communists in May 1949 on their
way from Nanking to Shanghai. Leftist students, who had earlier been
planted in the university, as they had been in all institutions, soon gained
control of the Student Association and brought increasing pressure on
the Executive Council. Requirements of indoctrination interfered more
and more with normal academic work. Government regulations became
more demanding and government control more rigid. In 1952, fifty years
after the start of Tungwu College, Soochow University had disappeared
from view.

After the fall of Shanghai in May 1949, St. John's continued to
function without serious official interference in spite of the presence on
the campus of Communist soldiers. However, radical students quickly
took over student organizations and attempted to dictate the content and
conduct of courses. Endless meetings began to interfere seriously with
classes. Administration shifted more and more into an organization in
which all groups on the campus—faculty, students, and laborers—were
represented. Finally, by 1952, St. John's, one of the first of the Protestant colleges of China and one of the best known, had become an
indistinguishable part of the Communist system of education.

At the University of Shanghai, the three years following the
Communist victory saw a constant struggle between directors, faculty,
and students seeking to maintain standards and a growing minority of
Communist sympathizers forcing new patterns on the university. In
June 1949 the university had to provide dormitory facilities for fifteen
hundred young people being trained as propagandists. The early religious liberty gradually disappeared under the requirements of Communist indoctrination. The assessment of heavy taxes and the closing of
channels of foreign support created an impossible financial situation. In
October 1951, President Lin, who had been living quietly at home, was

thrown in prison, where he died early in 1960. Finally, in the summer of 1952 the University of Shanghai was completely taken over by the People's Government.

When the Communists entered Foochow in August 1949, Fukien Christian University was under the control of a committee of six with "presidential powers." It was told to carry on, but administrative reorganization gave representation to almost every group on the campus. Classes reopened with nearly four hundred students and work continued fairly normally through the school year. For Hwa Nan the first year of Communist control brought few changes, but the second saw developments that made it necessary in the fall for Western staff to leave and in the spring for the university to terminate all communication with the West.

In January 1951 the government merged Fukien Christian University and Hwa Nan College with two other institutions, one private and one provincial, to form the National Fukien University. The Fukien campus was assigned to the new institution's college of agriculture, the Hwa Nan campus to its college of science. An administrative committee of which Dr. Lucy Wang was vice-chairman was replaced in 1952 by a president. Not quite forty years after the dreams of a Christian university and a Christian college for women in Fukien had taken concrete form, Fukien Christian University and Hwa Nan College were no more.

Yali came under Communist control in the fall of 1949. The year and a half following brought increasingly stifling government pressures and restrictions on those of the American staff who attempted to carry on. With the public trial and final expulsion of Dr. Dwight Rugh, last representative of the Board, in May 1951, the work of Yale-in-China at Changsha, started in 1904, had come to an end. Its College of Science at Wuchang disappeared shortly after with the absorption of Huachung into the new Central China Normal College. The Middle School was renamed Hunan Private Liberation Middle School. The Medical College was taken over by the government and quickly expanded until students numbered in the thousands. Yale-in-China was no more.

Communist forces occupied Chengtu late in 1949. For West China Union University, first orders were to carry on, but restrictions quickly began to limit the university's freedom. Hope persisted that it might carry on without great change, but conditions worsened until, on January 4, 1951, the military authorities took over the university. Indoctrination intensified, and in October a new president assumed charge in the name of the People's Government. After four decades of increasingly significant service, West China Union University came to an end.

Communist troops entered Canton on October 14, 1949. Prior to the establishment of order, the Lingnan campus suffered somewhat from bandits, but the University was soon functioning under a University Council to which had been added junior staff members and students and with a curriculum into which had been injected courses in the New Democracy and Maoist Political Economy. Campus life proceeded smoothly with little interruption except for meetings and conferences until Chinese intervention in Korea intensified anti-imperialist agitation. On December 14–15, the entire American group were branded as imperialists and their exodus began. The university continued as a private institution through 1951, but early in 1952 the government took over, making it the College of Arts of Sun Yat-sen University. President Ch'en Su-ching was made Vice-President.

The last fifteen years of the life of the China Colleges were a composite of struggle for survival, fresh hope, and final loss of identity. The storms of war drove them underground or into exile for eight years; an uneasy twilight provided four more years for rehabilitation and new dreams; two to three years of a new regime led to the final fall of night. By 1952 the story which began a century earlier and whose main thread covered some seventy years had ended. The China Colleges were no more.

22
Looking Back

When the day of Protestant higher education in China was drawing to a close, the China Colleges stood ready and competent to continue their service to China and its people. Their status was sound, as it had been ever since the fading of their foreignness and the recognition of their Chinese-ness two decades earlier. They had achieved true citizenship. They were a Chinese part of Chinese education, not only officially but in the popular mind and in academic circles. With a foreign flavor, to be sure—unavoidably so under the circumstances of history and economics—but not such as to stir up again the suspicion and antagonism of earlier years. They were truly and favorably recognized. In spite of the handicaps of foreign origin, religious purpose, and imperialistic association, the China Colleges had been a largely welcome, increasingly approved element in the life of China from the latter part of the nineteenth century to the middle of the twentieth. Initial suspicion had soon been replaced by acceptance and, finally, by a sincere welcome. They were never more at home than in their last years.

They also faced the future from a position of maturity, vigorous and confident, by no means free of problems, some of them such as to daunt even the most enthusiastic, but ready to meet the challenges of the future. Financial aid from overseas was still needed, but on a diminishing scale and no longer constituting a psychological millstone. Academically they stood well in China's growing circle of government and private colleges. Even at the height of the Anti-Christian Movement in 1923, Dr. Kuo P'ing-wen, President of National Southeastern University and later Vice-Minister of Finance, writing for the Chinese National Association for the Advancement of Education, stated that, "While open to adverse criticism from a national point of view, some of the institutions under mission control are among the finest and most efficient colleges in China today. And, because they made an early start, they have had much influence and prestige." And they had come far since then.

While standing ready to continue the important role they had played in the regeneration of the country and looking hopefully to even greater service, the colleges could review a remarkable history. If the story, as it has been told, seems to have been more concerned with obstacles than with achievements, that is only natural where there had been such radical changes in the setting and such need for adaptation on the part of the actors themselves. Awareness of shortcomings has tended at times to subordinate the many positive achievements of six decades of struggle. In reality, these far outweigh the negative aspects, however regretful those may have been. What, then, was the record? What had been the contribution of these institutions during sixty and more years of history? To the Church, in whose interests, broadly interpreted, they had been started? To the people who had been their concern and the nation in whose modern history they had been deeply involved? To the world, especially to those parts directly related to their existence and functioning? How sound had been the investment of lives and money? How justified the faith and hope?

Started at first primarily for purposes of evangelism and always with concern for Christian impact on Chinese society, the colleges had contributed notably, though not always to expressed goals or in the manner anticipated, to the development and strengthening of the Church. Except in the earliest stages, they had not concentrated on the training of clergy, but they had assisted, directly and indirectly, in the shaping of not a few outstanding church leaders. And they had fed into the Church a large number of educated and forward-looking members, and into society many highly motivated participants. Without the China Colleges, the Protestant Church in China would have been far weaker a body than that which, in spite of almost negligible numbers, contained so impressive a company of educated men and women.

The major contribution of the China Colleges to secular society was in the area of education. Especially at first, this was both crucial and distinctive. For one thing, the Protestant colleges provided almost the first modern higher education in a China greatly in need of and desperately striving to introduce it. Until well into the twentieth century, they constituted not only a major but a leading part of that education. For another thing, they were stimulators, encouraging the government and private groups to set up their own institutions. Through example and competition, they were goads to action by others. Meanwhile, they continued to fill as best they could the still largely unmet need. For yet another, they provided patterns, introducing new concepts and setting worthwhile standards and goals. These were not always accepted or closely followed, but they offered guidance and challenge. The China Colleges were notably pioneers.

The challenge continued even after some government and private institutions had caught up with the Protestant colleges academically. Honesty and efficiency in administration, emphasis on character, concern for the individual student, and the spirit and devotion of faculty continued to set them apart from others. Distinguished, though not always as clearly in fact as in theory, by an emphasis on moral and spiritual values as well as intellectual, they continued to bring to bear an important and badly needed influence on the life about them. Their numbers were not great, but the Christian colleges constituted a major factor in the early days of higher education and, even later, a force disproportionate to the size of the colleges themselves. It is doubtful if, during the first half of their history, a service of equal timeliness and effectiveness could have been rendered the nation in any other way. Nor did it disappear during the second half; at the end, the colleges remained a positive and important element in China's higher education.

In this process of providing higher education when needed, in stimulating and setting patterns for other institutions, and in continuing sound and distinctive programs of education, the China Colleges contributed to China and its development a highly influential group of trained men and women in all ranks of society at a time when the nation had great need of them. Through these men and women, the colleges provided Chinese society with much that it lacked in its transition from a traditional and no longer effective past to a modern and hopefully more creative future. Some of their gifts, not easily measured, were undoubtedly in the realm of the spirit, of ethics and morals. Others were matters of the intellect, an understanding of science and technology, an awareness of the rest of the world. Many lay in concrete service through the introduction of new ideas and their application in such areas as medicine, agriculture, and science. To these must be added the total of trained, educated, and often highly motivated men and women in almost all walks of life—business and industry, law and politics, education and social welfare, medicine and public health, and government service.

Among these were many graduates engaged in the direction, and in some instances the founding, of national organizations of social service. The Child Welfare Association of China, the National Anti-Opium Association, the Chinese Industrial Cooperative Movement, the Officers Moral Endeavor Association, and others drew heavily on graduates of the China Colleges. To government service, the colleges also contributed a surprising number of highly placed officials, especially graduates from the years before government institutions had fully developed. These included heads of ministries, ministers and ambassadors (Berlin, London, and Washington among others), and even a premier, in addition to many in lower but still critical posts. The fields of business and industry had many graduates, including founders and heads of important industries, presidents and managers of banks. The colleges also produced many college and university presidents. Eighty percent of the Chinese presidents of the China Colleges themselves were graduates of those institutions, though not always of the one they served. Graduates also headed government and private institutions. Among those were two presidents of Tsinghua University, Dr. Y.T. Tsur and Dr. Y.S. Tsao. Professors and heads of departments constituted a very considerable group.

These outstanding men and women of course made up only a small proportion of the total who graduated from the Christian colleges. Fully as important were the greater numbers playing less public roles who carried into that society, along with knowledge and skills, some of the ideals and values the colleges had stood for and had sought to impart. These enriched and enriching lives were an asset impossible to measure but making up no small part of of the contribution of the Christian colleges.

Not least important was the contribution of the China Colleges to international understanding and good will. In the largely unconscious role played by Christian missions as mediators of Western culture, in which they were possibly as successful as in their conscious work as disseminators of the Christian faith, the colleges played a major part through their offering of language, knowledge, values, and personnel representative of the West. Through them, much of the best of the West reached China; in them, Chinese and Westerner rubbed shoulders, not always without friction but generally without fire and to their mutual benefit; from them, knowledge of China, interpreted and exemplified, reached the West. As expressions of the concern of Christian people in Europe and North America, they served as spiritual and cultural ambassadors, helping to interpret West to East and East to West in spite of the impediments of imperialistic associations and foreign character. They represented the heart of the Christian people of the West responding to the plight of the Chinese people with a strength of emotion rarely if ever matched in other international and interracial relationships.

Forerunners of later foreign governmental programs of technical assistance, they pioneered and led the way in the encouragement of non-exploitative international cooperation.

Being introducers of Western culture, they were also *ipso facto* participants in the great revolution taking place in Chinese culture, society, and government. Through confronting the Chinese cultural heritage with Western civilization, they fed fuel to the fires of change and contributed to the shaping of China's future, greatly as that future differed from what most had foreseen. That they themselves were ultimately consumed does not negate their contribution to the awakening, modernizing, and transforming of an old society into a new.

So, as the first half of the twentieth century drew to a close, the China Colleges could look back with no little pride and view the present with considerable confidence. But the hoped-for future was not to be. Such service as they could render to the country of their adoption was over. With the start of the second half of the century, the story of the China Colleges came to an end. After some seventy years of increasing strength, growing public favor, and expanding public service, the Christian colleges and universities of China were quickly submerged in a spiritually alien system under which, whatever corporate and physical entities might survive, all spiritual identity would be erased. Buildings and their contents might remain, faculty might find a place in the new, but the Christian colleges would be no more.

The ending is tragic, but the tale itself is no tragedy. Rarely if ever has there been a comparable story of sometimes fumbling but often wide-ranging and generally effective service by Christian people of one culture to the people and society of another. To Church, to education, to modern knowledge, to various skills and professions, and even to government, these institutions had made contributions at times unique and out of all proportion to their numbers. After all deductions for errors have been made, the name China Colleges will be remembered as representing a notable and noble contribution from Christians on both sides of the Atlantic to a great people on the eastern shores of the Pacific, and a unique but integral element in their education through years of rebirth and change.

Appendices

Appendix A

CHRISTIAN INSTITUTIONS
OF HIGHER EDUCATION IN CHINA

1895	1905	1915	1925	1935	1945
PROTESTANT COLLEGES AND UNIVERSITIES					
		Fukien	Fukien	Fukien	Fukien
		Ginling	Ginling	Ginling	Ginling
Hangchow*	Hangchow*	Hangchow	Hangchow	Hangchow	Hangchow
	Boone	Boone	Huachung	Huachung	Huachung
			Huping		
		Hwa Nan	Hwa Nan	Hwa Nan	Hwa Nan
Canton*	Canton*	Canton	Lingnan	Lingnan	Lingnan
		Lutheran	Lutheran		
		Nanking	Nanking	Nanking	Nanking
N. China	N. China	N. China ⎫			
	N. C. Women's	N.C.W. ⎬ Peking (see below)			
Peking	Peking	Peking ⎭			
St. John's	St. John's	St. John's	St. John's	St. John's	St. John's
	Shanghai	Shanghai	Shanghai	Shanghai	Shanghai
Tengchow	Shantung	Shantung	Shantung	Shantung	Shantung
	Soochow	Soochow	Soochow	Soochow	Soochow
		West China	West China	West China	West China
		Yali	Yali		
			Peking	Yenching	Yenching

*Junior colleges.

PROTESTANT MEDICAL SCHOOLS

	Hsiang-Ya	Hsiang-Ya	Hsiang-Ya	Hsiang-Ya
Hackett	Hackett	Hackett	Lingnan	Lingnan
Peking	(Peking Union Medical College)			
Boone				
Soochow				
	Foochow			
		Moukden	Moukden	
St. John's	St. John's	St. John's	St. John's	St. John's
Shantung	Shantung ⎫			
Hangchow ⎱	Nanking ⎬			
Hankow ⎰		Shantung	Shantung	Shantung
N. China	N. China ⎭			
Women's	Women's			
W. China	W. China	W. China	W. China	W. China
		Woman's—	Woman's—	Woman's—
		Shanghai	Shanghai	Shanghai

CATHOLIC COLLEGES AND UNIVERSITIES

	Aurora	Aurora	Aurora	Aurora
		Tsinku	Tsinku	Tsinku
		Fu Jen	Fu Jen	Fu Jen

Appendix B

ENROLMENT FIGURES FOR THE CHINA COLLEGES

INSTITUTION	1899–1900	1910–11	1919–20	1929–30	1936–37	1944–45	1948–49
FUKIEN			111	142	169	591	574
GINLING			70	166	259	336	480
HANGCHOW	24	30	61	111	537	384	950*
HUACHUNG				28	207	215	572
BOONE		44	71				
HWA NAN			14	100*	96	120	300*
LINGNAN		24	81	315	560	500	1202
HACKETT MEDICAL				57	(53)		
MOUKDEN MEDICAL			70*	95	125*		
NANKING		29	88	508	908	1272	1145
ST. JOHN'S	16	119	256	279	578	2100	1479
MEDICAL			(19)	(37)	(82)		
SHANGHAI		14	120	449	629	1182	1349
SHANTUNG			232	336	567	400	350*
TENGCHOW	48	320					
MEDICAL		20	(80)	(88)	(115)		
TSINGCHOW	8	60					
SOOCHOW		27	163	708	667	750	1500*
WEST CHINA		10	97	170*	440	1300	1750*
MEDICAL			(28)	(30)	(157)		
WOMAN'S MEDICAL			39+	20	29	30*	30*
YALE-IN-CHINA (COLLEGE)			42++	49++	100*	250*	270
HSIANG-YA MEDICAL							
YENCHING	26		161	743	807	408	800
NORTH CHINA		109					
PEKING		45					
N. CHINA WOMEN'S		22					
OTHERS—HUPING		5	15				
LUTHERAN				11			
TOTALS	127	878	1,691	4,285	6,668	9,838	12,751

*Estimated.   + A peak of 184 was reached in 1922–23.   ++ Including premedical.   ( ) Included in total.

Appendix C

ACADEMIC ORGANIZATION OF THE CHINA COLLEGES*

INSTITUTION	ARTS	SCI.	PUB. AFF.	GRAD.	MED.	AGR.	LAW	ENG.	EDUC.	BUS.	THEOL.
FUKIEN	x	x									
GINLING	x	x				x					(x)
HANGCHOW	x	x						x-4			
HUACHUNG	x	x								x	x
HWA NAN	x	x							x		
LINGNAN	x	x		x-3	x	x					(x)
NANKING	x	x		x-4		x		x-3		x	(x)
ST. JOHN'S	x	x		x-4	x			x-1			(x)
SHANTUNG	x	x									x++
SHANGHAI	x	x								x	x
SOOCHOW	x	x		x-1	x		x				
WEST CHINA	x	x			x+++						
YALI		x+			x						
YENCHING	x	x	x	x-8							x
MOUKDEN					x						x
WOMAN'S					x						
TOTALS	13	13	1	5	7	3	1	3	1	3	5(4)

*Postwar Years 1946–50.

0 Independent but associated.

+Part of Huachung from 1929 on; not included in total.

++Division of Religious Studies.

+++College of Medicine and Dentistry.

Arabic numerals under GRAD and ENG indicate number of departments.

Appendix D

CHARTERING AND REGISTRATION
OF THE CHINA COLLEGES

CHARTERED			REGISTRATION
BY	WHEN		DATE
N.Y. (1918)	1934	Fukien Christian University	February 1931
N.Y. (1911)	1935	Ginling College	December 1930
D.C.	1920	Hangchow Christian University	July 1931
Conn.	1919*	Hsiang-Ya Medical College	**1914
N.Y.	1910	Huachung University	October 1931
N.Y. (1922)	1934	Hwa Nan College	June 1933
N.Y.	1893	Lingnan University	1927
		Moukden Medical College	
N.Y.	1911	Nanking, University of	September 1928
D.C.	1905	St. John's University	July 1948
Va.	1917	Shanghai, University of	March 1929
Canada	1924	Shantung Christian University	December 1931
Tenn.	1900	Soochow University	1928
N.Y. (1922)	1934	West China Union University	October 1933
D.C.	1924	Woman's Christian Medical College	
N.Y. (1890)	1929	Yenching University	1930

*Yale-in-China.
**Being a Chinese institution, Hsiang-ya was not required to register.
N.Y.   The Regents of the State of New York.
D.C.   District of Columbia.
Can.   The Dominion of Canada.
Va.   General Assembly of the State of Virginia.
Tenn.   State of Tennessee.
() Provisional or Limited Charter.

Appendix E

MISSION BOARD CONNECTIONS OF THE CHINA COLLEGES
(For full names of mission boards, see below)

	FUKIEN	GINLING	HANGCHOW	HUACHUNG	HWA NAN	LINGNAN	MOUKDEN	NANKING	ST. JOHN'S	SHANGHAI	SHANTUNG	SOOCHOW	WEST CHINA	WOMAN'S	YALI	YENCHING	TOTALS
AMERICAN																	
Baptist, North		x						x		x			x				4
Baptist, South										x							1
Brethren				x													1
Congregational	x										x					x	3
Disciples		x						x									2
Episcopal				x					x								2
Lutheran, United				x							x						2
Methodist, North	x	x			x			x			x		x			x	7
Methodist, South		x										x					2
Presbyterian, North		x	x			x		x			x					x	6
Presbyterian, South		x	x														2
Reformed in America	x																1
Reformed in the U.S.		x		x													2
Women's Societies														x			1
Yale-in-China															x		1
BRITISH																	
Anglican—C.M.S.	x										x						2
Anglican—S.P.G.											x					x	2
Baptist											x						1
Congregational				x		x					x					x	4
Friends													x				1
Methodist, Wesleyan				x		x					x						3
Presbyterian, Eng.											x						1
Presbyterian, Ire.							x										1
Presbyterian, Scot.							x										1
CANADIAN																	
Presbyterian											(x)						(1)
Methodist													(x)				(1)
United Church											x		x				2
EUROPEAN																	
Lutheran				x			x										2
TOTALS	4	7	2	7	1	3	3	4	1	2	11	1	4	1	1	5	57

242

Appendix F

MISSION BOARDS CONNECTED
WITH THE CHINA COLLEGES

AMERICAN

Baptist, North	American Baptist Foreign Missionary Society
	Woman's American Baptist Foreign Missionary Society
Baptist, South	Foreign Mission Board of the Southern Baptist Convention
Brethren	Division of World Mission of the Evangelical United Brethren Church
Congregational	American Board of Commissioners for Foreign Missions of the Congregational and Christian Churches
Disciples	United Christian Missionary Society of the Disciples of Christ
Episcopal	Domestic and Foreign Missionary Society of the Protestant Episcopal Church in the U.S.A.
Lutheran	Board of Foreign Missions of the Norwegian Lutheran Church of America
Methodist, North (see Methodist)	Board of Foreign Missions of the Methodist Episcopal Church
	Woman's Foreign Missionary Society of the Methodist Episcopal Church
Methodist, South (see Methodist)	Board of Missions of the Methodist Episcopal Church, South
	Woman's Missionary Council of the Methodist Episcopal Church, South
Methodist (1939)	Board of World Missions of the Methodist Church (Division of World Missions Woman's Division of Christian Service)
Presbyterian, North	Board of Foreign Missions of the Presbyterian Church in the U.S.A.
	Woman's Board of Foreign Missions of the Presbyterian Church in the U.S.A.
	(Consolidated in 1933 as a Board of Foreign Missions)
Presbyterian, South	Executive Committee of Foreign Missions of the Presbyterian Church in the U.S.
	Committee on Woman's Work of the Presbyterian Church in the U.S.
Reformed, in America	Board of Missions of the Reformed Church in America
Reformed, in the U.S.	Woman's Board of Foreign Missions of the Reformed Church in America
	(From 1934 part of the Evangelical and Reformed Church)

Women's Societies	Woman's American Baptist Foreign Missionary Society
	Woman's Board of Foreign Missions of the Reformed Church in America
	Woman's Missionary Council of the Methodist Episcopal Church, South
	Woman's Union Missionary Society of America
Yale-in-China	Yale Foreign Missionary Society, which in 1943 changed its name to the Yale-in-China Association.

BRITISH

Anglican—CMS	Church Missionary Society for Africa and the East, of the Church of England
Anglican—SPG	Society for the Propagation of the Gospel in Foreign Parts, of the Church of England
Baptist	Baptist Missionary Society
Congregational	London Missionary Society (interdenominational in character)
Friends	Friends' Service Council
Methodist	Methodist Missionary Society, representing the Wesleyan, United, and Primitive Methodist Churches
Presbyterian, English	Foreign Missions Committee of the Presbyterian Church of England
Presbyterian, Irish	Mission of the Presbyterian Church of Ireland
Presbyterian, Scotch	Church of Scotland Foreign Missions Committee

CANADIAN

Methodist	The Missionary Society of the Methodist Church, Canada (until 1925; see United Church, below)
Presbyterian	Board of Foreign Missions of the Presbyterian Church in Canada—until 1925
	General Board of Missions of the Presbyterian Church in Canada—after 1925 (see United Church, below)
United Church	Board of Missions, United Church of Canada (The United Church was constituted in 1925 by the union of the Congregational, the Methodist, and part of the Presbyterian Churches of Canada)

EUROPEAN

Danish Missionary Society
Swedish Missionary Society

Appendix G

PRESIDENTS OF THE CHINA COLLEGES

FUKIEN CHRISTIAN UNIVERSITY

1916–1923	Edwin C. Jones
(1918–1919	Roderick Scott, Acting)
1923–1927	John Gowdy
(1924–1925	Roderick Scott, Acting)
1927–1946	C.J. Lin
1946–1947	Theodore H.E. Chen
1947–1951	Yang Chang-tung

GINLING COLLEGE

1913–1927	Mathilda Thurston (Mrs. Lawrence)
1928–1951	Wu Yi-fang

HANGCHOW UNIVERSITY

1897–1911	Junius H. Judson
1911–1916	Elmer L. Mattox
1916–1922	Warren H. Stuart
1923–1926	Elmer L. Mattox
1927	Chu Ching-nung (elected but did not serve)
1927–1949	Lee Baen
(1927–1930	Acting)
1938–1943	Robert J. McMullen (in Shanghai)
1949–1950	Administrative Committee (Chow Cheng, Chrmn.)
1950–1951	J. Usang Ly

HUACHUNG UNIVERSITY

BOONE

1901–1916	James Jackson
1916–1924	Alfred A. Gilman

HUACHUNG

1924–1929	Alfred A. Gilman (Acting)
1929–1951	Francis C.M. Wei
(1934–1935	P'u Hwang, Acting)

(1937–1938   P'u Hwang, Acting)
(1945–1946   Richard Bien, Acting)

HWA NAN COLLEGE

1915–1925   Lydia Trimble
1925–1928   Ida Belle Lewis
1928–1951   Lucy Wang
(1946–1949   Doris Hsü, Acting)

LINGNAN UNIVERSITY

1887–1893   Andrew P. Happer
(1891–1893   President *pro tem*)
1893–1896   Benjamin C. Henry
1896–1899   Henry V. Noyes
1899–1908   Oscar F. Wisner
1908–1924   Charles K. Edmunds
1924–1927   James McClure Henry
1927–1937   Chung Wing-kwang (Jung-kwang)
1937–1948   Lee Ying-lam
1948–1952   Ch'en Su-ching
(1948–1949   Acting)

MOUKDEN MEDICAL COLLEGE

1912–1924   Dugald Christie
1924–1939   Soren A. Ellerbek
1939–1941   Peter D. Pedersen

UNIVERSITY OF NANKING

1910–1927   Arthur J. Bowen
1927–1951   Ch'en Yu-kwan (Y.G. Chen)

ST. JOHN'S UNIVERSITY

1888–1898   James Lester Hawks Pott (Headmaster)
1899–1937   James Lester Hawks Pott
1937–1946   William Z.L. Sung
1946–1948   Y.C. Tu
1948–1949   James H. Pott (Acting Vice-President)

UNIVERSITY OF SHANGHAI

1906–1912   J.T. Proctor
1912–1928   F.J. White
1928–1938   Herman C.E. Liu
1939–1945   T.K. Van
1945–1949   Henry Lin

SHANTUNG CHRISTIAN UNIVERSITY

TENGCHOW

1887–1895	Calvin Mateer
1895–1901	Watson Hayes

SHANTUNG

1901–1904	
1904–1906	Paul D. Bergen
1906–1907	Calvin Mateer (Acting)
1908–1913	Paul D. Bergen
1913–1915	William P. Chalfant (Acting)
1916–1920	J. Percy Bruce
1920–1921	James Neal (Acting)
1921–1927	Harold Balme
1927–1931	Li T'ien-lu
(1927–1929	Acting)
1931–1932	Chu Ching-nung (King Chu)
1935–1943	Liu Shu-ming
1943–1945	Edgar Chih-ho T'ang
1945–1952	Wu K'e-ming
(1948–	H.P. Lair, Acting)
(1948–1949	David Yang, Acting)

SOOCHOW UNIVERSITY

1900–1911	D.L. Anderson
1911–1922	John W. Cline
1922–1927	W.B. Nance
1927–1949	Y.C. Yang

WEST CHINA UNION UNIVERSITY

1914–1930	Joseph Beech
1931–1949	Lincoln Dsang
1949–1951	Fong Su-hsuan

WOMAN'S CHRISTIAN MEDICAL COLLEGE

1924–	Tsok Tsung Wang, M.D.

YALE-IN-CHINA, COLLEGE OF

1914–1924	Governing Board
1924–1927	Edward H. Hume
1929–1937	K.Y. Wang (Dean of Medicine)
1937–1940	H.C. Chang (Dean of Medicine)
1940–1947	H.C. Chang (Director, Natl. Hsiang Ya Med. Coll.)
1947–1951	M.Y. Ling (Director, Natl. Hsiang Ya Med. Coll.)

Appendices

YENCHING UNIVERSITY

PEKING

1888–1893 Leonard Pilcher
1893–1916 Hiram H. Lowry

NORTH CHINA

1889–1910 D.Z. Sheffield
1910–1916 Howard S. Galt

NORTH CHINA WOMEN'S COLLEGE

1904–1916 Luella Miner

YENCHING (PEKING in English until 1928)

1916–1919 Hiram H. Lowry (Acting)
1919–1948 J. Leighton Stuart
1929–1933 Wu Lei-ch'uan (Chancellor)
1933–1937 T.T. Lew, Y.T. Tsur, C.W. Luh (Acting)
1937–1946 H.H. K'ung (Chancellor)
1946–1948 C.W. Luh (Chrmn. Admin. Comm.)

248

Appendix H

CHINA COLLEGE HISTORIES

FUKIEN CHRISTIAN UNIVERSITY, by Roderick Scott	UBCCC 1954
GINLING COLLEGE, by Mrs. Lawrence Thurston and Miss Ruth M. Chester	UBCCC 1955
HANGCHOW UNIVERSITY, by Clarence Burton Day	UBCCC 1955
HUACHUNG UNIVERSITY, by John L. Coe	UBCHEA 1962
HWA NAN COLLEGE, by L. Ethel Wallace	UBCCC 1956
NANKING, UNIVERSITY OF, by William P. Fenn (in process)	UBCHEA
LINGNAN UNIVERSITY, by Charles Hodge Corbett	LINGNAN 1963
ST. JOHN'S UNIVERSITY, by Mary Lamberton	UBCCC 1955
SHANGHAI, UNIVERSITY OF, by John Burder Hipps	SHANGHAI 1964
SHANTUNG CHRISTIAN UNIVERSITY, by Charles Hodge Corbett	UBCCC 1955
SOOCHOW UNIVERSITY, by W.B. Nance	UBCCC 1956
WEST CHINA UNION UNIVERSITY, by Lewis C. Walmsley	UBCHEA 1974
YALE-IN-CHINA, by Reuben Holden	YALE 1964
YENCHING UNIVERSITY, by Dwight W. Edwards	UBCHEA 1959

UBCCC	United Board for Christian Colleges in China, New York
UBCHEA	United Board for Christian Higher Education in Asia, New York
LINGNAN	Board of Trustees of Lingnan University, New York
SHANGHAI	Board of Founders of the University of Shanghai, Richmond, Va.
YALE	Yale-in-China Association, Inc., New Haven, Conn.

Index of Proper Names

Index

Index

Maxwell, J. L., 144
McClure, William, 45
McCracken, Josiah C., 50, 86, 140
McMullen, Robert J., 201, 247
McNair, Harley F., 128
Medical Schools, 11, 15, 48, 51, 99, 139
    44, 159, 181–82, 188–89, 212–13,
    224, 240–44
Mei, Y. P., 127, 206
Menzies, James M., 127
Methodists, American Northern, 27, 31,
    47–48, 55, 59, 63, 65, 69, 79, 97–98,
    169, 217, 244–46
Methodists, American Southern, 53–54,
    69, 244–46
Methodists, Canadian, 65, 69, 182, 188,
    244–46
Methodists, English, 46, 63, 102, 181, 244–
    46
Methodist Woman's Foreign Missionary
    Society (see Woman's Foreign Mis-
    sionary Society, Methodist)
Miao, C. S. Chester, 154
Mills, Charles R., 145
Miner, Luella, 33, 67, 250
Moir, Duncan, 42
Monroe, Paul, 47, 88
Morse, Hosea Ballou, 128
Moukden Medical College, 11, 15, 141–43,
    159, 181–82, 189, 240–44
Murphy, Henry Killam, 162–63

Nance, W. B., 89, 149
Nankai University, 195, 208
Nanking, University of, 11, 14, 36, 52, 55–
    57, 70, 91–94, 117–18, 124, 126–130,
    132–33, 146–52, 155–56, 159–61,
    164–66, 168, 171, 174, 176, 178, 180,
    182, 184–86, 188–91, 199, 204–5,
    207–8, 213–14, 218–19, 228, 239–44
Nanking College of Agriculture and Fores-
    try, 57, 92–93, 146, 187, 190–91, 242
Nanking Union Medical College, 46, 55,
    240–41
Nanking Union Theological Seminary, 49,
    152–54, 176, 207
Nanking University Hospital, 57
Nanking University School of Nursing, 57
Nanyang College, 22, 40, 42, 55
National Christian Council, 154
Neal, James Boyd, 141, 144, 249
Nevius, Mr. and Mrs. John L., 24, 129,
    145

New York, University of the State of, 31,
    36, 48, 56, 58, 60, 62, 66, 70, 83, 94,
    97–98, 107, 142
North China Educational Union, 47–48, 68
North China (Union) College, 26–27, 31,
    33, 46–48, 67, 112, 123, 152, 155,
    169–70, 174, 187, 239
North China Union Medical College, 43
North China Union Theological (College)
    Seminary, 33, 48, 55, 152, 155, 227
North China Union Women's College, 43,
    48, 67, 70, 155, 192, 239
North China Union Women's Medical Col-
    lege, 48, 84, 141, 240–41
Noyes, Henry V., 248

Oberlin-in-Shansi, 206
Oriental Education Commission, 45

Park, W. H., 139
Parker, Peter, 137, 140
Pederson, Dr., 141, 248
Peiyang University, 22, 40–42
Peking Union Medical School, 48, 138,
    141–43, 150, 240–41
Peking University, 27, 31, 33, 36, 43, 46–
    48, 68, 70, 79, 83, 112, 122–24, 134,
    138, 152, 174, 239 (see also Yenching
    University)
Peking University, National (Peita), 70, 84,
    165, 208
Pennsylvania, Christian Association of the
    University of, 50, 61, 86, 99, 140
Pennsylvania Medical College (see St.
    John's Medical School)
Pennsylvania Medical College, Canton (see
    University Medical College)
Pennsylvania State College, 132, 134, 190
Permanent Committee (see Committee on
    Christian Colleges in China)
Pilcher, Leonard, 250
Planning Commission, China Postwar,
    180–81
Planning Committee, American Postwar,
    179–81
Planning Committee, British Postwar,
    180–81
Porter, Lucius, 47
Pott, Francis Lister Hawks, 30, 50, 85–86,
    131, 134, 201, 216, 248
Pott, James H., 216, 248
Presbyterians, American Northern, 30,

253

Index